The New Mom's Manual

The
New Mom's
Manual

Over 800 Tips and Advice from
Hundreds of Moms for Baby's First Year

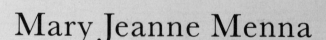

Mary Jeanne Menna

FOREWORD BY
Michael Shannon, M. D.

THREE RIVERS PRESS • NEW YORK

Published by Three Rivers Press, New York, New York.
Member of the Crown Publishing Group.

Random House, Inc. New York, Toronto, London, Sydney, Auckland
www.randomhouse.com

THREE RIVERS PRESS is a registered trademark and the Three Rivers Press colophon is a trademark of Random House, Inc.

Printed in the United States of America
Design by Fearn Cutler
Illustrations by Sally Mara Sturman

Library of Congress Cataloging-in-Publication Data
Menna, Mary Jeanne.
The new mom's manual: over 800 tips and advice from hundreds of moms for baby's first year / Mary Jeanne Menna; foreword by Michael Shannon.—1st ed.
1. Infants—Care. 2. Infants—Health and hygiene. 3. Parenting.
4. Child rearing. I. Title.
RJ61 .M575 2001
649'.122—dc21
00-050947

ISBN 0-8129-9070-6
10 9 8 7 6 5 4 3 2 1
FIRST EDITION

Author's Note

All the tips in this book have been reviewed by Michael Shannon, M.D., a pediatrician at Children's Hospital, Boston. I've also run all the nursing tips by La Leche League International. However, no book, including this one, can ever replace the advice of a doctor. I hope you'll share this book with your baby's doctor and use it to help you take the best care of your baby.

To Dave:

For helping me believe that anything is possible. *Ti amo.*

To Joseph and Matthew:

Two little guys who enrich my life in big ways.

Acknowledgments

A million thanks to all of the moms who helped make this book a reality. Words change lives, and your words will undoubtedly change the lives of thousands of anxious new moms, giving them renewed confidence, reassurance, and above all, comfort in the knowledge that they are not alone. Thank you for opening your hearts and sharing your practical wisdom—and sometimes very personal and private stories—so that other moms might benefit from your experiences in the challenging first year of parenthood.

My loving appreciation and a great big hug to my family: my husband, Dave, for your love, good humor, and steady encouragement; and my two sons, Joseph and Matthew, for teaching me to be a better mom. It is truly a privilege being your mommy.

A heartfelt thanks to Dr. Michael Shannon, who took time out of his hectic schedule to read my manuscript and offer his expert advice. My gratitude and appreciation to all of the creative talent at Crown and Three Rivers Press, especially to my editor, Betsy Rapoport, who embraced this project from the beginning and shared in my belief that there is enormous benefit to moms helping other moms. I appreciate her insightful direction and skillful editing. Thanks, too, to my literary agent, Anne Hawkins, for her guidance and helpful advice along the way. Finally, thank you to the numerous women's groups, clubs, and organizations that were kind enough to distribute my questionnaire to their members.

Contents

————— ❧ —————

Foreword

The magic of a first child is often dimmed by parents' anxiety about "doing something wrong." I cannot even begin to count the number of times in my twenty-five years as a pediatrician that a brand-new mother, ready to leave the hospital with her brand-new baby, has asked the question "So, where's the manual?" While it's traditional for new moms to receive some type of written guide with basic instructions on newborn care and the needs of a new-to-the-world child, I've found many of the available resources to be somewhat limited by the author's own viewpoint or bias. Consequently, many mothers have unnecessarily developed overwhelming anxiety and feelings of inadequacy because they've tried Dr. So-and-So's approach and it just didn't work. Was there something wrong with the baby? Were they bad moms? The end result is that child rearing, one of the most exciting events in life, becomes somewhat frightening. I am reminded of a close friend who returned her day-old child to the hospital nursery, hiding the fact that baby had a poopy diaper, because she had never changed a baby and was terrified by the prospect.

The New Mom's Manual is a welcome guide for the new parent. Written by other mothers, the book offers practical tips on the most important aspects of child rearing. You'll notice that the book sometimes offers conflicting recommendations: One mom will swear by one technique, and another will take the opposite approach. These differing voices are actually beneficial; because babies are so different, a new mom must learn to make decisions that work best for her own child. Becoming a good parent means learning through trial and error, combining common sense and imagination, and trusting your own instincts. *The New Mom's Manual* should not be taken as "this is the only way to do things," but rather as a useful guide, a source of inspiration and encouragement through the uncertainties of caring for baby. It is a one-of-a-kind, easy-to-read book that can help all new parents raise their babies more confidently. I hope it will help you appreciate that the real expert in caring for your baby is you.

MICHAEL SHANNON, M.D., M.P.H.
Children's Hospital, Boston
Associate Professor of Pediatrics, Harvard Medical School

Introduction

New moms have it harder today. You probably live far from your childhood home and don't have the same network of support—mothers, grandmothers, sisters, aunts, cousins, and lifelong friends—that women in generations past had available. Yet as a first-time mom, you need help and emotional support more than ever. Every year, millions of women face new motherhood alone, feeling isolated and lacking confidence, learning parenting skills chiefly through trial and error. Sure, you have lots of hefty baby encyclopedias to reach for, but what if that expert's advice doesn't work? Wouldn't it be great to sample lots of different tried-and-true techniques from the real "experts"—moms who've been through it all?

The New Mom's Manual was written to give you that helping hand. In it, hundreds of experienced moms pass along more than eight hundred tips, advice, anecdotes, observations, opinions, and words of encouragement for the new mom in baby's first year. These are the ideas that rescued us or that we moms dreamed up in moments of genius or desperation—advice that works from real moms who were once "first-timers" just like you. Here are their favorite tips on feeding, sleeping, crying, bathing, skin care, diapering, traveling, safety, teething, and more. You'll also get sound advice on making the emotional adjustment to having a newborn at home; gaining confidence in your new role as a parent; maintaining a strong marriage despite mounting tension and stress after the baby comes; connecting to other new moms with whom you can share your parenting trials and tribulations; making time for yourself; and getting help during the critical postpartum period.

Here are real-life solutions from real-life moms to the challenges of baby care, such as:

- The newborn who won't latch on
- The colicky baby who screams for hours
- The baby who has her nights and days mixed up
- Bathing baby for the first time
- Changing a dirty diaper in a crowded airplane, thirty thousand feet up

And other new motherhood concerns, such as:

- Feeling inadequate, incompetent, or overwhelmed—or all three—after baby comes home
- Feeling "blue" or depressed in the weeks following baby's birth
- Figuring out the changing ways to relate to your spouse
- Lack of interest in intimacy with your partner (that's code for "I'm so tired; will I ever want to have sex again?")
- Feeling a loss of identity at home with baby

Above all else, as you read this book, you'll feel reassured that you're not alone—no matter what dilemma or emotional hardship you encounter in baby's first year, another mom has been there. This book is packed full of practical solutions and encouragement from other moms. It's like a vast mothers' group between covers, with each mom contributing her best tip for caring for baby and easing the strife of new motherhood.

I wish I'd had such a book when my first baby was born. (I'm now the mother of two boys, ages three and four, born 12½ months apart—what was I thinking?) Like many expectant mothers, I'd received a couple of the big baby books—those hefty "definitive" guides—as shower gifts, but at six or seven hundred pages, they were pretty daunting, so I tended to use them more as an occasional reference than a front-to-back read. What I really needed was short, snappy, easy-to-read nuggets of wisdom—and lots of them, so if one idea to stop colic didn't work, I'd have a lot of other ideas to try. That's what you have in *The New Mom's Manual*.

As you'll hear echoed by moms throughout this book, it really helps to keep a sense of humor in the first year. There were many times when I did just that, especially in the early weeks when sleep deprivation got the best of me. On most days, I felt like I was walking around in a daze and was hardly able to form a complete sentence. In fact, one day, about a month after my oldest son was born, a neighbor telephoned with the good news that his wife had delivered a baby boy the night before. I asked him what name they had given their son and he replied, Ryan. My neighbor then asked me, "What is your son's name? I forget." But all he heard on the other end of the phone was silence. In my tired state, I had momentarily forgotten my baby's name! I told him that someone was at the door and could he hold for a moment. As I put the phone down, several names raced across my mind: *Ryan? No, that's his son's name. Patrick? No, that's my nephew. Hmmm . . . Jim is my brother, Dave is my husband . . .* I picked up the receiver and said I'd have to call him back. I hurriedly searched for my son's baby book and there in bold print was his name: Joseph Francis. *That's it!*

Having a baby will humble you, too. I remember visiting an expectant friend with my then six-month-old baby. I was showing him off a bit while touting the richness of motherhood. As I sat on the floor and chattered on, I playfully lifted my son up over my head and back down again. He loved it and it made him laugh, right up until the time he threw up his lunch—strained peas!—on my face. I tried to maintain my composure as I nonchalantly wiped my face with a burp cloth. Then I looked over at my friend, who just smiled and said, "It's all over your hair." We both burst out laughing.

To the expectant or new mom who reads this book, I want to emphasize that even though all the information was vetted by a pediatrician, it's not meant to replace the advice of a doctor; you should bring any medical problems your baby may experience to the attention of your baby's doctor first. You'll also find conflicting opinions from the moms. Just as in life, every mother and her child are unique, and what works for one mom or one baby may not be what works best for you. Like most parents, you'll probably want to try one thing, and if that doesn't work, try something else. I've also tried to represent both sides of key issues such as breast versus bottle and cloth versus diaper. You'll hear from moms who took each route and can help you succeed no matter which you choose. This chorus of voices confirms that there's no one "right" way to do anything. So no feeling guilty!

I hope you find this book helpful. Most of all, I hope that you enjoy your first year as a parent. Even though the first year involves a tremendous amount of work, babies give so much in return, and, given time, the work will pale in comparison. Then comes the day when your baby gets a bit older, when you'll look back on baby's first year with tenderness, remembering all the precious, fun times. It's at such a moment that you'll smile to yourself and think . . . *It's time for number two!*

Happy mothering!

The New Mom's Manual

CHAPTER I

Breast Is Best!

Breast-feeding for Success

Experts agree that breast milk is the best source of nutrition for baby, providing just the right amounts of carbohydrates, proteins, and fats, as well as critical enzymes and antibodies that promote immunities to fight disease in your baby. In fact, your milk contains over a *hundred* ingredients not found in formula. And, aside from the important nutritional and health benefits of breast-feeding, there are many other physical and emotional benefits for baby and mom. At a time when you may be feeling a bit anxious (or *completely overwhelmed!*) about caring for this new little person in your life, breast-feeding provides a quiet, relaxing time for you both—once you've gotten the hang of it.

Perhaps you've already made up your mind to nurse your baby. Now comes the tricky part: learning *how* to breast-feed. It's possible that you'll be one of the fortunate ones who find that breast-feeding presents no particular problem; you offer your breast, your baby latches on well and eagerly nurses. More likely, though, breast-feeding will require lots of practice and patience in order to get it right.

One challenge many new moms face is a newborn who is too sleepy in the first few days to stay awake long enough to nurse sufficiently. If this is your situation, try changing her diaper, partially undressing her, wiping her body with a wet washcloth, or tickling her feet to stimulate her enough to want to eat. Another common obstacle for the breast-feeding mom is failing to position baby on the breast properly, creating an improper latch. When your baby is latched on correctly, her nose and chin will touch your breast, she'll have positioned her mouth over your nipple and most of the areola (the darker circle surrounding the nipple), and her sucking motion will be smooth and the suction on the breast firm. If you find that your baby's mouth covers only the nipple, or that her sucking creates "dimples" on her cheeks, she is not properly latched on. You'll need to experiment with different positions and holds to see what works best for baby. The same applies if you find that nursing is especially painful, that you're experiencing persistent breast tenderness, or your nipples are sore, cracked, or bleeding; these are all indications that baby is not latched on correctly. As you'll hear from other moms, if you're having problems with breast-feeding, don't give up before you've consulted with a lactation specialist. The specialist will give you a variety of solutions to your breast-feeding problems, including optional holds and positions that will help baby latch on correctly and relieve your pain.

This chapter contains more than a hundred useful tips and words of encouragement from moms who've successfully breast-fed their babies. Nursing moms talk about the advantages of breast-feeding, what works and what doesn't, where to turn for help, solutions to the most common breast-feeding obstacles, diet tips for the nursing mom, breast-feeding after returning to work, weaning, traveling, and much more. Be sure to read the next chapter, too, which addresses bottle-feeding. It's important to be informed of all options available to you (sometimes breast-feeding just doesn't work out, even for the best-intentioned mom), and chances are, you'll give your baby a bottle sometime in the first year. Whatever choice you make, your baby will do fine.

Why Breast-feed

Benefits mom *and* baby. Breast-feeding is cheaper, easier, and more convenient than bottle-feeding, and the baby will get the nutrients and immunities that only colostrum and breast milk can provide at the most crucial time. It's always the perfect temperature and is easily digested by the baby, too.

Wendy R., Tooele, UT

Feeling close to you. For nine months, each of my babies lived inside my body—the physical closeness in the womb giving them a sense of security. Adjusting to the outside world must be difficult for a baby. Nursing allows us to reconnect, merging physically for hours each day . . . what a wonderful and gentle welcome to the world.

Kaleigh Donnelly, Memphis, TN

Mother Nature knows best. Why, if other animal species are born with the knowledge, ability, and initiative to feed their young in the wild, do we—the most intelligent of all animals—try to "manufacture" a substitute for mother's milk? Cow's milk is for *calves,* and human milk is for baby *humans.* It's as nature intended.

Tonya K. McCartney, Wilmington, NC

Go ahead, be selfish! If not for the health of your baby, how about breast-feeding for what I call "selfish" reasons:

1. *How badly do you yearn for your shape to come back?*

   I gained forty pounds during my pregnancy, and fit into my old blue jeans on the day my daughter turned three months old. (Most women find the prego-pounds come off more easily if they breast-feed.—MJM)

2. *Do you like having your period?*

   No? I don't either. You most likely won't get your period again until you begin to introduce solid foods at least twice a day. However, be sure to use birth control while you're nursing, as there is a remote chance that you may get pregnant.

3. *Are you lazy?*

   Well, then, I'm sure you would rather feed your baby the easy way than have to clean bottles and nipples, buy and mix formula, not to mention waking up to heat the bottles at two A.M.

4. *Are you cheap?*

   It's free!

5. *Want to spend less time in the pediatrician's office?*

   Studies show that breast-fed babies spend less time in the doctor's office: They experience fewer ear infections, allergies, rashes, digestive problems, diarrhea, and respiratory illnesses.

6. *Want to decrease your chances of developing breast cancer?*

   Studies show that breast-feeding actually helps prevent breast cancer as we age.

Alicia Beth Klein, Pittsburgh, PA

Just try it. Even if you're a little unsure about breast-feeding, at least *try* it—you can always quit and go to a bottle. But if you start with a bottle, it is difficult to change to breast-feeding.

Sheryl McCarthy, North Stonington, CT

Preparing Before the Birth

Get prepared *before* the birth. My advice to new moms is to hook up with a breast-feeding advocate or organization before the baby is born. I chose La Leche League and became educated about breast-feeding in advance. After the birth, whenever I felt like giving up, they were there to give me helpful advice and cheer me on.

Daphne Castor, Mililani, HI

Take a class. Call your local university or hospital to find out if they offer breast-feeding classes. I took a breast-feeding class at the local college prior to my baby's arrival, and I was glad I did. The instructor went over all of the various holds and thoroughly discussed the whole process—it helped me to feel more confident about breast-feeding.

Angela

Read a book. There are several good breast-feeding books on the market that you can read prior to the baby's arrival. Two that I would recommend are: *The Womanly Art of Breastfeeding*, by La Leche League International, and *The Complete Book of Breastfeeding*, by Marvin S. Eiger, M.D., and Sally Wendkos Olds.

Sonya Kasen, Jenison, MI

It's easier with illustrations. I highly recommend *The Nursing Mother's Companion*, by Kathleen Huggins. The author, a nurse, provides step-by-step instructions on the techniques of breast-feeding and includes many photos and illustrations to make it

❧ Breast-feeding Resources

LA LECHE LEAGUE INTERNATIONAL

For almost half a century, La Leche League (www.lalecheleague. org, or 800-LALECHE) has been a valuable source of information, support, and encouragement for breast-feeding moms. Contact them for advice and answers to your breast-feeding questions and to locate a local support group in your area where you can share your breast-feeding and mothering experiences with other nursing moms. La Leche League also offers a wide array of breast-feeding literature, a monthly magazine, and books.

INTERNATIONAL LACTATION CONSULTANT ASSOCIATION (ILCA)

Contact ILCA (www.ilca.org, or 919-787-5181) for a referral to a lactation consultant in your area. ILCA also sells breast-feeding publications and other helpful materials.

AMERICAN ACADEMY OF PEDIATRICS

The AAP (www.aap.org, or 800-433-9016) offers a wide range of free materials on breast-feeding on their Web site, including *A Woman's Guide to Breastfeeding.* ❧

easy to understand. There's also a section on safe medications for nursing moms.

Wendy L. Blumberg, Plano, TX

Get your nipples checked during pregnancy. Have your nipples checked while pregnant to determine if they are flat or inverted, so that you can correct the problem before your baby's birth. At the time my first son was born, I didn't know that my nipples were considered to be flat, and he had the hardest time latching on. I tried wearing breast shields after his birth, but they didn't correct the problem. While pregnant with my second child, a friend, who also happened to be a La Leche League leader, recommended that I begin wearing nipple shields for several hours a day, starting from about my seventh month of pregnancy. It worked! After he was born, he latched on great and I didn't have to wear the nipple shields anymore.

Nancy R., Ballwin, MO

At the Hospital

Ask for help *before* going home. Put aside your modesty and embarrassment and ask the nurses to show you how to latch your baby properly before you go home from the hospital. Don't wait until you get home to find that you're having problems—you may become frustrated and give up.

Angela

Request a lactation consultant or nurse. Ask specifically for a lactation consultant or lactation nurse at the hospital. My baby was premature and was kept in the NICU (newborn intensive-care unit); it would take her more than half an hour to latch on—I was in tears at every feeding. Finally, the NICU nurses called in a lactation consultant who was able to get my baby latched on in a minute. She even stayed with me for a couple of hours after her shift to make sure I had no more problems and gave me a wonderful pep talk . . . she deserves to be sainted!

Wendy R., Tooele, UT

Why didn't anyone warn me? My milk came in two days after my son was born. I had no idea it would be so painful. Suddenly I looked like Anna Nicole Smith, and my breasts were so hard you could've bounced quarters off them. It took two days for the swelling to go down (I lived in a hot shower) and it was hard for my son to latch on because my nipples were swollen almost flat. Ask your doctor to okay Tylenol.

Betsy, White Plains, NY

Speak up and stand firm. I made a big mistake in the hospital by not speaking up and letting the nursing staff know that I wanted to breast-feed exclusively. I delivered my son at nine forty-five P.M., and he was immediately taken away and not returned to me for *six hours;* the nurses offered no other reason than that the nursery was extremely busy that night. He was given a bottle of formula and a pacifier. Later that night the same procedure was repeated! My son never did latch on after that and I was, sadly, unable to breast-feed.

Dawn M. Oliveri, Saunderstown, RI

It's okay to supplement. You can do both—breast-feed *and* bottle-feed with formula—it doesn't have to be all or nothing. I had quadruplets and my daughters were extremely premature, requiring a lengthy stay in the NICU. Due to their size, they were unable to breast-feed, so I pumped my breast milk and froze it until I was able to feed them. As the babies grew, I was able to breast-feed for three of their daily feedings, then supplemented with formula for the balance of the feedings.

Gabriella Marshall, Houston, TX

At Home

"Things were great . . . until we got home!" My son nursed great in the hospital; in fact, the lactation consultant joked that she was going to wheel us around the floor to use as a model for other mother-baby nursing teams. Then we went home. The next week and a half were *miserable*!—I was in pain everywhere, especially in the nipples. I employed the breathing exercises I had totally forgotten about in labor and found that they helped a little. I kept telling myself, week after week, "*It's best for the baby, it's best for the baby* . . ." Then all of a sudden, things were really wonderful: The baby was gaining weight and I found that nursing did not hurt—in fact, it felt great! The bonding was so intense that as six months approached, it did not seem long enough, so I decided to nurse for nine months, then as nine months approached, I set a new goal of one year and beyond. My son is now eleven months old and we're still nursing strong!

Jennifer Metz, Tampa, FL

Keep a good attitude. Just relax and keep these thoughts in mind: Breast-feeding is the most natural and motherly thing you can do. You are helping another human being be the best, healthiest person he can be (who said ear infections are a natural part of babyhood?).

Carrie Bennett, Weirton, WV

Value the *work* you're doing. Surround yourself with women who have the same goals; this helps provide a support network for you. Take the time to enjoy nursing; don't get caught up in the *I don't have enough time to just sit here*—when you're nursing, you're doing some of the hardest work. Value that work!

Melanie Harper, WA

Patience is key to success. Nobody told me that breast-feeding would take soooo much time. It seemed like I had time for nothing else: feeding on one side, then the other; burping and diaper changes . . . only to start all over again thirty to forty-five minutes later! Be prepared for the time commitment required and for some degree of sleep deprivation for up to one year.

Holly Glennon, Anchorage, AK

Baby sling's an arm saver. I found breast-feeding to be exhausting, too! My baby would breast-feed for forty-five minutes on one breast, take a fifteen-minute break, then feed again on the other breast for another forty-five minutes! I gave up after two weeks, and now I wish I hadn't. Months later I learned of a great breast-feeding aid for moms of frequent feeders: a baby sling. A baby sling takes the place of your arms, allowing you to feed your baby while doing other things around the house. The baby is covered during feedings, so you can even go to the mall or the store while nursing as often as necessary. I will definitely breast-feed my next baby for a longer period of time with the help of a baby sling.

Kimberly Cushman, West Windsor, NJ

The remote is a godsend. I got so bored during nursing that I watched a lot of TV—with lights out and sound low at night—or chatted on the phone with a hands-free headset. Sometimes I surfed the Web. There's no law that says you've just got to sit there.

Ann R., NY

Hold off on the pacifier. Don't offer a pacifier or bottle for at least four weeks—this will prevent a lower milk supply and nipple confusion (an artificial nipple "confuses" baby). Also, breast-feeding requires effort on the part of the baby, whereas drinking from a bottle or sucking a pacifier takes much less effort—it's almost too easy. If the pacifier or bottle-feeding is established too early, baby may refuse to go back to the breast altogether. If baby really needs to suck, Mom or Dad can use a clean pinkie finger; it won't confuse her and is the best way to train her to suck properly if she is having trouble latching on.

Wendy Blumberg, Plano, TX

Give your baby a pacifier until next feeding. My son would nurse, then want to continue sucking practically until his next feeding! Although we were advised against using a pacifier, I gave him one immediately following his feedings. He rejected it at first, but then we found one that he liked (the bulb-shaped one), and it did the trick. He would suck for a while and then spit it out. He only needed it for about three months, and in the meantime, I got a little more time to myself.

Meghan Collins, Chelmsford, MA

Seek others with similar goals. Breast-feeding moms need a support system that encourages them, especially in the first few weeks, which can be the most difficult. Unfortunately, for the generation of moms now giving birth, most of their own mothers were not encouraged to breast-feed. My own mother could offer very little support for my breast-feeding goals; while her intentions were good, she was quick to say, "Maybe you don't have enough milk," or "If he's still hungry, give him a bottle."

Susan Sarnello-Harrison, Itasca, IL

Look for specialized training in breast-feeding. As a certified Lamaze and La Leche League leader, doula, childbirth educator, and mom, I can tell you that successful breast-feeding takes factual information, support, practice, and *lots* of patience. Although many people will give you "advice," look for individuals who have a background and specific training in breast-feeding, such as a lactation consultant or breast-feeding specialist. They will help you find solutions to your problems and help you to continue breast-feeding. Many women look to their obstetrician or pediatrician for advice when problems arise; however, many times these doctors have limited training or outdated information, and simply advise women to quit breast-feeding and give their babies a bottle. If this is the advice you are given, then find a lactation specialist.

Cindi Howard Castle, Lake Park, FL

"Where did I finish?" My sister taught me a helpful way to remember which breast to start on for my baby's next feeding: Wear the type of nursing bra that has three hooks at the top of each side. After nursing, hook the side on which you *started* on the first hook, and the side on which you *finished* on the second hook. Then, the next time you nurse, you simply feel for which side is on the second hook and start with that breast.

Jan Harrison Furlow, Alexandria, VA

YOU CAN ALSO MOVE A SAFETY PIN FROM ONE STRAP TO THE OTHER, YOUR WEDDING RING FROM ONE HAND TO THE OTHER, OR A RUBBER BAND, BRACELET, OR HAIR SCRUNCHIE FROM ONE WRIST TO THE OTHER.—MJM

Nursing on demand will increase your supply. Nurse on demand. It is the single best way to increase your milk supply: The more you nurse, the more breast milk your body makes.

Deanna Lloyd, Pembroke Pines, FL

Try increasing your water intake. Having problems achieving an adequate milk output? Increase your water input! By drinking eight cups of water a day, you will ensure an overflowing milk supply. To encourage drinking water, keep a full glass next to you while breast-feeding; also, fill a tall sports bottle with ice water and carry it with you throughout the day.

Christine Doolittle, Wexford, PA

An oasis for camels. I'm a camel; I hate drinking water. I set a timer every hour, and every time it went off, I drank a tall glass of water. My doctor told me that I had to drink an additional glass for every cup of coffee or cola because they're dehydrating, so I stayed away from those.

Stacy, NY

Is baby getting enough to eat? Unfortunately, our breasts don't come with ounce marks on them. However, you'll know if your baby is getting enough breast milk each day by keeping track of the number of baby's wet and dirty diapers. Six to eight wet diapers and two to four stools in a twenty-four-hour period is desirable—if you're getting this amount, or more, you're in great shape; if not, *don't give up!* As a lactation specialist, I have helped several women who were sure that their milk supply was too low, but through simple modifications in the positioning of their babies, as well as modifying their feeding schedules, they were able to nurse successfully after all. If you're concerned that your baby is getting too little to eat, talk to a lactation consultant or your baby's pediatrician.

Michelle Pool, Red Oak, TX

Supplement with breast milk. If you must give baby a bottle, don't supplement with formula; supplement with breast milk instead.

Jennifer Metz, Tampa, FL

Breast-feeding pillow offers good support. Buy a good breast-feeding pillow (the kind that wraps around your waist) to ease the strain on your back and hold your baby at nipple level. I couldn't have done without mine when breast-feeding my twins. It also helps to have a footstool of some kind to raise your legs a bit.

Allison DeWitt, Jacksonville, FL

As valuable as "liquid gold." While nursing, capture the milk leaking from the other breast into a cup. It's such a waste to lose what you'll later refer to as "liquid gold."

Andrea R. Cartwright, Stuyvesant, NY

Daddy's turn. I would suggest that once your milk supply is well established and baby is nursing well, pump at least one bottle's worth of breast milk per day and let Dad give it to baby in the evening. He'll enjoy participating in a daily feeding, and you'll have some time off to do something you want to do.

Angela

LIKE SLEEP!—MJM

Dad gets diaper duty. I made my husband do the diaper changing and burping for at least one after-midnight feeding every day. That way I could get a little more sleep so I wouldn't get too run-down, and he got bonding time.

Elizabeth, New York City

Vertical before horizontal. We wouldn't let our baby lie down until we got at least one major burp out of him following feeding on each breast. Otherwise, he'd lie down and burp out a huge amount of milk and we'd have to start all over. Burp early, burp often!

Betsy, White Plains, NY

Diet

Keep track of foods eaten. You'll know soon enough if your baby can't tolerate certain foods in your diet. It's a good idea to write down what you eat, so that if your baby has problems, you'll be able to tell if it was the result of something new or unusual in your diet.

Jennifer Terrell, Midwest City, OK

Eat for health and energy. A breast-feeding diet should include lots of fruit and leafy vegetables; also high-energy, complex carbohydrates like whole-grain breads, pasta, and cereals (and, of course, anything your husband is willing to cook for you!).

Rachel Martinez, Dededo, Guam

Don't forget the calcium. Be sure to include calcium-rich snacks like milk (whole, 2 percent, or skim), cheese, yogurt, cottage cheese, or ice cream, as well as veggies such as broccoli, and other foods like almonds. If you don't like the taste of milk, mix powdered milk into casseroles, soups, ice cream, or vegetables. Also, you can hide the taste of milk in homemade pudding or mashed potatoes.

Karen Rudolph Durrie, Calgary, Alberta

I PREFER LOW-FAT OR NONFAT (SKIM) DAIRY FOODS. TOFU IS ALSO HIGH IN CALCIUM.—MJM

Protein is important, too. Make sure you are eating enough protein; breast-feeding can cause a low-blood-sugar reaction, which is treated by increasing your *protein* intake, not carbohydrates. Some good protein foods include cheese, sliced turkey (and other meats), peanut butter, eggs, nuts, beans, and fish. My favorite protein meals are meat chili with beans and black bean soup.

Lee Firlus, Marietta, GA

Forget the diet! I know you're dying to get back into those jeans and banish that poochy belly. But nursing is the worst time to diet. Your milk supply will suffer, you'll end up with a cranky, hungry baby, and that means less sleep for you. It's just not worth it. Just cut out the sweets and the refined carbs, and those pounds will come off.

Liza, NY

Too much caffeine and sugar is bad for baby. Omit foods and beverages from your nursing diet that contain excessive amounts of caffeine and sugar—both are stimulants and can agitate babies and make them jittery. Become a judicious reader of food labels. Check fruit juices for added sweetener, and only buy 100 percent juice.

Berneda Wolfe, Mineral Wells, WV

OVER-THE-COUNTER MEDICATIONS CAN ALSO HAVE CAFFEINE. READ THE LABELS, AND CHECK WITH YOUR DOCTOR BEFORE TAKING ANYTHING.—MJM

Herbal remedy increases milk supply. As my milk supply waned in later months, I found that a daily combination of herbs worked best to increase my supply. I took blessed thistle, fenugreek, borage oil, mother's milk tea, and hops (in the form of one beer at dinnertime). I got this information from a book called *Wise Woman Herbal for the Childbearing Year*, by Susun S. Weed.

Angela J. Byrnes, Stanford, CA

See "No More Tears: Coping with Crying and Colic" (page 67) for additional diet tips related to breast-feeding.

Overcoming Obstacles

LET-DOWN

Quiet surroundings aid in let-down. It is very important that you are calm and relaxed when breast-feeding so that you'll have milk let-down (when the baby's initial sucking directs your pituitary gland to activate the hormone that produces breast milk). You'll know when you have let-down by a tingling sensation and by the ease at which your milk flows from your nipples. In fact, after you've breast-fed a number of times, let-down may occur from simply hearing your baby cry or just thinking about her. However, if you're stressed or uptight when breast-feeding, let-down may be hampered or not occur at all. If this is your problem, look around you and see what changes you can make emotionally and physically. You may only need quieter surroundings, additional privacy with your baby, or a more relaxed state of mind.

Amy Black, Hopewell, VA

Adding warmth helps. If I was pumping and could not achieve let-down, I would place hot washcloths over each of my breasts—it helped a lot.

Jamie Kennedy, Midland, MI

Cotton breast pads absorb better. If you have heavy let-down like I did (mine could spray past my toes!), use only cotton breast pads—not the synthetic or paper kind—they're much more absorbent and are less likely to leak.

Melanie Harper, WA

Disposable pads helped me. I didn't like the feel of soggy cotton nursing pads, and I could never wash out the sour milk smell (I was nervous about using bleach), so I switched to disposables. They were especially handy when I went back to work.

Elizabeth, New York City

LATCHING ON

Check baby's mouth placement. If you can't see your baby's jaw moving near her ear while she is nursing, she is most likely sucking on the nipple instead of the areola and is not latched on correctly.

Karen Rudolph Durrie, Calgary, Alberta

Nipple shields get milk flowing again. My son was much more interested in sleeping for the first weeks of his life than breast-feeding, which caused my breasts to become engorged and made it difficult for him to latch on. I called a lactation consultant, who gave me a "contact nipple shield," made from very thin silicone and containing four holes and an open area so that baby can press his nose to your skin. When I put it on my nipple, my milk began to flow and allowed my son to nurse without effort. After the engorgement decreased and he was more awake, I weaned him off of it so that he would learn how to latch on without it.

Catherine Rouse, Las Vegas, NV

Lamaze breathing helped. Both my kids latched on well, but in each case, it took about two weeks before my nipples stopped feeling sore. I used my Lamaze breathing, and it got me through.

Joan, NY

Excessive pain is not normal. If nursing really hurts, it is *not* normal! With my second baby, the nurses at the hospital told me that my cracked and bleeding nipples were a normal occurrence for a breast-feeding woman, and that my nipples just needed to "toughen up." They also commented that because he was sucking very hard and often he "sure is latching on well." But I knew that with my first child, although my nipples were a little sore at first, it felt nothing like this. Finally, I had a lactation consultant come out to my house, and she assured me that bleeding was *not* normal and that the reason my nipples were bleeding was that my baby was not latching on properly. Worst of all, because he was not latched properly, he was not getting enough milk (which explained why he was permanently attached to my breasts). If your nipples are cracked and bleeding, get help right away from someone who is qualified.

Deborah Baska, Kansas City, MO

Try nursing while lying down for inverted nipples. I had inverted nipples, so my son had trouble latching on, which also led to engorgement. To correct the problem, I first expressed a bit of milk by hand; this relieved the engorgement. Then, to help him latch on properly, I squeezed my nipple and, as he opened his mouth wide, pushed my nipple into the back of his mouth and held my breast for him. Feeding him while lying on my side was easiest.

Michelle Vittum, Garfield, NJ

Sometimes two is better than one. My baby had difficulty latching on and seemed to prefer the bottle to my breast. Then a visiting nurse gave me a tip that saved my life: She advised me to "trick" my baby by placing the bottle nipple on my breast nipple. It worked wonderfully well—he began nursing exclusively and didn't even seem to notice the difference.

Sylvia Morgado, Bronx, NY

SORE NIPPLES

Lanolin soothes sore nipples. For treating sore nipples, pure lanolin ointment is indispensable. Also, any clothing coming in contact with your nipples can be irritating in the first few weeks, so leave your bra flaps down and go without a shirt whenever possible. (I can still picture my poor husband coming home from work and there I was: baby in my arms, nearly naked to the waist—completely oblivious to the view that passing neighbors had into our house. No book *ever* told us that this was a possibility!)

Cathleen Phelps, Alexandria, VA

Preventive treatment helps avoid sore nipples. I used an all-natural lanolin on my nipples called Lansinoh for Breast-feeding Mothers. It's a medical-grade lanolin that's pure and hypoallergenic, and kept my nipples soft. By using it as a preventive, I completely avoided the dryness and cracking that so many other women experience. Also, you don't have to wash it off before feeding baby.

Meghan Collins, Chelmsford, MA

Breast milk is a natural healer. Rub breast milk on your sore nipples after nursing and allow them to air-dry for ten to fifteen minutes.

Amy Allred, Woodstock, GA

Tea bags are soothing, longer. My friend gave me good advice for relieving my sore nipples. She said to make myself a cup of tea and, while relaxing with the hot tea, place the tea bag under my breast pad to help soothe the pain. It worked nicely—compared to a hot washcloth, the tea bags stayed moister and warmer longer.

Andrea R. Cartwright, Stuyvesant, NY

Cold tea bag works nicely, too. I set my tea bags in cool water for about ten to fifteen minutes and then placed them on my nipples—it worked wonders for me.

Kelly Foster, Tacoma, WA

I RAN THESE TEA-BAG TIPS BY SOME EXPERTS AT LA LECHE LEAGUE INTERNATIONAL. THEY WERE CONCERNED THAT CAFFEINE IN THE TEA MIGHT MAKE ITS WAY INTO YOUR BABY. I WOULD TRY THIS WITH DECAFFEINATED TEAS FROM COMPANIES LIKE CELESTIAL SEASONINGS RATHER THAN WITH HERBAL TEA FROM BINS AT THE HEALTH-FOOD STORE, WHERE YOU CAN'T BE SO SURE OF THE INGREDIENTS.—MJM

Break baby's suction first. I wish someone had told me this: Don't *pull* baby off of your nipple (ouch!); instead, use your finger to gently release baby. Do this by inserting your fingertip into the corner of baby's mouth, breaking the suction, then pull your nipple away.

Dorothy Ingram, Laurel, MD

Tylenol is okay for relieving soreness. Don't be afraid to take Tylenol from time to time to relieve sore breasts—it will help take the edge off.

Marybeth Danielson-McElroy, Sherwood, OR

Stopping the biter. Don't feel like you have to discontinue breast-feeding because your baby's teeth are coming in. A stern *No!* and a minute's pause in nursing will deter baby from biting again.

Susan Flannery, Louisville, KY

ENGORGEMENT

Empty breasts at every feeding. Engorgement is a result of your breast holding too much milk. To keep your breasts from getting engorged, make sure that you are switching breasts during each feeding to adequately empty each one. I would switch my daughter from one breast to the other every ten to fifteen minutes. Once you have established the total number of minutes your baby nurses, simply divide the number by two and breast-feed on each breast for that amount of time.

Dorothy Ingram, Laurel, MD

Nursing and pumping relieves engorgement. To reduce engorgement, I would try to get my baby to suckle, and if that didn't completely take care of it, I would pump until the pressure was relieved.

Maria Lorena Maples, Odenton, MD

YOU CAN STORE EXPRESSED MILK FOR UP TO TWO WEEKS IN A REFRIGERATOR FREEZER AND UP TO THREE OR FOUR MONTHS IN A SEPARATE DOOR FREEZER. TO WARM OR THAW, PUT THE CONTAINER IN A PAN OF WARM WATER. NEVER MICROWAVE, AS IT CAN CREATE HOT SPOTS.——MJM

Hot-water bottle still reliable. A useful item to keep around the house in the early weeks of breast-feeding is an inexpensive rubber hot-water bottle. To relieve engorgement and make it easier for baby to latch on, "prep" the breasts prior to feedings by applying the hot-water bottle to the breast, then massage the breast from the outside toward the nipple. This technique will induce your milk to flow.

Susan Sarnello-Harrison, Itasca, IL

Pass the peas, please. If a warm compress doesn't work for you, try ice packs (or a bag of frozen peas) to help with engorgement.

Elizabeth Hewitt, Grinnell, IA

Cabbage leaves ease engorgement. I heard about this crazy tip that cold cabbage leaves placed on your breasts help to relieve engorgement. Well, it works! Apparently, the cabbage leaves exude a chemical that softens the breasts and relieves the pain—sounds like an old wives' tale, but you'll try *anything* when you're carrying cement-filled basketballs around!

Karen Rudolph Durrie, Calgary, Alberta

Learn to hand-express. I had to take a business trip and didn't discover until I was off the plane that my breast pump was broken. I got terribly engorged and couldn't figure out how to hand-express my milk to relieve the pressure. My advice is, learn this technique before you're desperate!

Betsy, White Plains, NY

CLOGGED DUCTS

Hot showers help unclog ducts. Clogged ducts (also called plugged ducts) occur when milk ducts are blocked and no milk is able to pass through—it's very painful and can lead to infection if not taken care of. If you get clogged ducts, get plenty of rest, drink lots of fluids, massage the infected breast, and take several hot showers. If a fever develops, seek medical attention (you may require an antibiotic). Keep trying to manually express the milk; you'll know the milk ducts are opened again when you see a stream of milk coming from your breast.

PoLee Mark-Yee, Kirkland, Quebec

Diaper makes a great compress. I found that the best way to relieve plugged ducts was to fill a disposable diaper with very warm water and use it as a compress. Then, allow baby to nurse on the affected breast and presto! . . . all better!

Jen Berger, Schaumburg, IL

Wear loose clothing. I developed clogged ducts when my daughter was five weeks old and ended up with mastitis—an infection in one of the ducts that gave me terrible headaches and caused me to have severe pain in my breast. As the infection worsened, I had to be hospitalized and treated with IVs and antibiotics. I was told to use a warm compress, holding it on and behind the area of the clogged duct to loosen the clog, as well as to periodically pump my breast. Both were effective in unclogging the duct. I believe I could have avoided clogged ducts altogether had I worn a looser bra. I couldn't find a comfortable bra for sleeping, so I wore something that looked like a sports bra, but with nursing snaps. As it turned out, it was too binding! Any nursing bra can be binding if it is too tight; be sure that *none* of your clothing is too tight when you're breast-feeding.

Sally Rowan, Baltimore, MD

MEDICATION

Request a nursing-safe drug. Many doctors are not educated on breast-feeding and medications, and they habitually prescribe the same drugs over and over again. If you are told that you need drugs and are advised to stop breast-feeding, tell your doctor that you wish to find an alternate nursing-safe drug instead. An excellent book that lists several optional medications for the nursing mom is *Medications and Mothers' Milk*, by Thomas W. Hale, M.D.

Nancy R., Ballwin, MO

Best Breast-feeding Aids

Twice as fast. The Medela *Pump In Style* worked great! It is a double pump with adjustable suctions, so I could pump both breasts at once and be done in just ten minutes. It also has a battery attachment for portable pumping, as well as an adapter for plugging the unit into the cigarette lighter in the car—it made pumping anywhere easy!

Lisa

It's like switching to high gear. Don't bother with a battery-operated pump—they don't work very well—invest in an electric pump instead.

Lynne F. Carlberg, Albuquerque, NM

Hospital-grade pumps most efficient. The Ameda *Elite* and Medela *Lactina* rentals are awesome! As a lactation specialist, I have tested several pumps, and I feel that both of these brands are comparable. Both offer double and single pumping features, as well as your choice of battery packs, car adapters, or electrical outlet plugs. Both are lightweight—weighing under seven pounds. The Medela has preset settings for suction (minimum, medium, and maximum), and a speed range of one to seven. The Ameda has a more variable suction with a dial setting you can set to whatever suits you, as well as variable speeds. I think that it is important to try out various pumps to determine which one you will be most comfortable with. Beware that most retail pumps are *not* hospital-grade. Some retail outlets will advertise a pump as hospital-grade, but most are not! The only hospital-grade pumps are: Ameda *Elite,* Ameda *SMB,* Medela *Classic,* Medela *Lactina Plus,* and Medela *Lactina Select* models.

Michelle Pool, Red Oak, TX

Insulated bag ideal for storing breast milk. Working moms many times feel too self-conscious to keep their pumped breast milk in the company refrigerator until it's time to go home, yet their milk must be kept cold for about ten hours. As a working mom and lactation consultant, I recommend that new moms tote an insulated bag or cooler to work (one large enough to hold four bottles), along with one frozen ice pack for every bottle of pumped milk. The milk will stay cool for up to ten hours and can be kept in your desk drawer. If you choose to purchase an electric breast pump, the Ameda *Purely Yours* and Medela *Pump In Style* breast pumps (ranging from about $250 to $275) come with their own tote bag and milk storage containers.

Sharon Birdseye, Atlanta, GA

Manual pumps are most economical. Since I'm a stay-at-home mom, I opted for the Medela manual pump. I needed to pump only occasionally, and I didn't want to spend a lot of money on an electric pump.

Daphne Castor, Mililani, HI

Traveling and Clothing

Tote fresh breast milk. Fresh-pumped breast milk is easiest to travel with; it holds for six hours at room temperature (72°F), whereas thawed frozen breast milk at room temperature must be used immediately.

Amy Jordan, Myrtle Beach, SC

❧ Breast-feeding Aids

AMEDA

For more than fifty years, Ameda (www.hollister.com, or 800-323-4060) has provided mothers with breast pumps and accessories. Contact their parent company, Hollister, to obtain information about Ameda manual and battery/electric breast pumps and other breast-feeding products and accessories, to place an order, to get free literature on breast-feeding, or to find an Ameda rental station in your area.

MEDELA

With more than thirty years of experience helping breast-feeding mothers, Medela (www.medela.com, or 800-435-8316) has a complete line of manual, battery/electric breast pumps, breast-feeding accessories, nursing bras and panties, and more. You can visit their Web site or call Medela to obtain product information, get help from one of their lactation consultants, or to purchase or rent Medela breast pumps in your area. Also, Medela is the first manufacturer in the U.S. to develop a workplace program to meet the needs of working mothers. Through the Corporate Lactation Program, businesses support breast-feeding employees by providing breast-feeding counseling and breast pumps in an accessible, private, and pleasant location. Your company's human resources department can learn how to be nursing-mother-friendly by contacting Medela.

AVENT

Avent (www.aventamerica, or 800-54-AVENT) imports a full line of natural-shaped nipples on their reusable and disposable bottles, designed to allow baby to suck as if breast-feeding. In addition to bottles, Avent offers the Avent Feeding System, an integrated line of manual breast pumps and bottle-feeding accessories, including trainer cups, nipple shields, nursing pads, storage sets, warmers, pacifiers, and sterilizers. This system enables mothers to use a combination of breast- and bottle-feeding. ❧

Nursing in public is no longer taboo. I traveled quite a bit during my son's first year, so I did a lot of breast-feeding in public; I've nursed on airplanes, at highway rest stops, at state fairs, in restaurants, at the mall . . . no place was off-limits. I never used a special covering, nor did I buy nursing clothing—honestly, I never felt uncomfortable breast-feeding in public. I think people are much more responsive to breast-feeding in general today.

Elizabeth Hewitt, Grinnell, IA

Carry a blanket everywhere. I hated how most nursing shirts looked, and I didn't like nursing in a dirty, smelly public bathroom. (Hey, would *you* eat your lunch there?) So I always took a lightweight baby blanket with me to fling over my shoulder and cover my daughter so she could nurse in privacy.

Beth, New York City

Practice nursing in public at home. I purchased a breast-feeding cloth specifically designed for draping baby while breast-feeding in public, but I quickly found that once we were out, my daughter did not like being covered and refused to feed. If you are modest about breast-feeding in public, I would recommend periodically covering up at home while breast-feeding to get your baby accustomed to it.

Natalie Tabet, NM

Dressing rooms aren't just for dressing. To breast-feed at the mall, find a dressing room—every clothing store has one. I would change my daughter's diaper, nurse, and just sit for a while.

Diane, Jersey City, NJ

Tank top hides midriff. Wear a tank top under your clothing, or carry one in your diaper bag. It will hide your midriff and the opposite breast while you nurse.

Valerie S. Turner, PA

Best bra. Nursing bras that open from the top are the best—you can unhook them one-handed!

Evelyn O'Donnell, Alameda, CA

Bras 24/7. I wore nursing bras nonstop for the first three months—no more waking up in the middle of the night with a milk-soaked nightgown, and the extra support felt good for my swollen breasts.

Joan, NY

Convert your turtlenecks. For easier breast-feeding in the winter months, buy some cheap turtlenecks at a discount department store and cut a slit in them for each breast. That way, you can wear them under your sweaters to keep warm, but it's one less piece of clothing you'll have to hike up in order to nurse.

Candace Youngberg, Woodstock, GA

Shop on the Web. If you don't have easy access to nursing clothes where you live, there are several good Internet sites which offer great nursing wear, and most offer clothing on clearance, too: Motherwear (www.motherwear.com), Motherhood (www.motherhoodnursing.com), iMaternity (www.iMaternity.com), One Hot Mama (www.onehotmama.com), and Abracadabra/The Mom Shop (www.momshop.com).

Berneda Wolfe, Mineral Wells, WV

Working and Breast-feeding

Preplan for pumping at work. I let my employer know before I went on maternity leave that I was planning to pump when I returned to work. Arrangements were made to convert a supply room into a pumping station. I purchased a Medela *Pump In Style*, which worked great, and my pumped milk could be stored right in the bag.

Kenyatta Thomas, Burke, VA

Human resources can help, too. If your manager isn't help-ful in finding a place for you to nurse at work, try talking to someone in human resources. Let them know that study after study shows that breast-fed babies get sick less often than for-mula-fed babies, and therefore, theoretically, you will miss less work. It's best to find a private place where you can feel relaxed (it helps to hang a DO NOT DISTURB sign on the door).

Lynne F. Carlberg, Albuquerque, NM

Flexibility is the key. Sadly, I stopped breast-feeding soon after I returned to work. I now believe that had I not thought of it as "all or nothing," I could have made it work. I would tell working moms that it's better to supplement with formula than to give up altogether in frustration as I did.

Faren

Easy nights. Having done both, breast-fed and bottle-fed my children, I can tell you that it is easier to breast-feed and work than to bottle-feed and work. It was the only way I could get any rest! Instead of waking up at night and waiting for the bot-tles to warm up, I could just lie down and nurse the baby, then fall right back to sleep.

Mary Czajkoski, Joliet, IL

Pack baby's picture. I keep a recent pic-ture of my son in a Ziploc bag and tuck it into the top of my pump bag. Looking at his picture at work helps with let-down.

Heather Petit, Newark, DE

Let-down camouflage. I was in a meeting when someone said the magic word "baby," and suddenly my blouse was soaked with milk. Now I always wear a blazer over my shirt to cover any stains, and I keep an extra stash of disposable nursing pads in my desk. Plus, I label my bag of breast milk with a sign that says BELIEVE ME, YOU DON'T WANT TO SWIPE THIS to discourage office refrigerator "borrowers."

Lisa, NY

Electric double pump extends nursing time. You *can* successfully work and continue to breast-feed; however, having done this two times myself, I strongly recommend that you invest in a good electric *double* pump. With my first child, I did not use an electric double pump and my milk supply dried up, but with my second, I did use one and had no problems keeping up with demand.

Deborah Baska, Kansas City, MO

Nurse on one, pump on two. While I nursed my baby on one breast at home, I pumped the other breast; by doing this, I was able to get enough milk to fill a bottle, which could then be given to my baby while I was at work. In fact, I found that pumping while breast-feeding at home actually produced more milk than I could get from *two* pumpings at work.

Nina Scanlon, Las Vegas, NV

Long-distance breast-feeding. After the birth of my second son, I worked as a regional sales manager and traveled extensively, yet I found that I was still able to breast-feed while "on the road" and did so for the first three months. If you travel for a living and wish to continue breast-feeding, be sure to pack a pump, breast-milk storage bags, an insulated cooler, and ice packs for your trips. Most hotels will allow guests to store items in their cooler or freezer during their stay (just be sure to mark your bag HOLD FOR GUEST—so that it doesn't disappear!). When you're ready to leave the hotel, place the ice pack in your bag for your trip home. You can also fill your bag with ice from the hotel if you want extra assurance that your milk will stay cold.

Kathy Stanton, Woodstock, GA

Polyester prints are best. I found that traditional maternity blouses are not that convenient for pumping at work, so I didn't spend the extra money for them. I work as a professional recruiter and am in a business suit on most days; I learned to steer away from flimsy or easily wrinkled fabrics and opted for polyester prints and polyester blends—they hide the leakage better. I also switched from wearing knee-length skirts and hosiery to dress trousers and longer, full skirts with a jacket, making it easier for me to get around at my baby's day-care center.

Lynne F. Carlberg, Albuquerque, NM

Home and away. Pumping at work really didn't work for me, but I found that I could "top off my daughter's tank" right before I left for the office, and pick up the feeding again when I got home. My breasts adjusted to the volume issue within a week or so, although I admit there were days I'd run home and clamp that baby to my breast before even putting down my briefcase, I was so full!

Joanne, NY

Recommended reading for the nursing, working mom. One book I would recommend for the working mom is *Nursing Mother, Working Mother,* by Gale Pryor. This book talks about every aspect of breast-feeding and the working mother, including how to get the support of your coworkers and child-care helpers, going on a business trip without having to wean your baby, milk supply and feeding schedules, and ways to store and transport milk safely.

Wendy Blumberg, Plano, TX

Weaning

Wean when you *and* baby are ready. Don't let anyone force you to wean—wean only when you feel that you *and* your baby are ready. Some people may try to tell you that after one year, breast-feeding offers no benefits to the child . . . that's nonsense! Remember that the breast isn't only a source of food (as well as vitamins and immunities) for your child, it is a source of great comfort and security. When you do decide that it's time to wean, do it slowly and with great sensitivity. My daughter was weaned when she was eighteen months old; my son is now the same age, and I am just beginning the weaning process.

Kathryn A. Varuzza, New Paltz, NY

Gradual weaning reduces engorgement. Wean *gradually*! Give your baby time to get used to the bottle, and give your body a chance to slow down and eventually stop milk production, otherwise your breasts will become painfully engorged. I first introduced my son to the bottle with breast milk, then, as his acceptance to the bottle increased, I steadily replaced the breast milk with formula.

Michelle Vittum, Garfield, NJ

Drop one feeding a week. We started weaning from breast to bottle by adding one bottle to our daughter's feeding schedule per week. She was completely weaned in six to eight weeks. This helped minimize my discomfort, and she hardly noticed the change.

Melissa Hill, Kent, England

Ready, set . . . switch! Weaning was extremely difficult for my daughter; she loved to nurse and refused a bottle. Then, one night, I tried something new: I switched to the Playtex nipples which most closely matched the size and shape of my own breasts and nipples. Then, when she was ready to nurse, I latched her on and let her nurse for about five minutes. After she was comfortable and rather sleepy, I unlatched her and quickly placed the bottle in her mouth. It worked! I kept this up for about a week, never changing the position in which I fed her. She still takes her nighttime bottle cuddled up in my arms.

Mary Waggoner, Ponte Vedra, FL

It's emotional. My son weaned himself at nine months, when he learned to walk—later for you, Mom!—and I had to wean my daughter at six months so I could take medication. In both cases, weaning wasn't really my choice, and I got very emotional. It's the end of some very special closeness and your hormones are in a stew, so don't be surprised by the odd crying jag. And it's great to get your body back.

Betsy, White Plains, NY

CHAPTER 2

The Next Best Thing
— ❦ —
Bottle-feeding with Love

Even though breast milk is best for your baby, that doesn't mean that breast-feeding is right for you. It requires a deep commitment of time and effort on your part and may prove to be too frustrating for you and baby. If you don't have a strong objection to nursing, you should at least give it a try, even if for only a few weeks. However, if you know that you don't want to nurse or have insurmountable problems breast-feeding, then feeding your baby formula may be best. Whether the problem is sore breasts, cracked nipples, insufficient milk supply, the need to go on medication incompatible with nursing, or a lack of support at work, it's good to know that today's formulas are better than ever; they contain most of the same key compounds found in mother's milk, as well as the correct amounts of carbohydrates, proteins, and fats that baby requires. Whether you make a conscious choice to feed your baby formula or the decision is made for you, you can relax with the knowledge that your baby will get adequate nourishment for growth and good health. Whatever you do, don't feel guilty about the choice to bottle-feed, and don't let anyone bully or lecture you.

In addition, there are several advantages to bottle-feeding that breast-feeding doesn't provide: For example, you'll be able to share the feeding responsibilities with your husband—which is especially nice in the early weeks when feeding can be every couple of hours—and you won't have sore and leaky nipples or tender breasts to contend with. Formula-fed babies eat less frequently, too, since formula takes longer for baby to digest than breast milk, and you'll know exactly how much food your baby is getting at every feeding, which will help you gauge if he's getting enough to eat. Also, unlike some moms who breast-feed, you won't have to feel self-conscious about feeding your baby in public.

In this chapter, moms who've bottle-fed talk about circumstances that led them to bottle-feed their babies (and why it's important to get rid of the guilt), how you can achieve a special closeness when feeding baby by bottle, helpful hints on choosing the right type of formula, bottle-feeding supplies and equipment, health and safety concerns for formula-fed babies, easy formula preparation techniques, making nighttime feedings easier, traveling and bottle-feeding, and weaning to a cup.

Why Bottle-feed

Good mothering is not defined by the breast. I had always planned on breast-feeding my baby—I knew that breast milk was best for her. However, once I began nursing my daughter, my attitude changed; my nipples cracked and bled, causing the most excruciating pain of my life—I had to bite on a towel during feedings to bear the pain. When I reached my breaking point, I decided to switch to a bottle. I was devastated with my decision—I felt like I had failed my beautiful child, and the guilt was indescribable. But eventually, I came to terms with my decision; switching to a bottle allowed me to regain my strength and to be a much happier mommy. I also came to realize that breast-feeding my baby did not make me a good mother; loving, caring, talking, kissing, caressing, singing, playing, teaching, watching, smiling, and a million other things made me a good mother.

Jenny Plakio, Belen, NM

Emotional closeness is important, too. I agree! It's far more important to feel an emotional closeness to your baby at feeding time than it is to breast-feed at all cost. After four weeks of pain and agony due to mastitis, among other things, I would find myself crying every time my daughter wanted to eat. I was not bonding with her the way I had envisioned and made the decision to quit breast-feeding. After that, my attitude improved *greatly*.

Sally Langehennig, Cedar Park, TX

A super-size appetite. I chose to bottle-feed my second son because he was so huge (over ten pounds at birth!) and wanted to eat constantly. I tried nursing him and was absolutely miserable. Then one day I went to the store to buy a breast pump and instead came home with a dozen bottles

and a case of formula! Bottle-feeding was much more convenient for me and allowed me to spend more time with my older
child as well.

Jayne Heilman, Lincoln, NE

Not the nursing type. Breast-feeding just wasn't right for me.
It's not that I found it repulsive; it just wasn't something I could
see myself doing. Today's formulas are very good, and babies
who are formula-fed do just fine.

Julie Anne Cooper, Roswell, GA

Nonlactating women are not alone. When it came time for
my baby's first feeding, I was very eager to get started, but was
dismayed to find that when she nursed, she got nothing . . . I
had *no milk*! After several attempts, the nurse at the hospital told
me that I was starving my baby, so she opened little formula
samples and ordered me to use them. But I still wanted to
breast-feed, so after returning home from the hospital, I scheduled a visit from a lactation consultant. She came to my home
and showed me how to use an electric pump; every couple of
hours, I obediently hooked up both breasts to the machine and
milked them for all their worth. The most milk I ever produced
was about two ounces, but I refused to give up. I continued to
visit the lactation consultant weekly for a month, and we tried it
all—including feeding my daughter through tiny feeding tubes
wrapped around my neck and taped to my nipple—and still, I
produced no more than two ounces of milk. Finally, she sat me
down and said, "You can't keep going on like this . . . you've
tried everything. It's time to switch to formula." She added that
while breast milk is best, today's formulas are quite good, and
my daughter would not suffer by being bottle-fed. Then she
gave me literature to read that said 10 percent of all women are
simply unable to produce milk! I was so relieved to know that I

was not alone in my failure to breast-feed; at the same time, I was angry that this factual information was not included in the widely distributed breast-feeding literature women receive while pregnant. I hope that by telling my story, other "10-percenters" might feel less pressured to perform.

Donna Schwartz Mills, Los Angeles, CA

Bottle-feeding gives Mom a rest. I think the biggest advantage to bottle-feeding is that Mom is not solely responsible for feeding baby. In my case, it meant that I could take the additional time necessary to recover from my C-section while my husband fed our son. Also, it allowed my husband to form a very strong bond with our son early in his life.

Lisa Locher, Kensington, MD

Getting Started

Stocking up. To get started, I recommend buying a dozen eight- to nine-ounce bottles and a half-dozen four-ounce bottles. Use the dishwasher to wash and sterilize bottles. I also recommend a plastic bottle-accessories basket for the dishwasher; the lid is designed to hold nipples upright for best cleaning, and the inside of the basket holds bottle rings, cup lids, baby spoons, bottle brushes, pacifiers, and even small toys.

Michelle Montague, PA

Proper positioning helps keep ear infections at bay. It's important to feed baby only in a semiupright position, *never* lying down. Babies' eustachian tubes are short and more horizontal than ours; feeding them in a horizontal position can cause formula to flow into the middle ear, creating a breeding ground for ear infections.

Donna Schwartz Mills, Los Angeles, CA

𝒲ater for 𝒥ormula and 𝒮terilizing 𝒷ottles

The American Academy of Pediatrics (AAP) recommends that tap water used in infant formula be sterile and contaminant-free (containing no lead). Boil tap water for five minutes, or use the terminal-heating method. In terminal heating, you begin with clean, but not sterile, bottles. Next, fill the bottles with formula and cap them loosely. Place the bottles in a pan of water (the water should reach halfway up the bottles) and gently boil for twenty-five minutes.

It is safe to wash your baby's bottles and accessories in the dishwasher, as long as the water in your house is chlorinated. If your water is unchlorinated or from a well, boil bottles and accessories in a pan of water for five to ten minutes.

Silence is golden. It's important in the early weeks to make feedings a time of peace and calm for baby *and* you. Choose a room away from noisy visitors, TVs, phones (let the answering machine pick up calls), and other distractions. If the family room is too busy, take baby to the nursery or your bedroom.

Michele Goodwin, Symrna, GA

A joyful noise. My daughter loved the hustle and bustle of the household while she nursed. It kept her engaged, so she would drift off to sleep before finishing her bottle. Some babies are sensitive to too much stimulation, though, so find out what makes your baby eat best.

Beth, White Plains, NY

Building a bond that lasts a lifetime. Be sure to hold your baby and his bottle close to your body while feeding. So many women think that a baby holding his own bottle is a milestone (or worse, they "prop" the bottle); they don't realize how critical holding, caressing, eye contact, skin-to-skin contact, and nurturing is to their newborn. Feed your baby the way a nursing mom does, and your baby will achieve the same great emotional benefits.

Nancy R., Ballwin, MO

It's a holdup. I got those four-ounce bottles with the hole in the middle so babies can grab them. My son loved the control of holding his own bottle.

Betsy, NY

Watch for signs of an allergic reaction. Talk to your baby's doctor right away if your baby has excessive gas or diarrhea, is spitting up a great deal or vomiting, or even if he's acting colicky. Among other things, these can all be symptoms associated with an allergic reaction to the formula you're using.

Lori L. Morton, Winnipeg, Manitoba

Switching formula may be best. When our daughter was about six weeks old, she started having extremely loose stools (not quite diarrhea). We tried switching to a soy-based formula, but she refused it. After a visit to her pediatrician, she was diagnosed as being lactose-intolerant, and her doctor recommended a lactose-free, milk-based formula. It took care of the problem.

Donna Schwartz Mills, Los Angeles, CA

Can differ from baby to baby. Intolerance to formula can differ from baby to baby; both of my twin girls came home from the hospital on Similac, which is a cow's-milk-based formula. One had no adverse reaction to it, but the other would immediately become gassy and cry, and her body would become stiff as a board after consuming just an ounce or two. Her pediatrician had us switch to Isomil Soy, a soy-based formula, and she was fine almost immediately.

Laura Witek, Milwaukee, WI

DON'T SWITCH FROM A COW'S-MILK-BASED FORMULA TO SOY, OR
ANY OTHER, WITHOUT FIRST CONSULTING WITH YOUR BABY'S DOC-
TOR.——MJM

The formula is simple: cost versus convenience. While
pregnant with my second child, I did a simple cost comparison
of the various types of formula and found that it comes down
to cost versus convenience. Here's what I found to be the pros
and cons of the most common types of formulas found in the
market:

Ready-to-feed: Four-ounce and six-ounce glass bottles of
formulas are premixed and ready to use. The glass bottles
require only a nipple; the cans require pouring formula into
a bottle. This size formula is just enough for one feeding and
is especially good for when you're on the go. The biggest disadvantage to this option is the high per-ounce cost. Also, it
can be difficult to locate this size in the grocery stores.

Ready-to-mix Powder Packets: Premeasured packets containing enough powder to make one four-ounce or eight-ounce
bottle when mixed with sterilized water. This option requires
no measuring and no scooping. The packets are lightweight
and make for easy toting in the diaper bag, but you have to
bring along your own bottles and water. Also, this single-
serve size has a higher per-ounce cost.

Ready-to-pour: One-quart cans and one-quart reclosable
plastic bottles are ready to pour and require no mixing. The
downside is that the cans can be difficult to travel with because
you have to carry a can opener, and both the cans and bottles require refrigeration for storing leftover formula. Also,
the cases (and you *will* be buying cases) are heavy and bulky.

Concentrated Liquid (or Ready-to-mix): Thirteen-ounce cans (makes twenty-six ounces when mixed with water). A more economical option, but requires mixing with sterilized water (though still less work than scooping and mixing powder). Once mixed, it makes enough formula to fill several bottles.

Ready-to-mix Powder: Economical fourteen-ounce, one-pound, and two-pound cans. This is by far the least expensive formula option, and it allows you to mix enough formula to fill bottle requirements for a two-day period. This option is convenient for traveling, too, since you can tote the can or take a quantity of powder in a smaller plastic container (just be sure to pack the scoop). The biggest disadvantage of ready-to-mix powder formula is that it is time-intensive, requiring you to measure the powder and mix with sterilized water. It takes some mixing effort to get the powder dissolved properly, too; if you mix it in baby's bottle by shaking it, unmixed powder can clog the nipple.

All things considered—particularly spoilage and cost—I think that the large cans of powder formula are still the best option.

Tammy W., Anchorage, AK

YOU CAN BUY ONE OF THOSE GIZMOS THAT WILL ALLOW YOU TO PREMEASURE FOUR OR MORE SERVINGS, THEN POUR THE POWDER INTO A BOTTLE WHEN IT'S TIME TO MIX IT.—MJM

Add more formula than needed. Put one ounce of formula more in baby's bottle than what you think he will eat. This way, you won't have to wonder if baby has had enough—he will stop eating when he's full and not when his bottle is empty.

Jean Capps, Cuyahoga Falls, OH

🐾 Baby-Club Memberships

Here are three national infant formula companies that offer toll-free numbers and Web sites for product information, home delivery, hard-to-find specialty products (such as two-ounce preemie formula bottles and other specialty formulas), and baby-club memberships that include periodic mailings and valuable coupons:

ROSS PRODUCTS (SIMILAC, ISOMIL, ALIMENTUM)
 Product information: www.ross.com, or 800-227-5767
  Similac: www.similac.com
  Isomil: www.isomil.com
Home Delivery: www.rosstore.com, or 800-FORMULA
The Welcome Addition Club: www.welcomeaddition.com, or 800-232-7677 for information regarding membership and 800-BABYLINE for enrollment.

MEAD JOHNSON (ENFAMIL)
 Product information/home delivery: www.enfamil.com, or 800-BABY123
Enfamil Family Beginnings Club: same as above

NESTLÉ/CARNATION (GOOD START, ALSOY)
 Product information/home delivery: www.verybestbaby.com, or 800-811-7500
The Very Best Baby Magazine for coupons: same as above 🐾

Baby knows when he's had enough. I agree, it's best to let baby eat as much as he wants to, but at the same time, allow baby to decide when he's had enough. If he decides to eat less than the amount in his bottle, then so be it—if you push him to finish his bottle, he may soon become overweight.

Paula, West Dundee, IL

Don't forget to burp. Even when using the best bottles on the market, some air will still get into baby's tummy when feeding. Burping her every few ounces (or half bottle) will relieve her of excess gas and the feeling of fullness, and she'll finish more bottle.

Kimberly Cushman, West Windsor, NJ

Less gas with disposable liners. I chose to use Playtex bottles with disposable liners because less air gets in baby's tummy, and as a result, baby has less gas. Also, there's less preparation and cleanup time involved; the bags are presterilized and tossed when baby is finished eating.

Laurie Dickan, Carmel, NY

Feeds from any angle. The other advantage to using bottles with disposable liners is that the baby can easily get the milk out regardless of how she holds the bottle.

Sheryl McCarthy, North Stonington, CT

Fill bottles the night before. I found that tears are spared if you prepare morning bottles the night before. This sounds simple enough, but every time I forgot to do it—or was too sleepy—I regretted it because it started an otherwise wonderful day with tears of anticipation and hunger.

Francine deFay, Rochester, NY

Discard unused formula. Be sure to use formula within an hour, or bacteria will grow rapidly. Your baby is new and so is his immune system, so it's better not to take any chances; after all, it's much less expensive to throw away unused formula than it is to treat a sick baby.

Ann Wells, San Diego, CA

Drying rack keeps it organized. A bottle-drying rack is a must for drying and/or storing bottles after they're washed. It keeps the bottles organized and within arm's reach of the sink.

An empty diaper-wipes container is great for storing the nipples and rings.

Dana

Milk can harm baby. It's important that you don't introduce whole (or *any*) milk too soon, which usually means not until baby is twelve months old. Babies under one year have an immature intestinal tract and can be harmed by ingesting whole milk. If you feel you need to give your baby milk earlier than one year, talk to your doctor first.

Amy Black, Hopewell, VA

✒ Why Cow's Milk Is Harmful to Baby

According to the AAP, although milk-based infant formulas are made with cow's milk, it is significantly altered to be digestible and safe for baby. Substituting regular cow's milk for formula, or giving baby cow's milk any time in the first year, can result in serious harm and improper nourishment. Here's why:

• Cow's milk contains too much sodium and protein, causing stress to an infant's intestines and kidneys, which can result in dehydration. The protein produces large curds that aren't digestible in baby's stomach and irritates the lining of the stomach. It can also lead to blood loss into baby's stools.

• Cow's milk lacks the proper amounts of vitamin C and iron that baby requires.

• Cow's milk can cause an allergic reaction.

• Cow's milk may be deficient in fat, which is crucial for baby's brain development and daily caloric requirements; in fact, fat makes up a full 50 percent of the calories in breast milk and infant formulas. ✒

Making Nighttime Feedings Easier

Coffeemaker warms bottles faster. I found the best way to heat a bottle at night was to use a coffeemaker. Before going to bed, I would fill the coffeepot with water but not turn it on. When baby woke up for a feeding, I would first go to the kitchen and switch on the coffeemaker, then go to my son's room to tend to his wet diaper. When the hot water was ready, I would pour it from the coffeepot into a tall thermal mug, then place the bottle in the mug. It only takes about a minute for the formula to warm. I liked using this method, as it was fast and hot water heats bottles more evenly than a microwave oven.

Lori L. Morton, Winnipeg, Manitoba

Crock-Pot works, too. I did the same thing with a Crock-Pot: I put water in the Crock-Pot before going to bed, then left it on the low setting all night. When one of my twins woke up, I would place the bottle in the water and it was warm in no time.

Kyra S. Miller, Floral City, FL

Bottle warmer most convenient. Even easier than fumbling around the kitchen in the middle of the night when you haven't slept in days is to keep an electric bottle warmer in the nursery. A bottle warmer will keep bottles cold until you're ready to heat them, and heating time takes less than two minutes. Having everything in the nursery with the baby is definitely the best way to go.

Dawn M. Casella, Westland, MI

Try using room-temperature bottles. I used room-temperature water in my baby's bottles. Before bed, I prepared one bottle with premeasured powder formula and one bottle with the correct amount of water; I kept both bottles close to the bed.

When my daughter woke, I would simply pour the water into the formula bottle, shake, and voilà!, the bottle was ready.

Jenny Plakio, Belen, NM

Prevent baby-bottle tooth decay. Never let the baby sleep with a bottle filled with milk, juice, or any liquid other than water in his mouth—it deposits debris on baby's teeth, which can cause tooth decay.

Katherine W. Manning-Pinotti, Houston, TX

Traveling and Bottle-feeding

Ready-to-feed cans easiest. Use the small, ready-to-feed cans of formula for traveling; they're a bit more expensive, but you can't beat the convenience and time saving.

Lisa Locher, Kensington, MD

Bottle warmer for car. I traveled with my son a lot in the car and carried premixed formula in bottles, storing them in an insulated bag with an ice pack. I bought a portable bottle warmer that plugged into the adapter in the car—it was great for on-the-go feeding!

Letha Fullbright, Malvern, AR

Thermos keeps water warm. My friend gave me the best travel tip when bottle-feeding: Carry a thermos filled with warm water and bottles with premeasured dry formula in them, then simply mix as needed.

Faren

Room-temperature bottles for traveling. I did the reverse and found it worked great: Pour the correct amount of room-temperature water into your bottles, then place the correct amount of scoops of formula into a Ziploc bag. When baby is ready to eat, scoop the formula into the bottle and shake. This not only serves the same purpose in eliminating the need to heat a cold bottle, it also eliminates the need to carry a thermal container.

Wendy Love Warfel, Crofton, MD

Stash extra. *Always* pack an extra bottle or can of formula when traveling. There will be times when you'll need it, and you'll be glad you did.

Tracy Murtagh, Long Island, NY

Tote your own drinking water. If you are unsure about the quality of the water at your destination or at stops along the way, bring along a gallon of purified drinking water for mixing with formula.

Rachel Martinez, Dededo, Guam

Weaning to a Cup

Don't offer juice in a bottle. Weaning will be much easier if you make it a habit to give your baby formula in bottles only, and strictly limit it to mealtimes. Put juice and water in sippy cups. If you don't do this, your baby will become dependent on the bottle as a source of security, and you'll find it even harder to wean him from it later. I learned this lesson the hard way with my first son—I gave him juice in a bottle for drinking during the day and at nighttime, and he would continually wake up throughout the night wanting his juice. This continued until he was two years old, and you can imagine how soaked his clothes would get after a night of drinking juice!

Carrie Massier, Airdrie, Alberta

NOT TO MENTION THAT JUICE ISN'T GOOD FOR BABY'S TEETH.—MJM

Cup tastes better to baby. When I weaned my children off of their bottles, I put only water in their bottles, and juice and milk in cups. They eventually chose to drink out of a cup instead of the bottle.

Lori Duncan, Yukon, OK

Leave yourself no choice but to succeed. When we were weaning our kids to a cup, we just did it cold turkey. We tried for many months to wean them gradually, but they never would accept the cup, so one day I just threw all of the bottles away! Because I gave myself no other choice, it worked.

Lara Joudrey, London, Ontario

Make it easy. Start with an easy-sip cup—the kind that doesn't contain a stopper at the opening. It's messier, but baby will catch on faster, and it's less frustrating than the spill-proof style.

Maria Lorena Maples, Odenton, MD

The no-mess method. Teach baby to drink from a cup in the bathtub; then there's no mess.

Diane, Jersey City, NJ

Don't buy twice. Buy only the spill-proof cups, but remove the rubber stopper; the cup will then be easy for baby to sip, and after she masters it, you can put the stopper back in to make it spill-proof.

Angie Wright, Charleston, OR

Wean *before* sibling arrives. If you find yourself expecting your second baby close to the first one, try to wean your first baby from the bottle before number two is born. On our first daughter's first birthday, we took her bottle away; our second child was born five days later. After the new baby comes home, you'll find it's much harder to wean for quite some time.

Patty Kartchner, Dayton, OR

CHAPTER 3

"And Now Introducing...Solids!"
— ✿ —
Baby's First Foods

Everyone seems to have their own opinion about when a baby can be started on solid foods. I have a friend who, after listening to my litany of complaints about the difficulties of having a newborn at home and getting too little sleep, suggested that I give my baby cereal in his bottle. She told me that she had done it with her baby at just two weeks and that it made him sleep longer at night. She went on to say that it was what her own mother did with her as a baby, and she "turned out all right." I have to admit, I contemplated following her advice: *Why not?* I thought. *I badly need more sleep at night, and what harm can come from giving my baby a little rice cereal?*

But after discussing the issue with my son's pediatrician, I learned that a baby's immature digestive system is simply not developed enough to process solid foods until sometime between the fourth and sixth months. Introducing them too early can trigger an allergic reaction. Furthermore, babies don't lose their tongue-thrust reflex, which causes them to reject solid substances placed on their tongue, until they're several months old. His doctor added that the idea of enlarging the hole of the bottle to get cereal into my baby's stomach was simply unacceptable (except in the case of a baby with special medical needs with the doctor's okay), and can lead to overeating and obesity in later years. So I followed his advice and waited until my son seemed ready to try cereal, which turned out to be in his fifth month.

You might find that your baby is ready for her first taste of solid foods (usually rice cereal, since it's easily digested and has a low risk of allergic reaction) as early as four months, or as late as six months, or older. Some breast-fed babies do not show an interest in solid foods until around the eight-month mark. You'll know when your baby is ready by her cues: Her feedings will become more frequent, you'll find that she consumes more breast milk or formula at each feeding, and she will readily lean her body toward food that she sees. It will help the first few times you attempt to feed your baby solids if you give her some breast milk or formula first, so she's not overly hungry and impatient. Also, she'll take to cereal more quickly if you thin it (with extra water, breast milk, or formula) until it's an almost runny consistency. It will take a few "practice" sessions before your baby masters eating solids, and they'll be messy ones at that. If you find that your baby rejects her first foods—turning her head, pulling back with her body, choking, or crying—it's best not to force the issue but rather wait a couple of weeks and then try again.

Moms who've dealt with the challenges of first foods pass along helpful hints on introducing solids, some of their own baby's favorite first foods, money-saving hints, preparing baby food at home, recommendations and safety tips on high chairs, feeding the self-feeder, aiming baby and toddler toward a healthy diet, and keeping messiness to a minimum.

First Foods

Go slow with cereal. Be *very* careful when introducing rice cereal—it tends to constipate a lot of babies. Start by giving baby a few ounces of breast milk or formula, then just a small amount of diluted cereal (don't expect baby to consume much; she may eat only one tablespoon or less of cereal a day in the beginning). If baby does become slightly constipated, giving her a few ounces of water during the day will help ease it.

Stephanie L. Becker, Traverse City, MI

Breast-fed babies may want solids later. Breast-fed babies may begin solids much later than formula-fed babies. It isn't necessary to start solid foods until after six months or even later. My daughter didn't show any interest in solids until nearly a year.

Jen Berger, Schaumburg, IL

Got water? Don't make my mistake; start your baby on water before it's too late! I didn't, and now she hates it. I have to force water into my daughter, who has severe constipation.

Cindy, Long Island, NY

No added iron for nursing babies. Nursing moms shouldn't give their babies cereal with added iron for the first six months, as it can inhibit the absorption of iron in breast milk.

Sarah L. Turner-Keeter, CA

Gauge baby's interest level. If your child seems to need more than breast milk or formula, and can sit up and reach for foods, then it's probably time to start solids. My breast-fed daughter wasn't interested in any food until she was nine months old; we gave her food right from our plates. My son, on

---

✒ Save with Baby-Food-Company Memberships

Laura Witek of Milwaukee, Wisconsin, gives us this money-saving tip:

Join baby-food companies' coupon clubs—membership is free and you'll receive periodic mailings and dollar-off coupons:

GERBER

Join the My Gerber Club (www.gerber.com, or 800-4-GERBER) and receive valuable information and coupons.

BEECHNUT

The Beechnut Label Saver offer (www.beechnut.com, or 800-BEECH-NUT) lets moms exchange labels for dollar-off coupons. Also, save the proofs-of-purchase from baby-food jars to get freebies or discounts on merchandise.

HEINZ

Heinz USA (www.heinz.com, or 800-872-2229) offers their *Heinz Feeding Booklet* free to new moms, which contains helpful information and introductory coupons. ✒

the other hand, showed an interest in food early, so we gave him cereal and baby food in a jar until he was a bit older and could handle table foods.

Tori Fugate, Asheville, NC

"Star bites." The transition from milk or formula to solid foods can be difficult because baby is used to getting the food in a constant flow, and having to wait between small bites can be frustrating. I found that spoon-feeding my baby as quickly as possible helped ease the frustration, as did creating a distraction overhead. I used a colorful, musical star that I would shake in between bites. It distracted my son just long enough for me to get in the next spoonful.

Tracy Murtagh, Long Island, NY

Fruits or veggies first? My son was a reluctant eater, so we tried sweeter fruits first. My daughter was born to be a chow-hound, so we gave her veggies first, which a lot of kids don't like as much.

Elizabeth, New York City

Busy hands at mealtime. Many babies will refuse to try new foods. I give my son a spoon and bowl to play with at mealtime; not only does it serve as a distraction while I feed him, but it keeps his hands busy so he can't interfere with the feeding.

Heather Petit, Newark, DE

Let baby help, too. Let baby help with her feedings; load up one spoon for her to use to feed herself while you feed her with the other spoon.

Elizabeth Vroom, Leiden, The Netherlands

Spoon trio. One for him, one for you, and one emergency backup when baby throws his on the floor.

Joanne, NY

One new food at a time. Introduce only *one* new baby food at a time, and wait one week before trying another new food. By doing this, your baby's tummy will better adjust to digesting the new food, and enough time will have passed if an allergic reaction were to occur. Food allergies usually show up soon after eating and may take the form of a rash, red bottom, diarrhea, or vomiting. I didn't know to do this, and I ended up with a real mess on my hands and a baby who was in a lot of pain. My daughter would eat, then projectile-vomit; this continued until she was ten months old, at which time her pediatrician finally figured out that it was a food allergy. We had to start her food cycle all over again—beginning with stage-one foods—introducing each new food one at a time.

Amy Black, Hopewell, VA

Safe feeding. When feeding baby, never feed directly from the baby-food jar because you'll contaminate the leftover food in the jar with bacteria from the saliva on baby's spoon. Instead, spoon only the portion you think you'll need into a bowl and return the jar to the refrigerator.

Ann Wells, San Diego, CA

Babies happy with homemade foods, too. Don't bother with baby food in jars. My children never ate it; not because I am a purist, but because they liked eating whatever the rest of the family was eating. You don't even have to puree the food, just mash it with a fork.

Nancy Burton-Vulovic, Toronto

There's no argument, it saves you money. Make your own baby food in a food processor—it's easier, healthier, and less costly. Why pay $.69 or more for two ounces of bananas in a jar when you can mash a banana yourself for a fraction of the cost?

Jen Berger, Schaumburg, IL

Easy on-the-go feeding. Making your own baby food is a breeze. Just cook or steam your vegetables and fruits until soft, then puree them and place in ice-cube trays. When the food is frozen, empty the cubes into plastic freezer bags and return the bag to the freezer. Now baby's meals away from home are cheap and easy. Place the frozen food cubes in a plastic container with a lid and you're ready to go; the food will thaw while you're out and baby gets a nutritious, homemade meal.

Barbara Legan, Riverside, IL

Take advantage of novelty. My baby was so thrilled to be eating solids that I got him used to tofu, yogurt, and other healthy food super-early. Fussier toddlers might balk at those foods if you don't introduce them.

Elizabeth, New York City

Papaya/banana slush is a treat for baby. I boiled chicken, peas, and carrots and blended them with some water. When my son was able to handle a bit more texture, I added cooked pasta to the mix. He also loved papaya with banana (which is also good for moving poopies through after eating too much rice cereal!). I microwaved the papaya (cut in strips with the skin on) with a little water in a bowl covered with plastic wrap (pull a corner back to vent) for about four or five minutes. Then I peeled off the skin and threw it in the blender along with a banana. It makes a great ice-cream alternative if you let it thaw until just slushy; or add apple juice for a nondairy smoothie.

Stephanie L. Becker, Traverse City, MI

Let baby set the pace. Remember that a full baby is a happy baby! Don't worry about overfeeding—when he's no longer hungry, he'll stop eating.

Christine Clark, Manahawkin, NJ

Try, try again . . . Don't assume that if your baby rejects a food once that she will always reject it—offer it again in a month. Favorite foods change frequently!

Kaleigh Donnelly, Memphis, TN

Frozen mixed vegetables are quicker. As a mom of quadruplets, I have to save time in the kitchen when I can. Rather than prepare different kinds of vegetables one at a time, meal after meal, I use this shortcut: I place a pack of frozen vegetables in the steamer and steam until soft, then puree it. This makes a good-size batch of vegetables and provides a load of nutrients and vitamins.

Gabriella Marshall, Houston, TX

High Chairs

"You get what you pay for." When it comes to high chairs, you get what you pay for. Your infant may not move much at all, but as your baby grows, he'll start to squirm and hang over the side. The cheaper ones have legs that are too thin and tend to tip more easily; also, they have less padding in the seat (and you'll find that if baby isn't comfortable, he won't sit for long). Look for overall sturdiness in a high chair—one that will withstand a lot of abuse. Also, the tray, seat, and legs should be easy to clean; if the chair contains too many folds and creases, food will pool and be harder to clean.

Sue Menna, Coastesville, PA

One-handy. When you're out shopping, look for high chairs with trays you can take on and off with one hand. You'll usually have one arm full with your baby.

Betsy, White Plains, NY

High-chair safety. Make sure your child's high chair has a wide, sturdy base and a seat belt that is relatively easy for you to buckle—then make it a habit to *use it every time*. Before you know it, your baby will be an active toddler and will be standing up or falling out of the high chair.

Paula, West Dundee, IL

Don't buy twice! We bought the reclining three-stage feeding seat by The First Years; it was a nice alternative to a high chair in that it attached to our kitchen-table chairs, saving space in the kitchen. In addition, it had a press-and-slide reclining feature that allowed us to feed our infant son at the table. It also converted to an upright high chair and a toddler booster seat.

Kelly Weaver, Aurora, CO

Get even more for your money. We wanted more value for our high-chair money. We invested in the Phases high chair by Evenflo. As the name implies, it follows the phases of your baby's development: It's an infant feeding seat, booster chair, youth chair, and even converts into a toddler table-and-chair set. We will get years of use out of this high chair.

Laura Witek, Milwaukee, WI

The Peg Perego high chair is the best! It folds up, so you can take it when you travel, and it is absolutely safe.

Cindy B., Island Park, NY

Feeding the Self-feeders

Caution: baby at work. Don't worry about the mess . . . baby is learning! I give my daughter chunks of avocado, banana, cheese, cooked spaghetti noodles with sauce, and scrambled eggs, and I let her feed herself. She eats until she's full, then she experiments with her food using her hands and fingers; squishing, smearing, and moving it around. Food is a great learning tool!

Angela J. Byrnes, Stanford, CA

✒ *Choking and Suffocation*

American Heart Association (www.americanheart.org, or 800-242-8721)

Choking and suffocation are among the most common causes of preventable death in children younger than one year. The most common objects that choke, strangle, or suffocate children are:

- Food items, such as hot dogs, grapes, nuts, popcorn, and hard candy
- Formula, milk, or juice can cause choking if these liquids are given to an infant who is lying down, especially from a propped bottle
- Toys and parts of toys that are small enough to place in the mouth. Uninflated balloons or pieces of balloons are frequent causes of choking and can be particularly hard to remove
- A variety of other small items like coins, marbles, buttons, beads, and safety pins
- Drapery and extension cords
- Plastic bags
- Cords from which toys and objects such as rattles, pacifiers, and jewelry are hung around the child's neck

Reproduced with permission © *Pediatric Basic Life Support,* 1997 Copyright American Heart Association   ✒

No food on the go. I took a baby-safety course, and our instructor told us not to give our babies snacks while they're in the stroller. The bumpy ride makes it easier for food to go down the wrong pipe, and since you can't see your baby's face, you might not know she's choking.

Elizabeth R., White Plains, NY

OTHER FOODS THAT CAUSE CHOKING INCLUDE: PEANUT BUTTER, RAW CARROTS, UNCOOKED PEAS, AND OTHER HARD FOODS. HOT DOGS SHOULD FIRST BE CUT LENGTHWISE, THEN LENGTHWISE AGAIN, AND THEN CUT INTO SMALL PIECES.

Cut it smaller! When in doubt, cut it smaller! My child choked one time, and that was enough to scare me for life.

Ann Wells, San Diego, CA

YOU CAN PURCHASE A "CHOKE TUBE" (A CYLINDER THAT SHOWS YOU WHAT SIZE OBJECTS ARE CHOKING HAZARDS) FOR A COUPLE OF DOLLARS OR LESS FROM MOST DISCOUNT RETAILERS, BABY STORES, HARDWARE STORES, OR CHILD-SAFETY CATALOGS. USE IT TO BE SURE YOUR BABY GETS PORTIONS OF A SAFE SIZE. IN ADDITION, HONEY, CHOCOLATE, EGG WHITES, FISH, AND NUTS ARE CONSIDERED TO BE HIGH-ALLERGY OR BACTERIA RISKS AND SHOULD NOT BE GIVEN TO BABIES IN THE FIRST YEAR.——MJM

Think fresh and natural. If you make your own baby food, don't salt or season it—salt and seasonings are an acquired taste, and one that baby has not developed. Also, canned vegetables and other packaged foods made for older kids and adults should not be fed to babies, as they contain high amounts of sodium and preservatives. Instead, boil chicken without added salt or broth, then grind it up—your baby will love it. Do vegetables the same way.

Daylle Schwartz, NY

Look at weekly consumption. Babies will not allow themselves to starve, so try not to get overly stressed when it seems as though your toddler isn't eating enough to keep a bug alive. At this age, children tend to eat more at one meal than another, so look at the amount of food he's eaten over the course of a week, rather than one day—you'll probably find that he's eating an adequate amount of calories after all.

Francine deFay, Rochester, NY

Make every bite count. Pushing your baby to eat more at mealtimes only discourages her from eating and trying new foods. Your child may begin to view eating as a negative experience. I'm going through this now with one of my twin girls; she is on the small side and doesn't eat as much as her sister. I've stopped trying to force her to eat larger quantities and instead offer foods that are high-calorie, high-fat, and high-protein. That way, she's getting the maximum benefit even when she eats small amounts.

Laura Witek, Milwaukee, WI

Aiming Toward a Healthy Diet

Offer healthier alternatives. Don't allow your baby to fill up on carbohydrates, sweets, or too much fruit juice between meals. If you do, you'll find that she'll eat less at mealtime, and her once-balanced diet will slowly become *un*balanced. Instead, offer healthy snacks, like fruit, cheese, vegetables, yogurt, and small pieces of sliced meat, and give her water or vegetable juice to drink. If your toddler insists on fruit juice throughout the day, dilute it by 50 percent.

Lee Firlus, Marietta, GA

Babies love variety. My daughter mostly "grazes" all day, so I place an ice-cube tray on her little table with all kinds of good things for her to eat: pretzels, cheese cubes, raisins, tiny pieces of turkey, commercial meat sticks, small bits of apple, banana, and strawberry, and so forth.

Amy Lanhardt, Orange, CA

Home-cooked goodness. A healthy diet for baby is easy to achieve with a little preplanning. Avoid overly processed foods such as hot dogs, canned pastas, and "fast food"; instead, make home-cooked meals ahead of time and freeze in small portions so that you will always have healthy foods on hand.

Allison DeWitt, Jacksonville, FL

Vegetable blends taste good. I had difficulty getting my daughter to eat vegetables. Then I learned a few "tricks" which worked beautifully: Pureed carrots can be added to spaghetti sauce; pureed sweet potatoes added to a fruit smoothie are

always a big hit; pureed cauliflower hides well in mashed potatoes. The same thing applies with fruit: Instead of candy, I gave
my daughter finely cut-up (soft) dried fruits; and I substituted
pureed fruit for jelly on bread.

Julie Zmerzlikar, Pacifica, CA

"Out of sight, out of mind." Minimize struggles of will by
keeping snacks out of sight, out of mind. Rather than trying to
explain to a ten-month-old why having a cookie before dinner
is inappropriate, keep the cookie jar in the cupboard.

Angela Harrison Miskimen, Bryan, TX

Give baby a small amount of juice. Juice can be introduced
at about four months but should be given only in small amounts
(two to four ounces per day) to ensure that it does not interfere
with the consumption of other foods, breast milk, formula, or
water. Two books that are great feeding and nutrition sources
are: *Feeding Your Child for Lifelong Health,* by Susan B. Roberts, and
Feed Me! I'm Yours, by Vicki Lansky.

Allison DeWitt, Jacksonville, FL

Keeping Messiness to a Minimum

T-bib. My son got to an age where he refused to wear bibs. We
found that oversized T-shirts were very effective and harder for
him to remove.

Kelly A. Foster, Tacoma, WA

Try this best bib "recipe." The best and most inexpensive
bibs were invented by a mother who raised seven children. Give
the instructions to Grandmom, who is more likely to have time
to make up a couple dozen for you. Here's what you do: Buy
packages of inexpensive kitchen towels, fold each in half, cut

a little crescent for the neckline, and finish the neckline with double-fold bias tape, including about five inches on each side of the neckline for a tie. They're a nice size and absorbent, too. After feeding baby, rinse the bib clean and use it to wipe baby's face, then throw it in the laundry.

Jane A. Zanca, Atlanta, GA

Head-to-toe coverage! I made full-body bibs out of vinyl tablecloths and sewed cuffs for my babies' arms to slide into. It sure made cleanup a lot easier! For the self-feeders, I bought the clear plastic carpet runners and placed them underneath the high chair.

Dawn M. Brus, Marion, IA

A clean catch. A truly useful bib I would recommend is a molded plastic one with deep pockets; it catches most of what baby drops and can be washed right in the sink. You can find it at most baby stores.

Kimberly Cushman, West Windsor, NJ

All-nude food revue. Sometimes we fed our baby in the tub. We'd sit her naked in her bath ring, let her make a huge mess while eating, then fill the tub and play some more in the water.

Betty, NY

Clean floors with a just a flick of a switch. As the mother of twins, to keep up with the messiness at mealtime (and keep a little sanity, too!), I purchased a Dustbuster Wet and Dry Vac. I have it hanging close to the high chairs and use it several times a day. Like the name says, it sucks up wet and dry messes and leaves the floor clean again.

Darcy McMahon, Midland, MI

Saves on laundry. We stripped off our son's clothes during mealtime and let him eat in his diaper—if he ended up with food all over his body, a wet cloth or a bath would take care of it. We also found that giving him small portions of food at a time helped; larger portions seemed to overwhelm him and cause him to play more than eat.

Tina Golden, Coldwater, MS

Tablecloth for easy cleanup. Buy a large square or round tablecloth and place it under the high chair. You can wipe it clean, or wait until the food dries, then sweep it or shake the food off.

Valerie S. Turner, PA

Shower curtains do double duty. I saw a vinyl floor covering for under the high chair in one of the baby catalogues. I used my old shower-curtain liner instead to save a few bucks. I toss it in the wash every few days.

Beth, New York City

Baby wipes save laundry time. Keep a box of pop-up-style wipes in the kitchen; it's easier and less work to clean up messy babies with a disposable wipe than dirtying and washing six washcloths a day.

Darcy McMahon, Midland, MI

CHAPTER 4

No More Tears
❧
Coping with Crying and Colic

Normal Crying

You probably know to expect your newborn to cry periodically throughout the day and night; after all, crying is the only means of "communication" your infant has of letting you know when he's hungry, in need of a diaper change, is too hot or too cold, overstimulated, overly tired, or in need of a cuddle. What you probably don't realize, though, is that your baby may communicate for a total of four hours or more a day! You may do everything you possibly can to comfort him yet find that he continues to cry and cry. The fact is, some babies cry more than others; crying relieves tension, which is why, many times, a baby will have a crying spell and then fall peacefully asleep. Whatever the reason for baby's cries, one thing is for sure, moms just aren't programmed to tune it out. What's a frazzled mommy to do?

Begin with a visit to your baby's doctor to rule out a medical problem. Barring that, you'll find lots of helpful techniques in this chapter to console a fussy baby. Try a number of different things to see which your baby responds to best. By responding to his cries now, by consistently and promptly meeting his needs, his crying will lessen in the months to come. Over time, he will come to feel more secure in his surroundings and will begin communicating in other ways to have his needs met. And don't forget to do what is necessary to relieve your own stress, too. An infant's crying, combined with your readjusting hormones, can make you feel as if you're being pushed to the edge. It's at times like this that you should seek reinforcements: Call your mom, a friend, your spouse—anyone—so you can step back, take a walk or warm bath, and collect yourself. You are not a bad mom if you feel frustrated because baby won't stop crying; on the contrary, you're a good mom who wants her baby to be comfortable and contented.

The first half of this chapter addresses normal crying, while the second half tackles the tortures of colic. Read on as moms who've been in the trenches impart dozens of useful tips for quieting baby, as well as the pros and cons of using a pacifier.

Picking up a crying baby won't spoil her. New moms shouldn't hesitate to pick up their crying newborn every time he cries. It won't "spoil the child"; rather, it builds trust and helps baby to feel secure in his strange—and sometimes scary—new world. A mother of seven children once told me that someone had advised her to just let her baby cry and he would eventually stop crying. "This is true," she replied. "But the baby stops crying only because he's learned that his cries will not be answered." That's a sad way for a helpless little person to feel, don't you think?

Deana Manganello, Commerce TWP, MI

"If I had it to do over . . ." I didn't pick up my son each time he cried. I was given "help" from a friend's mother who suggested I allow my baby to cry for twenty minutes in his playpen before picking him up, and if he didn't cry, to leave him there for one hour—she said this would build independence. My baby always seemed to stop crying at nineteen minutes and fifty-nine seconds, and I cried in the other room because I couldn't pick him up. Now, as a fifteen-year-old, he *is* independent, but if I had it to do over, I'd never do that to the little guy again.

Deb, Lititz, PA

Peekaboo, I'm here with you. Keep in mind that a baby cries out of loneliness, too. Peekaboo games are great for teaching "Just because you can't see me does not mean I am gone . . . I am here and you are not alone."

Michelle Pool, Red Oak, TX

Frequent breast-feeding may help. Try nursing whenever baby is fussy; often a baby is unsettled because he is being nursed only once every three or four hours. Breast milk digests in as little as twenty minutes, so babies can be hungry again within an hour or two.

Gaye Ward, Queensland, Australia

Deep breath in . . . deep breath out. An infant picks up on your emotions—trying to soothe a baby while you are frustrated and tense is an impossible task. Relax yourself first, and baby will follow your lead.

Lorrie

Take a breather. Don't be afraid to just put your crying baby in a safe place and go into the other room for a few minutes so you can get your sanity back!

Marie M. Bassili, Tucson, AZ

Swaddling quiets baby. Try swaddling your crying baby in a thin receiving blanket, keeping his arms close to his body. This mimics the close confines of the womb and makes baby feel more secure and calm.

PoLee Mark-Yee, Kirkland, Quebec

Vibrating bouncy chair hushes baby. Get a battery-operated, vibrating bouncy chair. It is priceless for soothing a cranky baby, especially during the times that you need to be doing other things. The vibration is calming to baby, and the chair easily carried from room to room. We set ours near the table at dinnertime so we could once again enjoy a family meal together.

Debra S. Fair, Waltham, MA

Exersaucer keeps baby busy. The Exersaucer was a godsend. It has a stationary base and a bouncy, swiveling seat. The interactive and musical toys (and snacks in the snack tray) keep baby entertained long enough for you to get something done around the house.

Michelle Coady, Daytona Beach, FL

Getting back to the basics. One mistake we made with our restless baby was to overstimulate him. My husband and I played with him all the time—always flashing some kind of award-winning infant-learning tool in front of him. We didn't know that our baby would have much rather had a soothing walk, or a little song sung softly to him, rather than a video of flying shapes and talking puppets.

Dawn M. Oliveri, Saunderstown, RI

Quieter surroundings are comforting. Sometimes a baby senses when mom is upset or when there is tension within the household. So look around when baby is extremely fussy and see if the environment can be made to be more soothing. Perhaps taking baby away from the stimulus can help her cope, as well as turning the lights down low, playing soft music, lighting the fireplace, and turning off the television.

Sue Coffman, Orange, CA

The eyes have it. Babies can't tell us if they've had enough. Watch your baby's eyes. If she constantly looks away, she may be saying she's overstimulated.

Liza, NY

It's worked for generations. I am a mother of twins, and I would tell new moms to get a good rocking chair. When my babies cry and I don't know what is wrong, I put them in my lap and rock . . . and sometimes cry with them.

Dina Dell Odom, Andalusia, AL

Hair dryer quiets fussy baby. The only thing that worked for us was the noise from the hair dryer—we went through a couple of them in the first two months!

Sheryl McCarthy, North Stonington, CT

Blow it. When our son was in a crying jag, we blew gently in his face. He'd be so surprised, he'd stop!

Joan, NY

Mommy's heartbeat is reassuring. Babies loved to be held and touched. To calm my crying babies, I would rock them or sway back and forth in a standing position and sing to them. Also, placing their heads on my bare chest gave them skin-to-skin contact, and they could hear their mommy's heartbeat—this was reassuring to them.

Michelle Vittum, Garfield, NJ

"Hush little baby . . ." A baby can't listen and cry at the same time, so break the crying cycle by talking or singing softly in baby's ear, and then keep it going. Eventually, he will forget why he was crying in the first place.

Sue Menna, Coatesville, PA

Rotating rattles. The white noise of a shaking rattle would stop our son's tears—but after a week, he'd get used to it and we'd have to find a new "miracle rattle." Keep a bunch on hand.

Joanne, NY

Try *wearing* baby. I wore my daughter in a sling, which seemed to cure a lot of her crying. A sling simulates the same comfort babies felt in the womb, and they maintain a quiet, alert state throughout the day. With less crying, babies are able to take in more of their environment, and mothers are better able to meet their immediate needs. Get a sling and you'll soon find that you have a happier, less fussy baby.

Amy Lanhardt, Orange, CA

Music soothes the soul. We find that soothing music always helps, and it doesn't matter what the category—almost any kind of soft country, rock, pop, classical, or lullaby works. Two of my daughter's favorites are: *Sleepy Time Songs* (Children's Book-of-the-Month Club), and *Sweet Dreams Classical Themes* (Designer Music Group).

Nancy Ablao, Kalamazoo, MI

Nature-made. Nature music—like ocean sounds, babbling creek, birds, flute, or Native American music—is calming, too. Most nature stores carry this kind of music, as well as most record stores (look in the specialty-music section).

Donna M. Condida, Archbald, PA

Be a baby librarian. Our daughter responded to rhythmical "shushing." We'd walk her up and down going "Shh, shh . . . shh, shh, shh" and patting her back. She'd go out like a light.

Betsy, White Plains, NY

White noise has a calming effect. White-noise tapes work great; my baby would stop crying and go right to sleep. If you have a tape recorder, you can make your own tape by recording static from the radio or TV, or by turning a fan on high and recording the humming sound.

Amy Allred, Woodstock, GA

Try soft lighting. My four-month-old sleeps better with a night-light on and his radio tuned to static.

Paula, West Dundee, IL

Burping relieves gas. A lot of times I found that my baby's stomach discomforts were caused by trapped gas. To relieve the gas—and get a good burp out of him—I would *firmly* pat and rub from the bottom of his spine *upward;* this pushed the gas bubbles up and out.

Sandie Fitzgerald, Lakeville, MN

None for me, thanks. Tummy problems lead to cries of pain, which can be avoided altogether by not giving your newborn *any* cereal. Too often, we listen to the generation that fed infants cereal at just two weeks, but today we know that an infant's stomach is not built to digest even the simplest cereals.

Debra Z. Ackley, Hammondsport, NY

More, please! I agree that most infants should not be given cereal, but some babies are bigger—and hungrier—than most. My son weighed ten pounds, three ounces at birth and was twenty-four inches long; he cried off and on for the majority of his first six weeks of life. I was breast-feeding every two hours, around the clock. After six weeks, and three separate discussions with our pediatrician on the subject, she suggested that we offer him diluted cereal in a bottle. It did the trick, and his crying quickly subsided. As our doctor told us, some babies are the exception to the rule.

Elizabeth Palmer Hale, Lorraine, Quebec

Pacifier Pros and Cons

It's surprising that such a small comfort aid like a pacifier can create so much controversy. If you choose to give your baby a pacifier, you may find that well-meaning friends and family members may become quite vocal in expressing their opinion— or even their strong objection—to its use. You may be told that a pacifier hurts a baby, becomes a crutch for the parents, looks bad, interferes with feedings, or is a poor substitute for parental attention.

On the contrary, the American Academy of Pediatrics reports that, when offered on a limited basis and used only for non-nutritive sucking (when you are sure that baby is not hungry), a pacifier does not cause any medical or psychological problems. In fact, a pacifier can be quite effective for comforting a fussy or crying baby after feeding, if the fussiness or crying is due to your baby's desire to continue sucking. Here's what other moms have to say about pacifier use:

Provides comfort and security. Anything that can provide the comfort and security that a pacifier does can't be all that bad. As long as you don't abuse it—using it only as a temporary substitute when you're tied up—I think it's okay.

Crystal Byrd, Deer Park, TX

Pacifies Mom, too! The way I looked at it, pacifiers calmed my daughter, which in turn kept me calm and functioning better, and *that* was good for her.

Daylle Schwartz, NY

Pacify now, pay later. If you don't start it, you won't have to stop it! Think twice before you decide to give your baby a pacifier.

Tracy R. Smith, Jackson, TN

If it's not one, it's the other! Both of my twin girls were pree-mies and were sent home from the hospital with pacifiers to help build up their muscles used for eating. Shortly thereafter, one dropped the pacifier and instead found her finger. In the beginning, the finger-sucking baby was easiest: no crying in the middle of the night, in search of a missing Binky. On the other hand, now that the "Binky Fairy" has come and gone, my finger-sucking child *still* sucks her finger.

Kathie Dell'Arciprete, Tewksbury, MA

Satisfies baby's need to suck. I'd recommend a pacifier to new moms for quieting a crying baby, as long as they are positive that the baby is not hungry. I swore I wouldn't use one, but our little boy sucked on everything, and I couldn't be a *human* pacifier!

Angie Wright, Charleston, OR

Try another style. My son wanted to breast-feed night and day. We wanted to use a pacifier but found he did not like the orthodontic-style pacifier we tried to give him. We thought he was rejecting the pacifier, but he was actually rejecting the *type* of pacifier; when we tried the one with the round nipple, he loved it.

Meghan Collins, Chelmsford, MA

Wouldn't use a pacifier again. We gave our daughter a pacifier for the first three months, but I don't think I'd use one again. I did some soul-searching and realized that I gave it to her for *my* convenience, not necessarily because she needed it. All she really needed was a diaper change, bottle, lullaby tape, or some extra snuggling.

Lisa

More work for Mom at night. I loved my daughter's pacifiers; she really loved to suck, and they kept her happy. However, I would caution moms against giving their baby a pacifier for falling asleep at night; if you do, and the pacifier falls out in the middle of the night, guess who gets to get up and put it back into her mouth?

Wendy R., Tooele, UT

"I'll have a case, please." If you're going the pacifier route, don't buy just a few, buy a dozen so that you'll have plenty on hand, plus a few more to stash for emergencies. Believe me, you'll be glad you did!

Kathy Thirtyacre, Richland, WA

Limit pacifier use for easier weaning. Try to limit pacifiers to naps and bedtime by baby's first birthday. That way, it will be easier to wean him from it by age two.

Paula, West Dundee, IL

Colic

I was exasperated: Just three weeks earlier, I had given birth to my second son—sweet and cuddly and perfectly contented when held in my arms. If he cried at all, the crying would quickly subside with a diaper change and a feeding. Then, beginning in about his third week—and persisting for ten *long* weeks—came the nightly doses of colic. His normal crying and fussiness would build and build throughout the day until they became screeches, lasting for several hours almost without pause. He looked as if he was in extreme pain and torment; his tiny face would turn crimson red, and his body would scrunch up and shake uncontrollably. From the first cry, every maternal instinct I had would go on alert, but I was at a complete loss as to how to relieve his suffering.

About 20 percent of all babies will develop colic in the first month of life. The inconsolable crying usually occurs in the late-afternoon or early-evening hours, lasting until midnight or even through the night in some cases—robbing you of valuable rest time at the end of an already exhausting day. If you believe your infant suffers from colic, begin with a visit to your baby's pediatrician to rule out other medical conditions. Unfortunately, when the diagnosis is colic, you'll find little comfort in the fact that there is no known cure, nor even an acceptable medical explanation. Widely held theories include: an immature digestive tract which can cause severe gas pains; food sensitivities in the mother's breast milk; allergies related to formula; and overstimulation in baby's environment. Colicky babies usually reach their "colic peak" at about six weeks of age, and colic usually disappears completely by the fourth or fifth month.

In this section, moms who've lived through colic talk about their own experiences with colicky babies and how it affected them and their families; share techniques for consoling baby; suggest useful equipment on the market, as well as helpful household items; and offer important advice on some ways you can reduce stress before it takes its toll on you and your spouse.

Baby prefers the night shift. Colic was hell! Our baby would scream from around four P.M. until midnight, and then was wide awake and raring to go until five A.M.! My husband and I had to eat—gulp!—our meals in shifts while the other tried to comfort the baby, mostly by walking her around the house for hours on end. We found that we couldn't take her out because of her screaming and felt trapped in our own home.

Angela

"I felt terribly alone." Colic was horrific. I had a newborn and a sixteen-month-old, and the baby cried constantly—starting up around noon and lasting until six A.M. the next morning. It caused a strain between my husband and me, and because I held the baby so much, it caused my older son to be jealous. My husband's mother could not understand why I couldn't calm the baby. I was nearly out of my mind with lack of sleep, and I felt terribly alone handling this problem.

Jenn Millington, Brampton, Ontario

A new face can be a soothing distraction. Colic was two and a half months of pure agony: nonstop crying for hours on end, and sleepless nights for my husband and me. It caused me so much stress—I thought I was a rotten parent and that the baby didn't like our house! Then I discovered that when my mother came to visit, my daughter would calm down. My mother would rock and sing to our daughter—like I would do—and for some reason the baby would stop crying for my mother, but not for me. It seemed a fresh face was all it took.

Daphne Castor, Mililani, HI

Time for a shift change. When faced with a colicky infant, you really do need help from other people. If you don't have family nearby, recruit your partner, friend, or neighbor to watch baby during the most difficult times. A shared colicky baby is only half as bad. Take that time to do something to relieve your stress: Take a walk, lie down, do a chore, or visit your local coffee shop for a decaf.

Peta Gjedsted, Perth, Western Australia

Take ten. Remember, when you get frustrated, put the baby down! I've always been thoroughly disgusted by any parent who would hit, shake, or hurt their child in anger. Then, after listening to my six-week-old daughter cry for five hours straight, I found myself ready to shake her—I wanted to do *something* to get her attention so that she would stop crying. Luckily, I put her down in time and was able to cool off. Until you're facing it, you don't realize how distressing constant crying can be.

Kathryn Hennessy, Simpsonville, SC

"But, Doc, you've just gotta do *something*." My baby's colic began in his second week. We took him to the pediatrician five times in four weeks trying to find an answer; it's hard to accept that there is no explanation or cure. Now, at three months old, he is growing out of it like everyone said he would. I can't say that any of the remedies we tried worked—they just made us feel better for trying them. We never found a miracle cure, only a baby swing!

Catherine Rouse, Las Vegas, NV

Hardwired to cry. We had a hard time; our son had colic for four months, and I wanted to throttle all the experts who told us it would peak at six weeks and end in three months. It wasn't allergies or gas; our son was just very intense. Ten years later, he still is. The cliché holds true: "This too shall pass."

Elsa, NY

Walking (a lot!) worked. After a long day of work, my husband was treated to our daughter crying every night, from about seven till ten P.M. We were both tired, and at the end of a long day with her, I was depressed. The only thing we found that worked was to walk, and walk, and walk, and . . . well, you get the idea.

Diane, Jersey City, NJ

"And there's the Big Dipper . . ." If you can't go for a long walk, scoop up your baby in your arms and take her outside, even if it's just in the backyard. The fresh air and nighttime "noise" was a soothing distraction for my daughter.

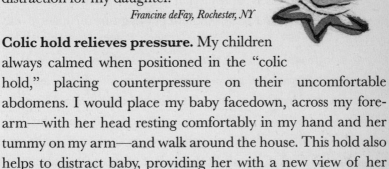

Francine deFay, Rochester, NY

Colic hold relieves pressure. My children always calmed when positioned in the "colic hold," placing counterpressure on their uncomfortable abdomens. I would place my baby facedown, across my forearm—with her head resting comfortably in my hand and her tummy on my arm—and walk around the house. This hold also helps to distract baby, providing her with a new view of her surroundings.

Susan Sarnello-Harrison, Itasca, IL

Try a gym ball. The one thing that really saved my sanity with my colicky daughter was a large gym ball. I would throw a towel in the dryer to warm it up, then drape it over the ball. Then I laid my baby on her tummy on top of the ball and gently rocked her back and forth—it worked almost every time. You can also hold your baby and gently "bounce" on the ball.

Dawn M. Brus, Marion, IA

"Hold the pepperoni, Mom!" Experiment with your diet if you're breast-feeding; the culprit could be the foods you're eating. Avoid gassy foods like garlic, onions, and broccoli, as well as spicy foods and caffeine. If you're using formula, ask your baby's doctor about switching to soy or a hypoallergenic formula—it may offer some relief.

Debra S. Fair, Waltham, MA

Try putting dairy foods on hold. Mommy eating *any* dairy turned out to be our biggest culprit. Once I cut out the dairy, things went a lot smoother.

Heather, British Columbia

Cut out the food sensitivity and cut out the gas. For me, it was vitamin C, wheat, and chocolate. After I cut these out of my diet, I found that my son did not get as gassy.

Jeanette, Burnaby, British Columbia

Cleans your carpeting at the same time. Run the vacuum! I rocked and carried my crying baby for hours before I learned this trick. My mother-in-law was visiting one day and began vacuuming; just like *that,* the crying stopped. Off went the vacuum, on went the tears; on went the vacuum, off went the tears. We ate a lot of meals in those days with the vacuum running, but it was worth it!

Amy L. Burrell, Sharon Hill, PA

Burp early, burp often. I know it's hard to save any energy for burping baby after the effort of feeding, but it really gets those gas bubbles out. Five minutes of burping could save hours of crying.

Johanna, White Plains, NY

Extended play. If you don't want to burn out the motor on your vacuum over and over again, just do what I did: Record the vacuum cleaner on a ninety-minute tape. It saved my life! My daughter never slept; she was up all day and all night. Then I placed the tape recorder by the head of her bed. When she would start to fuss after I had put her down, I would sneak into her room on my hands and knees so she wouldn't see me, and reach up and start the tape. It would buy me at least another hour and a half of sleep time.

R.M.S.

Dries tears, too. My son was colicky for about three months. I found that laying him on a fluffy towel atop the clothes dryer while it was running kept him warm and calm and even put him to sleep.

Alysha Goodsell, Brighton, MI

KEEP YOUR HAND ON BABY SO HE WON'T ROLL OFF.—MJM

Peppermint—a natural gas reliever. Try essence of peppermint . . . yes, the oil! You can buy it in a health-food store. Peppermint is a natural soother—helps to eliminate gas bubbles in baby's tummy and tastes good, too. Just take a toothpick and dip it into the oil, then swish the toothpick around in your baby's four-ounce bottle of water. If you can't find the oil, use a round peppermint candy and dip it in warm water a few times.

Kelly Bathke, Colfax, CA

Take a drive. My husband and I would take long scenic drives in the afternoons on the weekends. Our colicky son would almost always sleep in the car, allowing us some much-needed time to talk and relax. It really helped us deal with our very beautiful—but very loud—son.

Carol M Smith, Williamsburg, VA

Heating pad helps hurt tummy. Try wrapping a heating pad in a towel and placing it on your chest. Position baby's tummy on top of the towel and gently rub his back. The heat will help his hurt tummy to feel better, and the close physical contact will make him feel more secure.

Hsiu-chen Lin Classon, Streamwood, IL

Rubs me the right way. Infant massage was a lifesaver for our colicky baby. The class was offered by the local hospital's parents program and was taught by a certified massage therapist. The therapist played soft classical music in class and used only natural lighting. After laying my daughter on a soft blanket, I would rub almond oil on my hands and massage her. The best time to do massage at home was an hour before the colic would start, which for me was about six P.M. I found it *very* helpful; it taught us both to relax and was a wonderful quality time for us each day.

Sonya Kasen, Jenison, MI

"Chiropractor worked wonders . . ." I am an NICU nurse and found that taking my baby to a chiropractor worked wonders. However, you need to find someone who's really qualified in his or her field and who treats infants on a regular basis; my baby's chiropractor has twenty-one years of experience in treating infants and pregnant women. She treats colic by palpating a baby's spine from the neck to the sacrum to "feel" which areas are out of alignment, then adjusts them back to their proper position. Each part of the spine affects different areas of the body. The thoracic area affects digestion and, when adjusted, relieves the colic. Check with your baby's pediatrician first, but be aware that medical doctors may not believe in this type of treatment, as they may feel that the research is not academic enough. All I know is it worked great for me.

Carrie Massier, Airdrie, Alberta

Sound sleep with gas drops. My daughter was waking up with gas in the middle of the night. I've since discovered simethicone drops (I like the Mylicon Drops brand)—0.3 milliliters after her final feeding and she sleeps soundly through the night. Hard to believe that something so small can make such a *huge* difference!

Sally Rowan, Baltimore, MD

Generic-brand gas drops save money. Buy the generic brand of infant gas drops; it contains the same ingredients but costs half the price.

Paula, West Dundee, IL

Colic tablets helpful. One homeopathic remedy that made a world of difference in relieving our colicky baby was Hyland's Colic Tablets—they've been around for generations and are 100 percent natural. You can find them at health stores, like GNC, as well as most large discount retailers, like Wal-Mart.

Tina Golden, Coldwater, MS

Chamomile soothes naturally. Try using chamomile drops or weakened chamomile tea. Chamomile is a natural herb that soothes and relaxes the senses. I grow my own in my garden and love sharing it with new moms. You can also purchase the drops in health-food stores and the tea in most grocery stores.

Laura Heinzel, Ketchikan, AK

Fennel tea works, too. I used a family favorite for calming all three of my children when they were babies: fennel tea. You can purchase fennel tea bags from most health-food stores, as well as drugstores. I'm not sure why it works, but fennel is an herb that has been known to calm upset tummies for many generations. I would prepare it the same as I would prepare a regular cup of tea, except I diluted it by adding twice as much water, making it weak enough for baby. Then I would allow it to cool before giving baby an ounce or two (older babies and toddlers can have two to four ounces). I was never quite sure if it was the fennel or the warm liquid that would relax all three of my babies' tummies, but it did make them feel better, and they would eventually pass gas bubbles, either through burps or toots!

Alexia Weber, South Lyon, MI

Caution: JUST BECAUSE SOMETHING IS HERBAL OR NATURAL DOESN'T MEAN IT'S SAFE, SO ACT ON THE SIDE OF CAUTION. ASK YOUR DOCTOR BEFORE YOU TRY ANY HERBAL OR NATURAL REMEDY.—MJM

Roll away colic. My daughter had only a mild case of colic, which my husband would help relieve by making what he called a "roll." He rolled up a blanket, then laid our daughter over it on her stomach. For some reason, it worked—she always seemed to calm down.

D. Walker, San Diego, CA

"Kneesies" get rid of excess gas. A friend who survived colic with her three babies showed me how to do kneesies, an exercise that helps baby expel excess gas: Lay baby on her back and hold her legs together by the back of the calves. Bend baby's legs up toward the tummy on the left side, roll her legs across to the right side, and then straighten them out. Repeat as often as necessary. This exercise helps move the gas in baby's tummy—as the colon moves from the left side to the right— and push out the gas. I did this with my daughter and found that I would get a string of toots out of her and she was much happier.

Angela

Finding support on the Web. Our baby developed colic around six weeks of age; she would cry uncontrollably for two or three hours during the day and again in the evening. To make matters worse, other people would say things like: "What's wrong with her? My baby doesn't cry like that" and "She sounds hurt." It got to the point, if other people were around, I would take the baby into another room. I would recommend that new moms with colicky infants get positive support where they can find it. I found that the colic message boards on the Internet were a good place to commiserate with others going through it. Some good ones are: Parentsoup (www. parentsoup.com), Family (www.family.com), StorkNet (www. storknet.org), and the Labor of Love (www.thelaboroflove.com).

Faren

Don't stop loving the ones around you . . . My best advice to other moms facing colic is this: Don't stop loving the ones around you, because when it ends—and it *will* end—hurtful words and raised voices will have a lasting effect. It seems that all my two-year-old daughter heard in our household during her baby brother's colic period was yelling and screaming between Dad and Mom—we took our frustrations out on each other to relieve the stress. My daughter screamed and yelled at my husband and her baby brother for quite some time after that and took even longer before she began loving her brother again . . . it's guilt I've had to live with for two years. If you find yourself facing a similar situation, please seek a friend, counselor, or anyone else you can think of to help you and your whole family through the colic months.

Brenda Antonich, Superior, WI

CHAPTER 5

To All a Good Night
Helping Baby Sleep

It's one of the most frequently heard complaints by new moms: *I just can't get enough sleep!* Unless you've lived through it, it's hard to fully understand the depth of a new mom's sleep deprivation or even comprehend why mom isn't sleeping enough when a newborn sleeps for an average of fourteen to sixteen hours a day. The problem isn't so much the number of hours baby sleeps, but a newborn's sleep pattern and round-the-clock feeding requirements that so directly affects mom's sleep. Your baby's sleep cycle in the early weeks will be whatever it was for the past nine months, which means waking off and on throughout the day and night. And just as she was unable to distinguish between day and night in the womb, she still won't be able to after birth. The other problem is related to your baby's size, or more correctly the size of her stomach. An infant's stomach is too small to hold more than a few ounces of breast milk or formula at each feeding; therefore, hunger will arouse her every two or three hours.

Fortunately, time and encouragement from you will solve both problems over the weeks and months to come. For the first few weeks, there is little you can or should do to affect baby's sleeping pattern. Your newborn will need nourishment every couple of hours and should be allowed to sleep when she wants for as long as she wants—this will help her transition more smoothly from the womb to the outside world. After the first month, however, you can do plenty to foster more favorable sleeping habits. Begin by limiting your baby's daytime naps to no more than three or four hours, and allow her to sleep in the natural light and noise of the day. Be sure to provide plenty of daytime stimulation, too, like playing, singing, reading, stroller rides, and visits to friends and family. At night, make your visits as calm and unstimulating as possible: Keep the lights low, don't play with baby, change wet or soiled diapers in the crib, and promptly return baby to the crib following her feedings. This will help encourage her to sleep longer at night. As your baby continues to grow and her stomach becomes bigger, she'll gain the capacity to hold larger quantities of breast milk or formula, and she'll be sustained for longer periods of time.

Read on as veteran moms talk about the best places for baby to sleep, cultivating good sleep habits while steering clear of the bad ones, getting baby back to sleep after waking at night, baby sleep aids that really work, sleeping tips for the older baby, and establishing a sound napping schedule.

Best Places for Baby to Sleep

Cozy comfort. Newborns like sleeping in small, cozy spaces— try a bassinet or cradle for the first few weeks.

PoLee Mark-Yee, Kirkland, Quebec

Sound sleeping for baby and Mom. Position the bassinet or cradle next to your own bed for the first month or two; not only does the baby sleep better, but you will, too. It will give you peace of mind knowing that your baby is safe in the room with you, and it makes nighttime feedings easier—you hardly even have to wake up.

Lori Peters, PA

Get a better night's sleep. Having your baby in a crib or bassinet next to you as a newborn is fine, but after a couple of months, I would advise moms to get the baby out of your room. When my daughter slept in our room, she would wake up every hour and a half during the night, but as soon as I put her in her own room, she began sleeping for longer periods of time.

Anonymous

Long-distance listening. A baby monitor gave us peace of mind, although sometimes I caught myself straining to hear every one of my baby's breaths. Sometimes it helped to mute the sound and let the light bars let us know if the baby was awake or crying. Ask your pediatrician what he or she thinks of baby monitors.

Elizabeth, New York City

Side bed is handy. There's something on the market I would recommend called a "side bed," which connects to the parents' bed and is the same height. This allows your baby to be only an arm's reach away.

Lauren McMenimen, Tempe, AZ

You're the expert. I got so sick of people insisting we should move the baby in or out of a bassinet, crib, or parents' bedroom on a predetermined schedule. Who knows what your baby will need? You do!

Ann, NY

Encouraging Sleep

Swaddling helps baby feel secure. My second baby was a nightmare to get to sleep, then my mother-in-law came up with a routine that worked like a dream. Every night we would take a big terry-cloth towel and swaddle her tightly, making sure she couldn't get her legs free (otherwise, she would kick and scoot until she woke herself up). Then, we played classical music that had a great deal of violin. She would whimper or cry for only about five minutes, then fall fast asleep.

Tonya K. McCartney, Wilmington, NC

Lullaby and good night. With my newborn, I found that singing put him peacefully to sleep. I would give him his bottle in our favorite chair and then sing to him as he ate; by the time he finished his bottle, he was asleep.

Kimberly Cushman, West Windsor, NJ

Keep it strictly business. Keep a night-light on in the hallway so that you don't have to turn on a light in the nursery. Make your nighttime visits with baby as low-key as possible, so that she doesn't associate them with attention; don't hold, hug, or kiss the baby. If she has a wet diaper, change her in the crib. She'll soon learn that when it's dark, it's time to sleep.

Daylle Schwartz, NY

Soft landing. In the first few months, make sure baby's mattress is placed in the highest position, so that you are able to gently put baby down—not drop him—into his crib. This will keep a sleeping baby from waking up.

Angela Dove, Singapore

JUST BE SURE TO LOWER THE MATTRESS AS BABY GROWS. I FORGOT TO DO THIS WITH MY SECOND SON AND HE FLUNG HIMSELF OVER THE SIDE OF HIS CRIB HEADFIRST!—MJM

Diaper-change first. For nighttime feedings, change baby's diaper *before* feedings, so that when he's full and begins to fall asleep, he won't be woken up again by the interruption.

Nancy Wilson, Abilene, TX

Drawstring gowns are quick and easy. Dress baby in gowns with drawstrings for bedtime. Don't put him in anything with snaps. The last thing you'll be coordinated enough to do after a middle-of-the-night diaper change is resnap in the right order.

R.M.S.

Layering bedding saves laundry. Babies tend to spit up a lot, and as a mom of twins, I found that I constantly had to change their sheets—this was especially difficult at night because the light would wake them. Then I started layering my twin's bedding: sheet, blanket, sheet, blanket. When the bedding was wet, I would simply pull the first layer off; the bedding underneath remained dry, and my babies stayed asleep.

Kyra S. Miller, Floral City, FL

Vibration lulls baby to sleep. If your baby is particularly gassy, like mine was, try a vibrating bouncer chair, allowing baby to sleep in a semiupright position. I found the bouncer would take the pressure off of my daughter's back, making her stomach feel better. I used it for about two weeks and then she was fine in her crib. I highly recommend the Fisher-Price Deluxe Soothing Bouncer—it worked great!

Laura Witek, Milwaukee, WI

It's worked for generations. I'm a mom of eight children, and I did it the old-fashioned way—I nursed or rocked each of my babies to sleep. I loved it and so did they. Now that they're too old to be rocked, I miss it. I wonder if they do, too.

Jana McCarthy, Lake Forest, CA

Music lulls baby back to sleep. Musical crib toys worked well for my son. Try to find one that's sound-activated, playing soft music when baby starts to cry.

Michelle Coady, Daytona Beach, FL

Good vibrations. A handy tool for new moms is a crib vibrator. We found that our baby would fall asleep easily in her vibrating bouncy chair, but when we moved her to the crib, she would wake up. Then we found the crib vibrator—it clips directly onto the bedding and gently vibrates baby to sleep.

Deborah Baska, Kansas City, MO

Nature sounds are soothing. Here's a good way to get a newborn to sleep: Buy an inexpensive sound machine that plays peaceful sounds like the ocean, a light rain, a rushing stream, or white noise—there's even one that mimics a mother's heartbeat. It's a soothing way for a tired mommy to get to sleep, too. If $19.99 is too steep a price for the machine, buy a $2 tape from a baby store with only the heartbeat sound.

Sarah, Owensboro, KY

Low lighting is best for nursery. Keep a night-light on in the baby's room, or use low wattage (25-watt) bulbs for night feedings. Also, run a humidifier in the winter; it will keep the air moist, while the constant humming will lull baby to sleep.

PoLee Mark-Yee, Kirkland, Quebec

Limit the baby swing to early months. Allowing your newborn to fall asleep in the baby swing is fine, but don't let it continue past five or six months of age, otherwise baby will rely on the swaying motion to sleep (and what will you do when baby's too big for the swing?).

Laura Witek, Milwaukee, WI

Night rider. Possibly the worst advice I ever received on helping my infant fall asleep came from a pediatrician who was speaking to the prenatal class I attended. She informed the class that babies often fall asleep in their car seats, so if baby just won't go to sleep, try taking her for a ride. So we tried it. Although this method did work for a few days, our daughter soon lost the ability to comfort herself to sleep altogether. We found ourselves with a twelve-month-old who needed to be driven around in order to take a nap or go down for the night—we probably put an additional ten thousand miles on the car that year! We finally realized just how ridiculous we were being when, while on vacation with all three of our children, we ordered everyone out of our hotel room and into the car at two A.M. just to get our daughter back to sleep.

Susan Sarnello-Harrison, Itasca, IL

Right from the start. Put baby to bed drowsy but not quite asleep. That way, she'll learn to put herself to sleep, and you'll be giving her a gift that will last a lifetime.

Judy Fleck, Tigard, OR

Teach baby to calm herself. In the early months, when our daughter cried at night, I would pick her up right away; after I swaddled her on my chest and rocked her, she would calm down. Then, starting at about four months, I would let her fuss for a minute in her crib—never crying hard—before picking her up. She is now nine months old and has learned to put herself back to sleep with no crying.

Laurie Dickan, Carmel, NY

Be firm about sleep schedule. Babies should start forming a regular sleep pattern at about four to five months, and by six months, you should be able to lay baby down to fall asleep on her own. With three girls fairly close in age, I went through various methods of "sleep training," and I learned that each child can be taught to sleep, no matter what the circumstances. What's important is that you're firm about it. I did not lull my girls to sleep—when it was time to nap, or sleep for the night, I put them down and walked out.

Tina Pavich, Noblesville, IN

Breast-fed babies feed more frequently. As new parents, we felt cheated after listening to other new parents tell us that their babies slept through the night at three to six months of age. If you're breast-feeding, do *not* expect your baby to sleep through the night at such a young age—breast milk does not stay with the baby as long or digest as quickly as with formula-fed babies. Our breast-fed baby did not sleep through the night until she was fourteen months old, and this is not unusual.

Elizabeth Vroom, Leiden, The Netherlands

THERE'S A WIDE VARIATION IN WHEN BABIES ARE READY TO SLEEP THROUGH THE NIGHT.—MJM

Consistency is the key. Routine, routine, routine. Whatever you do, be consistent, and your baby will begin to associate the routine with going to sleep. With our two boys, our nightly routine is bath, treat, story, and book on tape.

Jayne Heilman, Lincoln, NE

Wean baby from nighttime feedings. When you feel baby is ready to begin sleeping through the night—around three or four months of age—middle-of-the-night feedings should gradually stop. Taking a bottle throughout the night becomes a habit for baby and not a necessity.

Tina Golden, Coldwater, MS

Three's a happy crowd in the crib. If you have multiples, try putting them to sleep in the same crib. My triplets slept together for the first six months and never seemed to be bothered by one another's wiggling and noises—in fact, they really seemed to enjoy being together. We had a schedule from birth, which is essential for higher multiples; all three babies had a diaper and clothing change (if necessary) at the same time, then to bed to drift off to sleep. As much as I would have liked to rock them and play before sleep time, it wasn't practical, and believe me, with triplets the name of the game is survival!

Stephanie Parrott, Knoxville, TN

Practice preventative measures for SIDS. Sudden Infant Death Syndrome (SIDS) is the number-one cause of death in infants between one week and one year of age. My second son died from SIDS when he was only four months old. I foolishly thought that it was something that happened to "other" people, but now I am one of them. Get educated on how to reduce the risk of SIDS (www.sids-network.org):

1. SIDS occurs most often to babies who are male, premature or low birth weight, or whose mothers smoke, and occurs most often during the winter months.
2. Babies should sleep on their backs for the first few months. Some studies show that babies who sleep on their stomachs do not expel enough carbon dioxide or do not take in enough oxygen.
3. Do not expose baby to cigarette smoke either during pregnancy or after birth.
4. Soft bedding may cause baby to asphyxiate; do not use pillows, thick blankets, comforters, or soft toys in the crib.
5. New research suggests that bed sharing (co-sleeping) may be hazardous. Suffocation may occur by overlying by an adult; also the mattress may be too soft.
6. Dress baby lightly for sleep and cover baby with a thin blanket. Keep the temperature in the room comfortable.
7. Breast-feed for the first few months or more. Many stud-

ies show a relationship between breast-feeding and a lower SIDS risk.

In memory of my beautiful son, Christopher W. Beno, 11/23/97–3/23/98.

Mary K. Beno, WI

YOU'LL FIND PASSIONATE ARGUMENTS FOR AND AGAINST CO-SLEEP-ING. ASK YOUR PEDIATRICIAN FOR ADVICE.—MJM

Sleep and the Older Baby

Don't extend napping time. If your older baby has trouble falling asleep at night or staying asleep during the night, don't overcompensate by allowing him to take additional, or longer, naps during the day (even if it's for *your* benefit); it will only reduce his nighttime sleeping hours even more. By the same token, *no* nap during the day will make him restless at night and affect his sleep pattern, too. Encourage healthy sleep habits by maintaining a sleep routine (bed at the same time each day, using transitional objects, on a full belly, and so forth) while recognizing that the older the baby gets, the less his total required sleep time will be.

Kay Florea, Blanchester, OH

Crib comforts. Many older babies sleep better with a transitional object in the crib. My daughter slept with her favorite lamb; she would cuddle it and suck her thumb until asleep. Some babies have a special blanket or favorite toy. Transitional objects will help reassure and comfort your baby when she's away from you.

Nancy Ablao, Kalamazoo, MI

Comfort baby only in his room. Stand your ground—if you take your crying baby out of his crib once during the night, he will expect you to do it over and over again. I allowed my oldest son to sleep in our bed one time, and he continued it until he was three years old. What a nightmare! I vowed never to make that mistake again. With my second son, I refused to take him out of his crib until morning. He slept through the night at one month of age.

Christine Clark, Manahawkin, NJ

Consistency pays off. Routines are important for naptime. Around four or five months of age, my son started giving me cues that he was tired: rubbing his eyes, becoming fussy, and so forth. I would take him to his crib, kiss him, tuck him in, and walk out. He would fall asleep without a whimper, and he's continued to do so ever since.

Tammie Weidner, Flower Mound, TX

Dr. Ferber's method is effective. We "Ferberized" our son at six months, and it really worked. When he would cry—and we would allow him to cry for about five minutes—we would go into the nursery to reassure him that we were nearby, but did *not* pick him up. Each time he cried, we waited an additional five or ten minutes before going in again; we repeated this until our son stopped crying and went to sleep. After three nights, the crying stopped completely. Although his crying was painful to hear, my son was able to get himself back to sleep, and once asleep, he slept through the night. He was a much happier baby.

Jodi Detjen

THIS BOOK IS *SOLVE YOUR CHILD'S SLEEP PROBLEMS*, BY RICHARD FER-BER, M.D. THIS IS A CONTROVERSIAL APPROACH, BUT LOTS OF MOMS SWEAR BY IT.—MJM

Sometimes it's hardest on the parents. When my first baby was about ten months old and still not consistently sleeping through the night, we finally did the "cry it out" method. It was a difficult decision for us to make; we decided to do this only after we were completely exhausted from getting up throughout the night and were barely able to function during the day. It took several attempts before we finally willed ourselves to not answer her cries. Surprisingly, after only two nights of crying, she began sleeping through till morning.

Deborah Baska, Kansas City, MO

There's no escaping . . . We placed a crib tent over our son's crib starting at about five months—this got him used to having it over him when sleeping and prevented him from climbing out in the middle of the night when he got older. This also lets Mommy and Daddy sleep peacefully, too.

Kimberly Cushman, West Windsor, NJ

Bigger is better. When transitioning from a crib, don't go the toddler-bed route; go directly to a twin bed and use safety rails, or place the mattress on the floor. Toddler beds are too small, and you'll find that your toddler will outgrow it quickly. Also, it's one less transition for your child.

Kelly Weaver, Aurora, CO

Establishing a Napping Schedule

Follow baby's lead on naps. Most infants nap from about nine to eleven A.M. and again from about two to four P.M., with bedtime around seven or eight P.M. When baby begins to stay awake during his morning nap, it's time to go to one nap a day, which can be around noon and last until about three P.M. It's important to try to keep the same schedule each day.

Sue Menna, Coatesville, PA

Babies have different sleep needs. It took us months to realize that our daughter simply needed less sleep than most babies; she rarely went down before ten-thirty P.M. but woke up cheerfully every day at six A.M. We put a safety gate on her door and baby-proofed her room to the max so she could play quietly while we got our son to bed.

Elizabeth, New York City

Prepare for the crankies. Babies can have a few rocky weeks when they're consolidating two nap times into one. Be prepared!

Joan, NY

Put baby in the crib for naps. Unless you want to hold your baby every time she naps, start putting her in her bassinet or crib for naps when she is very young. From the time my daughter was a newborn, I would rock her to sleep and then hold her and watch TV while she slept. What a mistake! Now, at seven months old, she still won't nap unless someone is holding her.

Marie M. Bassili, Tucson, AZ

Get baby accustomed to noise. One tip I would give to moms of newborns on napping during the day is to get the baby accustomed to sleeping through noise. With my firstborn, I tried to keep things as quiet as possible and regretted it later.

We found that we could not have people over to the house because our baby would wake up and stay awake until it was silent again.

Lisa Carlson, Lester Prairie, MN

A NUMBER OF MOTHERS HEARTILY RECOMMEND VACUUMING NEAR A NEW BABY'S CRIB.——MJM

In the still of the night. It also helps to have a different location for baby to sleep during the day than where he sleeps at night. During the day, keep baby in the room where the activity is, teaching him to sleep through noises when everyone else is up. At night, put baby to sleep where it is dark and quiet. This method quickly teaches him the difference between day and night.

Mary Czajkoski, Joliet, IL

Once around the block. If you wish for baby to have a set napping schedule, it isn't hard to establish one: Nurse or bottle-feed baby at the time you want him to fall asleep. If he won't sleep, then take him for a car ride. Do this at the same time for a few days, and the napping time will become established (then stop the car rides).

Kathryn A. Varuzza, New Paltz, NY

You've heard it before . . . One piece of advice: Never, *ever* wake a napping baby (and don't let anyone else either, like a visiting mother-in-law).

Dawn M. Casella, Westland, MI

CHAPTER 6

Scrub-a-dub-dub
Bathing and Skin Care

Bathing

In the beginning, both my firstborn son and I dreaded bath time—I was a nervous new mom and lacked confidence; he was so tiny and seemed so fragile. What I hoped would be a pleasant, relaxing time for us both was anything but tranquil. From the initial immersion into the water—invariably followed by a wail of distress from my son—bath time became a race against the clock. I worked furiously, soaping him down, shampooing his hair, and rinsing. At the time I didn't know that for the first several weeks or more, my baby really didn't need to be bathed in a tub; a simple sponge bath would have been sufficient. But somehow we got through it, and everything seemed right again after the bath. There was nothing sweeter than the sight of my baby wrapped up in a towel, peacefully peering up at me from underneath the hood and smelling wonderfully fresh. A feeding immediately following his bath, and within minutes he was back to sleep in my arms once again!

Although it may be hard to believe the first few times you attempt to bathe your baby, bath time will soon become one of his favorite activities. Your baby will love splashing and playing in the water and will delight in this special time spent with you. You'll find lots of good tips in the first half of this chapter as experienced moms guide you through the bathing process, best bath products to have on hand, the easiest ways to bathe your baby, tips on making bath time go more smoothly, making shampooing less traumatic, and bath safety tips. Be sure to read the second half of the chapter, too, to learn about caring for baby's delicate skin.

Bathing the Newborn

Practice with a baby doll. Bathing a baby for the first time and changing a diaper can be anxiety provoking. Have a relative or friend give you lessons, or buy a baby doll and practice on it. Believe it or not, you will learn a lot from your doll when you go through the motions of undressing, bathing, diapering, swaddling, holding, and so forth. It's one way of reducing stress before the birth.

Sheila Billick, Gillette, WY

Frequent bathing is too drying. Newborns don't need to be bathed daily—two or three times a week is fine. If you bathe him every day, his natural oils will be stripped, leaving his skin too dry. Also, the best time to bathe baby is in the morning, when neither of you is too tired.

Mirka

Easy as 1-2-3. If you're a nervous new mom, relax and write down the bathing steps on a piece of paper, then just follow the list. Have everything you need next to the tub before you run the water:

- Baby bath soap
- Baby shampoo (or use baby soap)
- Two cotton balls
- Two washcloths (ones made especially for babies are softer)
- Hooded towel
- Regular towel to line the baby tub (and prevent slipping)
- A clean diaper and clothes
- Diapering ointment, lotion, and powder (optional)

Start by wiping baby's eyes with cotton balls dipped in clean water (*no* soap) from the inside corner of her eye to the outer corner. One cotton ball per eye, one swipe only. Then, with a wet washcloth, gently wipe baby's face. Next wash baby's body with soap from the neck down and rinse with clean water. Wash baby's hair next, and rinse with the second washcloth soaked in clean water. After the bath, wrap baby in the hooded towel; now he's ready for diapering ointment and lotion.

Berneda Wolfe, Mineral Wells, WV

Prepare a bath bag. I teach baby-care classes, and I suggest to new parents that they prepare a "bath bag" containing all necessary bathing supplies for the baby. Then, whether the parents decide to bathe the baby in the bathroom, kitchen, or wherever, they will have everything necessary. After each bath, the bag should be restocked for the next bath.

Myra Lowrie, Sugar Land, TX

Check the neck. Remember to clean baby's neck twice a day; babies have folds in their necks where milk can accumulate and smell bad. If you're not bathing baby every day, periodically check and clean behind the ears, under the arms, and, if your baby is a girl, in her genital area. Wipe baby clean with a warm washcloth or baby wipes, then apply a small amount of powder or cornstarch.

Faren

Beneath the folds. I have a boy and a girl. You wouldn't believe how much poop can hide under the scrotum or work its way up inside the vulva. Be gentle, but be diligent in cleaning out all those nooks and crannies.

Betty, NY

Sink is the ideal height. I bathed my daughter in the kitchen sink when she was a newborn (after her cord fell off); most of the newborn tubs will fit across the sink, or you can just line the sink with a thick towel. The sink is the perfect height, which was especially helpful since I was recovering from C-section and would have had trouble bending over a tub. The sprayer makes rinsing easy, too.

Heather, British Columbia

No more shivers. To keep baby warm during a sponge bath, wrap her body with a towel, then unwrap only one body part at a time. Wash the head last, then cover it right away.

Sarah L. Turner-Keeter, CA

Bathtub sponges are versatile. I bought a large bathtub sponge and put a towel on it to bathe my daughter. When she graduated to the tub, I used the sponge as a cushion for drying and dressing her.

Natalie Tabet, NM

Use a wrist to test bath water. To test the temperature of baby's bathwater, I would feel it with my wrist. If I couldn't tell what temperature it was—it didn't feel too hot or cold—then I knew it was right.

Maria Lorena Maples, Odenton, MD

Bath thermometer takes the guesswork out. Try a bath thermometer for an accurate bathwater temperature reading; I like the Safety 1st Bath Duck best.

Heather Petit, Newark, DE

❦ Hot-Water Scalding

According to the Consumer Product Safety Commission (CPSC), each year approximately 3,800 injuries and 34 deaths occur in the home due to scalding from excessively hot tap water. The majority of these accidents involve children under the age of five and the elderly. Set your hot-water heater to 120°F and use your wrist and arm (never your hand; your hand is not as sensitive to heat) to test the water before exposing baby. ❦

Big tub pays dividends for Mom, too. I found that the easiest way to bathe my baby when he was small was to put him in the big bathtub with me. He relaxed in my arms and stayed warmer covered with water than he did in his tiny bathtub, where most of his body was exposed to the air. I had more control over him, too. The bonus came when I handed him off to my husband to dress—I got to stay in the tub for a nice relaxing soak!

Carrie Massier, Airdrie, Alberta

Skin-to-skin feels best after bath. Wear a large, roomy bathrobe and, after baby's bath, hold her against your bare skin, wrapping the robe around her—she'll nurse right to sleep.

Anonymous

Dilute bath soap. Add baby bath soap to a bowl of water, rather than directly to the baby's skin. If you dilute the bath soap, it will be easier to rinse and won't dry baby's skin as much. Rinse with a second bowl of clean water.

Stacie L. Bryant, Two Rivers, WI

Bath moisturizer is best for dry skin. If baby has dry skin, don't use baby soaps—they're too drying. Instead, use a moisturizing body wash made for babies with sensitive skin. I really liked the Johnson & Johnson line of sensitive-skin baby bath soaps, shampoos, and lotions.

Heather Allen, Lemon Grove, CA

Number one with pediatricians. Don't spend the money on expensive baby bath soaps; Dove is best—mild and a whole lot cheaper ounce for ounce. They also have a line called Sensitive Skin, which is hypoallergenic and fragrance-free.

Sue Menna, Coatesville, PA

❧ Baby Bath and Skin-Care Products

Johnson & Johnson (www.yourbaby.com, or 800-526-3967) offers a wide array of baby skin-care products under the Johnson's baby-products line. Contact Johnson & Johnson for their free New Parent's Pack, containing information on bathing baby and skin and hair care, as well as free product coupons. ❧

A kinder, gentler bath. I found that the health-food stores offer better baby bath products than the supermarkets. The natural soaps and lotions are gentler on baby's skin and contain fewer dyes, perfumes, and detergents.

Kathryn A. Varuzza, New Paltz, NY

Drip, drip, drip. I always kept a slow stream of water running while I bathed my daughter. The sound seemed to soothe her, and she seemed mesmerized by the sight. Wet, white rain!

Johanna, NY

Castile soap still popular today. I love Dr. Bronner's castile soap—it's still as gentle as ever.

Jen Berger, Schaumburg, IL

Washcloth offers security. Bath time can make a newborn feel vulnerable. A tip my mom gave me for bathing my infant son was to lay a warm, wet washcloth on his torso during bath time. This gentle pressure from the top made him feel more secure—like he did in the womb—and he didn't flail about. It really works!

Ann Wells, San Diego, CA

Thinner foam is better. I recommend buying a baby tub with a thin foam insert, not the thick kind. When the thick foam inserts get wet, the foam located above the water line continues to hold water even after the water gets cold, making the baby cold. The thin foam drains the water much more quickly. My girls hated bath time and would cry from the start until I got rid of the thick foam pad—now they love their bath.

Laura Witek, Milwaukee, WI

Saves an aching back. We put our daughter's bathtub right on her changing table. It's a good height, and we have everything we need right there.

Andrea R. Cartwright, Stuyvesant, NY

EuroBath versatile for bathing. When our baby was ready for a larger bathtub, we used the Primo EuroBath and absolutely loved it! It has a one-piece design that fits inside your family bathtub. One end of the tub has molded "arms" to keep a younger baby from rolling around; the other end of the tub is open, which allows an older baby to sit up for bathing. The best part was that it freed both of my hands for washing baby.

Hsiu-chen Lin Classon, Streamwood, IL

Wet washcloth best for shampooing. When shampooing baby's hair, don't apply shampoo directly to baby's scalp or it will be hard to rinse out. Instead, put a small amount of shampoo on a wet washcloth, and rub baby's head with it. To rinse, tilt baby's head back and use a second wet washcloth squeezing the water from it onto baby's head.

Karen Rudolph Durrie, Calgary, Alberta

Shampoo visor works great. A bathtime "must have" is a shampoo visor (found in any baby-supply store) to keep water and shampoo off of baby's face—it's one of the greatest inventions!

Kathy Murphy, Monsey, NY

Get hubby to help. If you can get hubby to help you bathe baby, take advantage of it. It makes it easier. My husband and I still bathe our son together, and it's a special time for all three of us every day.

Rachel Martinez, Dededo, Guam

Get your morning shower back. I have seven children and teach childbirth classes, and I frequently hear new moms complain that they don't have time to take a relaxing shower in the morning anymore. I tell them taking a morning shower *is* still possible, and here's how: Undress baby and place him in a baby seat lined with a big fluffy towel. Wrap baby with the towel and place him outside the shower on the floor, where he can hear you. Jump in and take a luxurious shower while talking or singing to your baby. When finished with your shower, turn down the water temperature and pressure until it feels like a gentle waterfall. Reach out, slip off baby's towel, and hold him in your arms while showering. When you're done, place baby back in the baby seat and wrap him in the towel; he'll stay warm while you get dressed. If you want your baby to get accustomed to the shower, begin soon after the cord falls off and he'll quickly learn to love it. Older babies who are new to the shower are many times frightened of it, but can still learn to like it over time.

Patty Kartchner, Dayton, OR

BE SURE TO HOLD YOUR BABY SECURELY WHEN SHOWERING; BABIES ARE VERY SLIPPERY WHEN WET!—MJM

Washcloth gloves keep a good grip. Buy a pair of washcloth gloves—they make washing baby in the tub or shower a whole lot easier, and baby is a lot less likely to slip out of your hands.

Kylene Nickerson, Bayfield, CO

Keep baby toasty-warm after bath. To keep your baby warm after the bath, put a heating pad on the changing table, turn it to the medium setting, and lay the baby's towel and jammies on top. After baby's bath, the towel and jammies will be nice and warm.

Angie Wright, Charleston, OR

Never leave baby unattended. Never leave your child unattended in a tub, sink, or anywhere there's water, no matter how quickly you will be returning or how safe you presume baby will be. Let the doorbell or phone ring. If you've forgotten something, let it go. Nothing is worth risking your baby's life, and baby can drown in a minute.

Denise Campbell, North Providence, RI

✒ Drownings in the Home

The CPSC warns that young children can drown in as little as two inches of water. Accidental drowning is the third-leading cause of death for children under five years of age. About a hundred children drown each year in bathtubs; including many children who were sitting in bath seats or bath rings. *Never* leave your baby alone or with a young sibling in a bathtub, even if you are using a bath seat or bath ring. Keep young children out of the bathroom unless you are watching them closely; keep bathroom doors shut and use a door-handle safety cover to prevent children from opening the door. ✒

Empty baby-wipe containers store and organize. Use empty baby-wipe containers for storing baby's bath products—they don't take up much space and stack easily in your bathroom cabinet. Also, I use empty containers to store baby's medicines, thermometers, and other items. Use a marker to write the contents on the outside of the container.

Licia Croft, San Leandro, CA

Bath Time and the Older Baby

Wetter is better. For older babies, bath time is playtime. Like the sign says at our local water park: YOU *WILL* GET WET, YOU *MAY* GET SOAKED! Make it fun and don't rush it—just throw in some toys and enjoy!

Danielle Furr, Belmont, NC

A clear view of your little splasher. If your baby likes to splash, you can reduce the amount of water that ends up on the floor (and you) by buying a clear plastic shower curtain. That way, baby can splash all she wants, and you can still see her.

Laura Gazley, St. Catharines, Ontario

Bath ring props up baby. We use a baby-bath ring in our bathtub when bathing our son—it props him up for easier washing, yet keeps him confined while in the tub. A couple of words of caution, though: Place the ring on the tub bottom and not on a rubber mat. The suction cups won't stick well to the rubber mat. Also, it is crucial to keep a hand on the ring at all times, especially as baby becomes interested in splashing in the water and going after toys. There's a real danger of baby spilling out of the ring, or tipping over completely if the suction cups on the bottom become disengaged.

Lisa Locher, Kensington, MD

Run cold water last. Run the cold water last when giving your baby a bath, for two reasons: One, if the baby happens to touch the spigot, he won't get burned; and two, if the water trickles out of the spigot after the water is shut off, it will be cold and not hot.

Deborah Baska, Kansas City, MO

Cover your faucet. We love those foam-rubber faucet covers; you never have to worry about your baby grabbing a hot faucet or banging his head on the metal.

Beth, New York City

Make your tub nonslip. I was a nervous wreck bathing my daughter. I would tell her to sit down, which she would do for about a second—then she would stand up again and end up slipping. Finally, I bought an extra-long bath mat, so that no matter where she stood, she wouldn't slip. Now bath time is much more pleasant.

Laurie Dickan, Carmel, NY

Skin Care

Baby's skin is delicate and requires tender care, but be careful not to overtreat it. You may be surprised to learn that many pediatricians recommend that moms of infants use no lotions, baby oils, or powders—they're usually not necessary. If you choose to use these products, apply them sparingly. If your baby has dry skin, a true moisturizer, one that adds moisture to the skin—like Lubriderm or Eucerin—is best. Never use adult products on your baby; the chemicals and perfumes in the product can irritate his skin.

Here's what moms have to say who've cared for their own

baby's skin, including umbilical-cord and circumcision care, as well as the best home remedies for treating common skin problems like cradle cap, eczema, and dry skin.

Cord care made easy. If you're squeamish about umbilical-cord care and cringe at the thought of having to handle it, just soak a cotton ball in alcohol and squeeze over the umbilicus. The alcohol will run into the nooks and crannies without your having to touch it.

Cathleen Phelps, Alexandria, VA

Cotton swabs easiest. The little prepackaged alcohol squares that the hospital sends home with you for umbilical-cord care are too small and too hard to use. I found that dipping cotton swabs in alcohol was much easier.

Diane, Jersey City, NJ

Keeping circumcision area clean. I'm a nurse, and after having two girls, I was still nervous about caring for my son's circumcision. New moms should be aware that for a few days the penis will look red and may be swollen; there may be some yellow crusting as well. Some pediatricians direct parents to use petroleum jelly, while others advise using nothing at all. The most important thing is to keep the area as clean as possible; if stool gets on the penis, use soap and water to wipe gently. Also, for both circumcised and uncircumcised boys, gently push back the foreskin (only as far as it freely goes, which may not be much) for cleaning during baby's bath.

Lori L. Smith, NE

Pure and simple is best for sensitive skin. If your baby has delicate skin, try using all unscented, hypoallergenic skin-care products, such as wipes, soaps, and lotions.

Sally Rowan, Baltimore, MD

Generics save money. Buy the generic brand of baby skin-care products—they work as well as the national brands and will save you money.

Lisa Sullivan, Largo, FL

Home remedy for cradle cap. To clear my daughter's cradle cap, my doctor recommended putting olive oil on her scalp and scrubbing it with a soft toothbrush—it cleared up in just two days.

Lee Firlus, Marietta, GA

Baby oil works, too. Just apply baby oil to the scalp and leave it on for fifteen minutes. To avoid messiness, you can place a shower cap on baby's head while waiting. Then comb with a fine-tooth comb and shampoo as usual. Two of my sons had cradle cap, and I can assure you that it *will* go away.

PoLee Mark-Yee, Kirkland, Quebec

Dandruff shampoos irritate baby's scalp. Don't use adult dandruff shampoos on your baby to treat cradle cap. We used one on our daughter and it made her scalp break out; it was too strong for her delicate skin. We ended up slathering her head with baby lotion after her baths and put a cap on her head; that took care of it.

Valerie S. Turner, PA

Preventative treatment for eczema. My son was diagnosed with eczema when he was a baby. Instead of treating outbreaks with cortisone cream, my doctor recommended a preventative treatment: I switched to a soap called Basis and applied Der-masil body lotion every night—both products worked very well. In addition, I used a wonderfully effective lotion called Lanalor on his face, which is an over-the-counter synthetic lanolin lotion (you may find the pharmacist has to order it). This treatment kept my son's eczema under control.

Tracy Murtagh, Long Island, NY

Tea-tree oil for rashes. For minor rashes in the first year, a fifty/fifty mix of tea-tree oil and olive oil works great. You can buy tea-tree oil at health-food stores.

Lisa Troop, Folsom, CA

Mix A&D and baby lotion for driest skin protection. To prevent dry, chafed skin in drier weather, we use a mixture of A&D Original (amber-colored) Ointment and baby lotion on our babies' skin.

Ann Wells, San Diego, CA

Chap Stick soothes chafed skin.
For a baby with dry, red skin from a runny nose or cold, try putting a little Chap Stick on her nose and upper lip. That's what we did and it really soothed our nine-month-old's nose, and allowed us to wipe with notears.

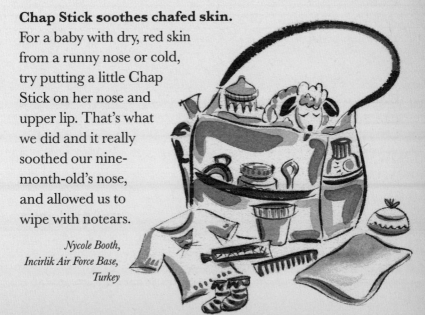

Nycole Booth,
Incirlik Air Force Base,
Turkey

Clipping nails while nursing is a good distraction. I nurse my son on a Boppy pillow, leaving my hands mostly free. As he nurses, I clip the nails on the hand and foot facing me. When I switch breasts, I clip his nails on his other hand and foot. Baby nail clippers are good because they give you lots of control. Once I got the hang of it, I switched to using adult clippers because they're sharper and give a cleaner cut.

Cathleen Phelps, Alexandria, VA

Nails softest after bath. Try clipping baby's nails after she's had a bath, when they're the softest.

Debra S. Fair, Waltham, MA

Clipping's easier when baby's asleep. When my daughter was a newborn, I would wait until she was asleep to clip her nails.

Angela J. Byrnes, Stanford, CA

CHAPTER 7

Bottoms Up!

Diapering, Clothing, and Laundry

Diapering

If you had to guess the number of times you'll be changing your baby's diapers before she's potty-trained, what would you guess? A thousand times? Two thousand times? Would you believe more than *five thousand* times? It's true, and you'll change more diapers in a day (ten or more) when your baby is a newborn than at any other age.

You'll want to investigate your diapering options now, before baby is born, so that you can stock up on diapers and supplies. Take cloth diapers. As you'll hear from other moms, today's cloth diapers are *not* your mother's cloth diapers. There are compelling environmental, financial, and health reasons why cloth diapers at the very least warrant consideration. Disposable diapers, on the other hand, are certainly the fastest, most convenient diapering option and will save you time spent diapering and laundering. Disposables aren't cheap, however— over time they can cost twice or as much as four times as much as cloth diapers. And some studies show that babies are more prone to diaper rash with disposables, since they work almost too well: The higher the absorbency, the drier your baby will feel, even if she is not. And less frequent diaper changes can result in diaper rash.

Diaper rash is a painful rash that leaves baby's bottom red and sore, and sometimes with small bumps. Most babies get diaper rashes sometime within the first year, when baby's skin gets irritated from a wet or soiled diaper left on too long. This is especially true if a soiled diaper is left on all night; the acidity in baby's stools attacks the skin, and makes things worse. Although it isn't necessary to change a wet diaper at night, unless it's soaking clothes or sheets, a soiled diaper should be changed as soon as possible. Diaper rash also commonly occurs in babies being treated with antibiotics or starting solid foods, and as the result of an allergic reaction. It's easier to prevent diaper rash than it is to treat it, and the first step in prevention is to change your baby's wet diapers often—every two to three hours during infancy—and soon after a bowel movement. It's important, too, to wipe baby's bottom clean after each diaper change and, if desired, apply a diapering ointment (ointments containing zinc oxide are most effective) after changing soiled diapers. As one mom points out, "airing out" baby's bottom through the day clears up diaper rash fast, too.

The first half of this chapter contains lots of good diapering tips, including the pros and cons of cloth and disposable diapers, saving money on diapers and supplies, organizing the changing area, and preventing and treating diaper rash. The last half of the chapter addresses clothing and laundry, including making money and saving money on clothing, and some of the best stain removers touted by moms in the know.

Cloth Diapers

Take another look at cloth diapers. When my husband suggested cloth diapers for our expected baby, my jaw almost hit the floor. I was horrified at the thought of cleaning and scrubbing poopy diapers and pricking my baby's lovely skin with pins. But my husband felt strongly about the harmful impact disposable diapers have on the environment, not to mention the high cost. The next day I searched the Web and, to my surprise, found that cloth diapers have come a long way—they now come with plastic snaps or Velcro closures, rather than pins; elastic waist and leg bands to prevent leakage; and biodegradable, flushable liners that keep the poopy cleanup to a minimum. And the cloth diaper covers no longer have to be the old-fashioned plastic pants. My favorite diaper covers are called Air Flow, by Mother-ease—they're made from a breathable, brushed knit fabric and have a laminated waterproof interior and elasticized waist and legs. They also have several snaps along the sides to adjust the fit. We found that once we got the hang of cloth diapers, we really liked using them, and our daughter has never had a diaper rash because it's easy to tell when she's wet and we change her right away. Three of my favorite cloth diapering sites are: Mother-ease (www.mother-ease. com, or 800-416-1475); Kooshies (www.kooshies.com/kushies. html, or 800-841-5330); and Wee Bees (www.weebees.com, or 888-342-7373).

Angela J. Byrnes, Stanford, CA

It's more money in your pocket. You would be surprised at the amount of money you'll save with cloth diapers; we estimate that we save over $1,000 per year over disposables. I use Diaper Service Quality (DSQ) prefolds (flat third-folded diapers; most economical) with a special polar-fleece diaper cover, at a cost of about $22 per dozen. Prefolds are the sturdiest in the wash, and you can use them over and over again. I also use some All-in-One (AIO) diapers—a cloth diaper that combines the diaper and diaper cover. AIO diapers are quite a bit more expensive than prefolds, but still cheaper than disposables. We use them along with a couple of diaper doublers (absorbent liners) for nighttime use and for times when we get a baby-sitter. About the only problem I found with the AIO diapers is that they tend to break down faster in the wash and take longer to dry. I buy all of my diapers and accessories on the Internet. To find dozens of cloth-diaper sites, go to keyword and type "cloth diapers," or visit the extensive cloth-diaper products-review site: Born to Love (www.borntolove.com).

Kimberly Cushman, West Windsor, NJ

AIOs are more user-friendly. I used the Bumkins All-in-One Diapers (www.bumkins.com, or 800-338-7581) for both of my children. Because they were so very easy to use, my husband was willing to go along with using cloth diapers. They work just like disposables, except you place the dirty diapers in a laundry bag instead of the garbage can. I used the disposable diaper inserts for a while, too, but found that it was easier to just scoop out the poop with a baby wipe at the same time I wiped my baby's behind. I kept about twenty-four to thirty-six AIO diapers on hand in each size.

Heidi Sloss, St. Louis, MO

Easy handling of soiled diapers. Handling wet and poopy diapers before wash day is really pretty easy if you have two diaper pails on hand. I kept the one pail in the bathroom for soaking poopy diapers (put cold water in the pail along with a scoop of borax, baking soda, or vinegar); I kept the other pail in the nursery placed near the changing table to hold wet diapers (nothing else is added to the pail).

Lori L. Smith, NE

Diaper Duck makes it easy. A must-have for all cloth-diapering moms is a Diaper Duck. It hangs from the toilet and holds the dirty diaper in the toilet water. When the diaper has been soaking long enough, you just pull one corner of the diaper through the Diaper Duck, and it wrings it out for you. You hardly have to touch a dirty diaper at all. It's great!

Tori

Laundering isn't so hard. Washing cloth diapers is easier than you may think. I own three dozen diapers, so I wash about every six days. I use regular laundry detergent containing no bleach (bleach weakens the cotton fibers); Arm & Hammer baking soda, which neutralizes the alkaline in the urine and removes odors; and vinegar to remove excess detergent.

1. Start the washer on the hottest water temperature and use the two-rinse cycle option.
2. Add one scoop laundry detergent and one scoop baking soda.
3. Place soiled diapers in the washer (the poop previously dumped in the toilet).
4. Fill a fabric-softener ball with vinegar and drop in at the beginning of the wash (if your washer does not have a two-rinse cycle option, you'll still need to rinse the diapers twice; add the ball the second time you rinse).
5. After the wash is complete, place the diapers in the dryer on medium heat (don't use fabric-softener sheets, as they reduce the absorbency of the diapers), or hang in the sun to dry (the sun will take out the stains, too). If you hang

your diapers outside, after they've dried, place them in the dryer for a few minutes to soften them up.

I buy the one-gallon size of vinegar and the ten-pound box of baking soda for less at Sam's Club, a discount warehouse store.

Kimberly Cushman, West Windsor, NJ

Diaper service is most convenient. I found that cloth diapers really aren't hard to use, especially if you have access to a diaper service. The service rents the diapers to you and then comes to your house once a week to pick up the dirty diapers (no rinsing of poopy diapers!), leaving behind a fresh supply. They provide the diaper pails and liners, too. A service is more expensive than if you were to wash your own diapers, but still costs less than using disposables (averaging about $10 to $15 per week). The best part is, unlike moms who use disposables, I never have to worry about last-minute rushes to the store for diapers. Visit the official Internet site for the National Association of Diaper Services (www.diapernet.com, or 610-971-4850) for more information and to locate a service in your area. You can also look in your phone book or a local parenting publication.

Cynthia, Palo Alto, CA

Try using a combination of the two. You can also use a combination of cloth and disposables. With my first two children, I used cloth diapers at home and disposables for outings or when the baby-sitter watched my kids. With my third child, I was working full-time and just didn't have the time to spend on cloth diapers. But even if you primarily use disposables, it's good to have cloth to fall back on for times when money gets tight.

Lori L. Smith, NE

It really works! Place a block of coal in the diaper pail to absorb odor.

Kelly Weaver, Aurora, CO

Keeping baby drier at night. If you do choose to use cloth diapers, I suggest using disposables at night to keep baby drier; otherwise, your baby will most likely get diaper rashes.

D.B.

Disposable Diapers

Disposable diapers are easiest. I vowed that I would be conservative and use only cloth diapers; that was until my newborn pooped and wet for the first time. I used only disposables after that.

Donna M. Condida, Archbald, PA

Stock up before baby's arrival. Since we knew we were having twins, we clipped coupons months ahead of our babies' births and bought a couple of packs of diapers each time we went to the grocery or drugstore. We didn't buy too many newborn sizes, mostly size one and larger sizes. We also bought gift cards from Wal-Mart so that we could buy diapers and clothing after the babies arrived. By the time the twins arrived, we had tons of diapers and over $200 in gift cards. Now that they are five months old, we still haven't had to buy any diapers! Buying diapers and gift cards in advance is a good way to beat the stress of a new baby, since living expenses can skyrocket after he arrives.

Laura Witek, Milwaukee, WI

"Super Bowl Shower" a great idea! Here's another good tip for stocking up on diapers: Host a Super Bowl Shower and have your husband invite all of his male friends and relatives. We hosted one and sent out invitations that indicated that we would supply the food and drinks, and the invitee had to bring one package of diapers (we listed the specific sizes of the diapers we wanted on the invitations). The shower was a great success—the guys had fun watching the Super Bowl, and we netted about thirty packages of diapers!

Laura Witek, Milwaukee, WI

Notch diapers perfect for newborns. Try the disposable diapers made specifically for newborns; they have a notch cut to keep the diaper off of the cord. No more trying to fold the bulky diaper band two or three times.

Ann Wells, San Diego, CA

Moms love Luvs. You don't have to buy the most expensive diapers, especially if you change your baby often. By the same token, don't buy the cheapest brand, either—they tend to leak. Luvs is the brand I found to be the most reasonably priced, and they work as well as the higher-end brands.

Tracy R. Smith, Jackson, TN

Clip 'em, save 'em, trade 'em. Collect diaper coupons for brands you use and also for those you don't; trade the ones you don't use with other moms.

Julie Zmerzlikar, Pacifica, CA

Cheaper to buy in bulk. If you don't already have one, consider a membership to Sam's Club or Costco. I found diapers, formula, and wipes to be cheapest there, especially if you buy off brands; you can save as much as 40 percent over the national brands sold in supermarkets.

Tammy W., Anchorage, AK

Diaper Genie cuts diaper odors. I would recommend the Diaper Genie to all new moms; it does a great job of keeping diaper odors to a minimum. It's more than a trash bin; it tightly twist-seals each diaper individually

OTHER DIAPERING TIPS ~ 127

✿ Save Money with Diaper-Club Memberships

Tina Golden of Coldwater, Mississippi, gives us this money-saving tip:

Apply for free club membership with as many of the diaper companies as you can—you'll appreciate those dollar-off diaper coupons on diapers and wipes, plus free products, more than you could ever know. Be sure to cut out the UPC codes on diaper packages, too; lots of companies offer freebies in exchange—it's another great way to get something back from what you spend on baby essentials. Here are some diaper companies to start with:

Pampers: 800-699-7916 (www.pampers.com)
Luvs: 800-374-5887 (www.luvs.com)
Huggies: 800-990-4448 (www.huggies.com) ✿

in plastic and holds about twenty diapers total. It's a great invention!

Lori Peters, PA

Diaper Genie veto. I could never figure out how to use the Diaper Genie and finally went to a regular diaper pail.

Cindy B., Island Park, NY

Recycle grocery bags at home. Recycle those plastic grocery bags by using them for disposing of wet and dirty diapers. Store the clean bags in empty paper-towel tubes.

Licia Croft, San Leandro, CA

Other Diapering Tips

Put clean diaper in place first. Always put the new diaper under baby before changing him. You'll save your furniture!

Linda Alderman, Kanab, UT

One-handed wipies. I prefer the baby wipes that come in a tub over the ones in the canister. You can grab a wipie out of the tub with one hand, but the canister takes two hands, which is tough with a squirmy baby.

Betsy, White Plains, NY

Sponge on diapering cream. I found diapering cream to be messy and hard to get off of my hands without first getting it all over my baby's skin, her clothing, and the furniture. So I started using disposable makeup sponges to apply the cream. They're inexpensive, and a single sponge can be used several times as long as baby's bottom is clean before applying.

Tammy W., Anchorage, AK

Supermarket baby clubs a good deal. Check with your local supermarkets for a free baby-club membership—you'll get great savings on all kinds of baby products, as well as related grocery and health and beauty items, too.

Lee Firlus, Marietta, GA

Save yourself some money. And the number-one waste of money? A changing table! You'll be changing diapers for the better part of two or three years, and your child will fit on the changing table for only about ten months. Ask any mom where she changes her baby, and she'll tell you she changes him on the floor, the couch, the bed, or even standing up—unless she's a mom of a newborn, she probably won't say that she changes baby on a changing table. Put up a shelf in the nursery for holding diapers and wipes, and save yourself the $60 to $150 you would otherwise spend on a changing table.

Barbara Thomas, Newport News, VA

Wipe warmer makes baby happier. Changing a newborn in the middle of the night with cold wipes upsets them and can fully wake them. One of the best items given to me at my baby shower was a diaper-wipe warmer—it's wonderful for warming their little tushes.

Shannon Waters, AZ

I FOUND THAT THE HEAT FROM THE WIPE WARMER TENDS TO DRY OUT THE WIPES, SO SPRINKLE SOME WATER ON THE STACK OF WIPES ONCE A WEEK.—MJM

Helps baby boys to stay drier. During the first few days at home, my son would wet himself and his clothes no matter how frequently I would change his diaper. Then we realized that we needed to tuck his penis down when putting his diaper on.

Meghan Collins, Chelmsford, MA

Diapering surprises keeps baby occupied. To keep diapering battles to a minimum, put several small toys inside an empty tissue box—making it a grab bag—then let baby grab a toy each time you change his diaper.

Kelly Weaver, Aurora, CO

Toothbrush is good, too. Try giving a squirmy baby a toothbrush to chew on during a diaper change—it keeps baby *very* occupied.

Nicole, Kissimmee, FL

Make diaper-changing tub for key rooms. Use a basket or plastic tub to put all of the diaper-changing items you'll need at changing time, and keep it close to where you keep baby during the day. That way, you won't be constantly running upstairs to the nursery. The diapering basket should be large enough to hold a protective pad, diapers, a clean Onesie, diaper-rash ointment, alcohol pads, wipes, cotton swabs, and a toy to serve as a distraction.

Lisa Troop, Folsom, CA

Homemade wipes at a fraction of the cost. One day I was visiting an old friend who runs two day-care centers, and I complained to her about the cost of diapering wipes, especially with my twins. She gave me this recipe for homemade wipes, which has saved me a lot of money:

Homemade Baby Wipes

1 roll Bounty Big Roll paper towels
2 tsp. Johnson's Baby Oil
2 tsp. Johnson's Baby Bath
2½ cups water
1 plastic round container with airtight lid (large enough to hold a vertical half roll of paper towels)

Cut paper towels in half with a sharp knife. Place the half roll in a plastic container. In a large bowl, mix water, baby oil, and baby bath. Gently pour liquid over and all around the paper towels. Cover and let stand for fifteen minutes. Next, remove the inner cardboard tube (it will be soft and easy to take out). Then just pull a wipe from the middle of the roll whenever one is needed. These wipes work great for baby's bottom, face, and hands, and even for removing Mom's makeup!

Kelley Raney, Marvell, AR

Or use a washcloth. I keep a spray bottle on the changing table that contains a mixture of 75 percent water and 25 percent baby bath. I then spray a washcloth with this solution, and this becomes my wipe—no more buying expensive wipes!

Kimberly Cushman, West Windsor, NJ

Wipes are good stain removers, too. I found that baby wipes get most stains out of clothing instantly. They work well on fresh spills on carpeting, too.

Jaki Thomas, South Australia

Keep necessities at arm's reach. Always pick out baby's clothes before the diaper change, making sure you can reach everything without having to step away from the changing table. Hanging travel organizers—the ones with the clear plastic pockets of varying sizes for holding stockings and jewelry—are great for hanging near the changing table. Tubes of ointment, cotton balls, cotton swabs, thermometer, toothbrush, and clothing items fit nicely in the pockets, and the plastic gives you a clear view.

Heather Petit, Newark, DE

Treating Diaper Rash

Prevention is best. I applied a thick layer of A&D Ointment in the morning and a thick layer of Desitin at night. My daughter probably qualified for an oil hazard, but she never got a diaper rash!

Amy L. Burrell, Sharon Hill, PA

Balmex rules. Balmex was the *only* ointment that ever helped my daughter's rashes! I never used perfumed diapers, as they irritated her.

Cindy, Long Island, NY

Petroleum jelly more economical. The cheaper preventative treatment is good old Vaseline; apply it generously after every diaper change and each bath.

Tameka Green, VA

Save more with generic. Buy generic-brand diapering creams—they're a lot cheaper than leading name brands and have the same ingredients.

Debra S. Fair, Waltham, MA

One-pound size less money. My pediatrician advised me to use Balmex, which I ordered in the more economical and convenient one-pound tub. He said that when a diaper rash develops, I should "frost" my baby's bottom like I would frost a cake—the results proved him right. You can order Balmex, Desitin Ointment, or A&D Original Ointment in the one-pound size from almost any drugstore or supermarket pharmacy, or buy it at most Babies "R" Us and Toys "R" Us stores.

Cindy A. Morris, Sarasota, FL

Clears it up fast. There's a simple and very reliable solution to mild diaper rash: Add baking soda to baby's bathwater. It works!

Sharon Roe, St. Andrews, Scotland

Gentle rinsing for baby's sore bottom. In the case of diaper rash, if baby's bottom is really messy, rinse her under the faucet in the sink. The water (and gentle baby soap if you wish to use it) will gently rinse away the stool, whereas the wipes can be irritating and sting. Gently pat baby dry and leave the diaper and the diapering cream off, allowing her bottom to "air out." This method will clear up diaper rash fast.

Jana McCarthy, Lake Forest, CA

YOU CAN ALSO WIPE AWAY STOOL FROM A RASHY BOTTOM WITH A WIPIE COATED WITH PETROLEUM JELLY.—MJM

Air baby's bottom at night, too. You can put baby to bed with no diaper (and no diapering cream), too, to further promote healing. Keep the bedding dry by placing a waterproof pad underneath the sheet.

Julie, Moorpark, CA

Switching to another brand may help. If your baby is prone to diaper rashes, try switching to another brand of disposable diaper. It helps, too, to buy the most absorbent (although they're the most expensive) diapers on the market; they pull more moisture away from baby's skin (just be sure to change baby as often as you normally do). Our son got rashes from the diapers that have plastic on the outside, so we switched to the ones with the paper covers, and that seemed to help.

Michelle Coady, Daytona Beach, FL

Try hypoallergenic diapers. If your baby gets rashes from disposable diapers, try using a brand without perfume.

Nancy Burton-Vulovic, Toronto

Vitamin E capsules. I poked a sterilized pin into a capsule of vitamin E and squeezed it right onto my son's diaper rash. It cleared right up.

Jo, NY

❦ When It's Time to Call the Doctor

Most diaper rashes are minor and clear up within two or three days. If your baby's diaper rash persists, becomes worse, or turns into a bright red rash (possibly signaling a yeast infection), consult your baby's doctor. The doctor will help you determine the cause of the diaper rash and the most effective treatment for your baby. ❦

Passed down for generations. For treating diaper rash, straight cornstarch applied to baby's bottom is best.

Andrea R. Cartwright, Stuyvesant, NY

Neutralize the acid. One tip that our doctor gave us when our daughter had a diaper rash from a nasty bout of diarrhea was to apply a mixture of Kaopectate and cornstarch to baby's bottom. Apparently, the Kaopectate neutralizes the acid in the diarrhea. It worked like a charm!

Jenny Plakio, Belen, NM

Maalox mixture is a good option, too. As a certified doula, the diaper-rash treatment I recommend most to moms is the following: Mix one part (about twenty tablets) finely crushed tablets of quick-dissolve Maalox with a regular-size tube of diaper-rash cream. Apply with each diaper change.

Cindi Howard Castle, Lake Park, FL

Clothing and Laundry

I remember wondering why my newborn son was so fussy once I brought him home from the hospital. Then I got my answer from the visiting home-health-care nurse (my son was born premature); she took one look at the way I had dressed my baby and asked, "And just when were you planning on leaving for that Alaskan cruise?" She wore a knowing smile as she removed layer after layer of clothing from my baby, while tactfully commenting, "Lots of new mommies overdress their babies, making baby hot and grumpy." After shedding my son of all except his T-shirt, he seemed much happier (and several degrees cooler!). As one seasoned mom in this chapter will tell you, it's easy to overdress baby; after all, you want her to be warm enough, but in actuality, she will be most comfortable dressed in the same amount of clothing that you are wearing, or at most one layer more. This is especially true in the summertime, as I learned, when a T-shirt or light cotton one-piece outfit is sufficient.

Keep reading for useful tips on baby clothing and laundry, including buying tips, dressing baby, and getting extra life out of infant clothing; as well as getting clothes their cleanest, best home remedies for removing the toughest stains, and earning some extra money on clothing resale.

CLOTHING

Hold off on newborn clothing. Until the baby is born, you won't know if he will be tiny or huge, so don't invest in a lot of newborn clothing that may not fit. A few Onesies and a couple of T-shirts for the first couple of weeks will suffice. Do you think you won't want to get out of the house and take baby shopping a couple of weeks after giving birth? Think again!

Barbara Thomas, Newport News, VA

Keep tags on new clothing. Don't take the tags off of those wonderful baby clothes you received from your shower until baby is the right size to wear them. You may find that your baby has outgrown smaller-sized clothing before he's ever had a chance to wear it, or that the clothing isn't right for the current season. Keep the tags on baby's clothing and you'll be able to exchange it later.

Barbara Legan, Riverside, IL

Simple is better. Try dressing your baby in the early days in outfits for sleep *and* play. In the summer, dress baby in T-shirts—they're most comfortable for warmer weather.

Lori L. Smith, NE

You get what you pay for. Quality all-cotton clothing is more expensive than cotton blends or synthetics, but it wears much longer. My favorite clothing for babies and toddlers comes from the kids' clothes line at Lands' End (www.landsend.com, or 800-356-4444); you'll find that "better" clothes don't shrink as quickly and fade much less than the cheaper alternatives. The clothing holds up better through multiple children, too (we bought one set of short-alls that have been through at least six kids in the family in twelve years!). An added bonus is that name-brand clothing commands a higher price and sells quicker in the resale shops.

Heather Petit, Newark, DE

Clothing with buttons or snaps easier. It is best to buy clothing that doesn't have to be pulled over baby's head, because it's very hard to do. Also, socks are difficult to keep on a newborn. I prefer dressing my baby in one-piece outfits that snap up the front and have feet.

Jan Harrison Furlow, Alexandria, VA

Check the neck opening. If you buy clothing that requires being pulled over your baby's head, make sure that the neck is stretchy. I had some outfits that had neck openings that were too small, and I couldn't get them over my baby's head at all. Also, outfits that button or zip up the back, or have no crotch snaps, are difficult for diaper changes—you have to undress baby almost entirely to get to his diaper.

Deborah Baska, Kansas City, MO

The amazing sleeve trick. It's hard to put a floppy newborn's arm into a sweater. Try this trick: Put the sweater sleeve, inside out, over your hand. Grab your baby's hand, then slide the sleeve right side out over baby's arm. Much easier!

Bessie, NY

"You put your right arm in, you put your right arm out . . ." I would play a game with my daughter when it was dressing time, otherwise she would cry and fuss. I did whatever came to mind: singing, peekaboo, or some other interesting distraction. Dressing baby in the quickest possible time helps, too—I think new moms could enter baby-dressing marathons!

Donna M. Condida, Archbald, PA

Drool bibs keep clothes cleaner. Use lots of bibs! Keep a bib on baby throughout the day; they save baby's clothes from drool and food stains and will save you laundry time.

Jaki Thomas, South Australia

Skip the shoes. Don't bother putting shoes on your baby's feet; babies don't need them until they're walking, and then only when walking on surfaces that can hurt their feet. It makes me sad to see little babies with the latest clunky shoes on their tiny feet. How uncomfortable!

Natalie Tabet, NM

Rotate clothing. Most people will give new moms baby clothing for newborns or infants. I had tons of clothes and would stress out trying to make sure my baby wore each of the adorable little outfits. Finally, I started a rotation system. After my baby wore an outfit, I would hang it in the back of the closet, then pull a new outfit from the front of the closet.

Deborah Baska, Kansas City, MO

Consignment saves on clothing bill. Consignment, consignment, consignment. Consignment stores saved me an enormous amount of money. I found the clothes to be in good or excellent condition, and they often cost less than half that of new. Also, because the clothing is broken in, it's softer on baby's skin.

Sharyn Lonsdale, Englewood, FL

Save on baby supplies and equipment, too. Consignment stores and church bazaars are also great places to shop for baby equipment, like strollers, cribs, and changing tables, as well as toys. You can also pick up good deals on books, cassettes, and videos.

Laura Bell, Roseville, CA

Tag-sale savvy. Come during the last hour of the tag sale and you can scoop up all the baby booty for even less. No one wants to take all that stuff back inside!

Elizabeth, New York City

Why pay full price? When I shop for clothes at the better department stores, I always go to the clearance racks first. In addition, I buy at the end of the season, when clothing prices are lowest (in the sizes I think my daughter will be wearing a year later). By shopping this way, I never pay full price.

Amy L. Burrell, Sharon Hill, PA

Separates make more sense. Take it from the organizer queen: Organize your dresser in the order you dress your baby. Undershirts and socks in the top drawer; shirts, jumpers, and sweaters in the middle drawers; pants and shorts in the bottom drawer. And it's best to buy coordinating separates, not matching outfits. If you buy separates, you can mix and match virtually every piece of clothing. If you dress your baby in outfits, when one piece of clothing gets dirty, you have to change the entire outfit.

Lara Joudrey, London, Ontario

White-sock stampede. Don't buy colored socks—they take too long to match. Instead, buy only white socks that are all the same style. As your child grows out of smaller-sized socks, store them away for the next baby. There's nothing worse than running late for an appointment and digging through the sock drawer only to discover that all of the socks are too small.

Amanda Battles, Asheville, NC

Don't overheat baby. New moms tend to overdress their babies in the winter. Dress them as you would dress yourself: If you're comfortable in a sweater, they will be comfortable in a sweater, too. Babies should be dressed the same as you, or at most in one additional layer.

Christine Clark, Manahawkin, NJ

Layer baby's clothing. Dress baby in layers to adjust for changing temperatures throughout the day and night.

Dawn M. Casella, Westland, MI

Less is best in summer months. My daughter was born in July, and it was one of the hottest summers in a long time. Being a new mom, I had purchased cute little outfits that made my baby look like she belonged in a television commercial. Then one day, she began to cry, and she cried for six hours straight. I thought I would go crazy! I called my mom and asked if she could offer any help. She immediately asked me what I dressed my daughter in that day . . . I was dumbfounded. After hearing how I dressed her, she suggested that I strip her down and put her in the bathroom sink filled with cool water. Sure enough, she calmed right down; my daughter was extremely warm and only needed to cool off! For the rest of the summer, I dressed her in only a diaper at home and a Onesie when we went out.

Donna M. Condida, Archbald, PA

Homemade nonskid socks. Nonskid socks are expensive, but you can make your own for a fraction of the cost. Buy regular socks and decorate the bottom with 3-D fabric paint. Let the paint dry for twenty-four hours. This makes a good personalized gift for your expecting girlfriends, too.

Licia Croft, San Leandro, CA

LAUNDRY

Keep laundry basket in baby's room. We keep a laundry basket in our daughter's room just for her laundry. It really helps in keeping up with her clothes and makes it easier if you use a different laundry detergent for your baby's clothing than the rest of the family's.

Angela Allen Willner, Christiansburg, VA

Portable hamper. We used a lightweight hamper for our son's room and carried it back and forth to the laundry room. No more little socks ending up in my husband's shirtsleeves!

Bethany, New York City

Wash socks in lingerie bag. Wash and dry your baby's itty-bitty socks in a nylon lingerie bag—you won't lose them, and it will make matching the socks after the wash easier.

Tammy W., Anchorage, AK

A load a day keeps the laundry blues away. Do at least one load of laundry a day; that way you won't feel so overwhelmed. I would rather do one load a day than six loads all at once.

Laura Witek, Milwaukee, WI

Stain relief. Pretreat, pretreat, pretreat those stains. You can keep your baby's clothing looking picture-perfect, despite the many episodes of spit-up, pureed carrots, and blowouts. Soak soiled colored garments in cold water, then spray with a stain remover—my favorite is Mother's Little Miracle Stain and Odor Remover, which can be found at most baby stores. For whites, soak with detergent and bleach in hot water before washing.

Deborah Baska, Kansas City, MO

Sun it out! What is the best stain remover for poop stains on cloth diapers or clothing? The *sun!* Hang the damp items in the sun to dry and watch the stains magically disappear.

Sarah L. Turner-Keeter, CA

Try using a stain stick. I found that stain sticks—I liked Wisk—worked best for removing stains.

Paula, West Dundee, IL

Treat stains in the nursery. Keep a stain remover stick in the nursery to treat clothes as you throw them into the hamper to prevent stains from setting. Also, use the "soak" cycle on your washer prior to washing.

Allison DeWitt, Jacksonville, FL

Soak soiled clothing overnight. Put two big scoops of Biz into a small bucket of the hottest water possible for the clothing material and soak overnight. Most stains will be gone in the morning.

Juliana Russo, Encinitas, CA

Stains out with Zout. Use Zout on stains. It's absolutely the best stain remover I've ever used!

Susan Flannery, Louisville, KY

Cleans glassware, too. Bleach can irritate baby's skin, so I didn't use it when washing my babies' clothes. Instead, I would wet the clothes, then take an old toothbrush and scrub the stain with a small amount of automatic dishwasher detergent— that's right, it takes the stains right out!

Sue Menna, Coatesville, PA

Fabric softener can irritate. If your baby has sensitive skin, skip the fabric softener, as it can be an irritant to baby's skin. Also, use a mild detergent specifically formulated for baby, such as Dreft.

Lori Peters, PA

Try sensitive-skin detergent. Two of my children got rashes from regular laundry detergents, but rather than spend extra money on the baby detergents, I switched to a hypoallergenic, perfume-free, dye-free detergent called Fab Sensitive Skin. No more rashes.

Kyra S. Miller, Floral City, FL

CHAPTER 8

Dribble, Drip, and Drool
The Teething Months

Most new parents don't think twice about the teething months . . . until they arrive. Trouble can begin months prior to that first tooth, which will appear at about seven months, although some babies pop a tooth much earlier or later. You may find your baby getting fussy throughout the day and drooling more than usual. For some babies, this is the extent of their teething pain; for others, it's just the beginning.

Teething can be tough on baby. Although my firstborn son's teething period was uneventful, his younger brother ran the teething gamut: One minute he was happy and the next irritable. His gums would swell, and he drooled nonstop, soaking the front of his clothing in saliva. From time to time he developed low-grade fevers and diarrhea. I tried the numbing gels on the market for his sore gums, but they didn't have staying power (and as you'll hear from one mom, they're not even considered safe by many doctors). The best treatment I found was a combination of several of the effective home remedies recommended by moms in this chapter. Here are some great tips for relieving your baby's irritability and tender gums during the teething months:

Teething

Frozen washcloth is soothing. For teething, dampen a terry washcloth and place it in the freezer for thirty minutes or so. The cold helps to numb baby's gums, and it's safe for her to chew on. It's a good idea to keep three or four washcloths in the freezer (storing them in individual freezer bags)—that way, you'll always have one available when baby needs it.

Shari Osmon, Roanoke, TX

Mom's knuckles are good for chomping. I would allow my daughter to "chew" on my knuckle, and I would rub her gums gently with my finger.

Sheila Billick, Gillette, WY

Chill teething rings. Refrigerate water-filled teething rings— they soothe baby's pain and help with swelling. (Some teething rings can be frozen, too, but check the instructions first.)

Alysha Goodsell, Brighton, MI

CHECK FROZEN TEETHING RINGS FOR ICE CRYSTALS; ICE CRYSTALS ON A TEETHER CAN DAMAGE BABY'S DELICATE GUMS.——MJM

Socksicles are a hit! Teething rings are great, but I found that after my baby's teeth came in, she would bite through them.

Instead, I filled a small clean sock with two ice cubes, then tied the end in a knot. She loved sucking on it!

Marion G. Griffith, Pearland, TX

Try washcloth with crushed ice. We tied off a burping cloth with a rubber band and filled it with crushed ice. My girls would suck on it like a pacifier and get relief.

Janice Michael, Phoenix, AZ

Homemade teethers are the best. I wouldn't waste money on store-bought teethers. Some cheaper, but very effective, homemade teethers are: chilled celery, frozen bagels or waffles, frozen bananas, cold carrots, chilled cucumbers, or just about anything that's cold and hard that baby can hold. Just be sure to give baby whole uncut foods—no sticks or slices. Also, babies like to "gum" their plastic-coated baby spoons.

Marie M. Bassili, Tucson, AZ

Caution: FREEZING FOODS CAN BE A CHOKING OR FREEZING HAZ-ARD. CHECK ALL FROZEN-FOOD TEETHERS FOR FREEZER DAMAGE AND SUPERVISE CLOSELY IN THE EVENT THAT A PIECE OF FOOD BREAKS OFF IN BABY'S MOUTH.——MJM

Fruit and yogurt pops work great, too. For teething, our daughter loved homemade fruit pops made with water and a little juice concentrate. She liked sucking on frozen baby yogurt, too. The yogurt also provided calories on the days her gums were too sore for her to eat.

Elizabeth Vroom, Leiden, The Netherlands

Why not breast-milk pops? If you're breast-feeding, try breast-milk pops! Just freeze your breast milk in Popsicle trays—you can buy the trays and sticks at most large discount retailers.

Laura Gazley, St. Catharines, Ontario

Frozen Binkies provide relief. Put pacifiers in the freezer! The cold feels good on baby's sore gums, and in hot weather it's great for cooling a cranky baby.

Ann Wells, San Diego, CA

Numbing gels don't last. Over-the-counter numbing gel isn't worth the money; the relief it provides is only momentary because it washes out of baby's mouth in just a couple of minutes.

Debra S. Fair, Waltham, MA

Numbs the throat, too. I was surprised when my second child was teething and my pediatrician advised against numbing gels, saying that they numb the throat, too, and can cause baby to choke on her own saliva.

Denise Campbell, North Providence, RI

Hyland's tablets work well. The only over-the-counter teething medicine that I found that really worked was Hyland's Teething Tablets. They are all-natural and significantly relieved my son's pain without side effects. I would give him several crushed tablets a day. The tablets can be found in health-food stores and some drugstores.

Christine Doolittle, Wexford, PA

Use pain relievers when necessary. My daughter had an extremely hard time with her teeth, and I got all sorts of advice, from rubbing whiskey on her gums to offering various teething rings. At first I was hesitant to give her Infants' Tylenol, but after talking with my baby's doctor, I learned that a little pain reliever would allow us all to get some sleep.

Anonymous

Knobby teether feels good. There is a knobby toothbrush on the market for teething babies. It has tiny nylon knobs that wrap around the head of the toothbrush. My daughter loved chewing on it, and the counterpressure felt good against her gums.

Julie Zmerzlikar, Pacifica, CA

Teething cookies tasty, too. My girls liked the teething cookies available at the grocery stores. The cookies were very hard and it took a while to "gum" their way through one.

Sheila Billick, Gillette, WY

Clothespin teether. My son got teething relief by chewing on wooden clothespins (the kind without the springs, of course).

Dana

WATCH FOR SPLINTERS!—MJM

Pretreat for diaper rash. Be sure to change baby's diaper more often when she is teething and use extra diaper-rash cream. Teething can cause baby to have diarrhea, leading to diaper rash, and it's easier to prevent than it is to treat.

Laura Witek, Milwaukee, WI

Petroleum jelly prevents drool rash. My teething daughter would break out in a drool rash on her chin from the saliva. I found that the best way to prevent the rash from developing in the first place was to first wipe her chin dry, then apply a dab of petroleum jelly.

Tina Evans, Marietta, GA

Sheet Saver saves laundry time. There is a handy item available at most baby retailers called a Sheet Saver: It's a rectangular-shaped, quilted cotton pad made for absorbing excess saliva while baby sleeps. It lies on top of the crib sheet, under baby's head, and attaches to the crib rails with ties. Not only does it save sheet changes, but it's much easier to remove and wash than all of baby's bedding. If you have a sewing machine handy, it would be easy enough to sew a couple yourself.

Sue Menna, Coatesville, PA

CHAPTER 9

Have Baby, Will Travel
✆
Traveling with Baby

Local Travel

After a few weeks of being cooped up at home with my new baby and staring at the same four walls of our family room, I was looking for *any* excuse to get out of the house; even one hour of fresh air a day was enough to recharge my batteries and make me feel like my old self again. The biggest problem was figuring out where I could tote my newborn and get some exercise at the same time. Since he was born in the wintertime, my options were rather limited. Then one day I decided to trek to the local shopping mall and discovered that it was a virtual mecca for new moms. I soon fell into step with the stroller brigade—cutting the same circular path each week around the mall, breaking to chat at the visitors' center and feed my baby. Then, when my son was about four months old, I joined a baby gym class, which I found to be especially rewarding and fun. We enjoyed playing on the foam equipment and singing songs, and I made several new mom friends in class. The moms would meet afterward for an early lunch and adult conversation. It was just what I needed at the time: other new moms who were going through the same things I was.

When you're ready to take your baby out, take it slow and don't expect too much; this isn't the time to run five errands in a row, or try to pick up where you left off before the baby came. Babies tire easily in the early weeks and do better when they're not overstimulated. And don't be surprised by the inordinate amount of time it takes to get your baby out of the house. The time it will take you to get yourself and baby ready to go (including gathering up all of baby's necessary supplies) may be more than the total number of minutes you will actually spend away from home! Or, as one mom in this chapter points out, you and your baby may get all ready to go only to find that baby has suddenly become fussy or that you're just too tired to make the trip after all. Don't worry, though, you'll find that as your energy level increases (which most often is directly related to the number of hours of sleep you're getting at night) and you become more organized, you'll come to be much more efficient in all aspects of traveling with baby and be out of the house in only minutes instead of the better part of an hour.

The first half of this chapter addresses local travel, and the last half long-distance. Here's what moms who've toted their own babies around town have to say about the trials and tribulations of toting baby, getting organized for your outings, what to include in baby's diaper bag, what to look for in a stroller, tips and advice on places to go and keeping baby happy when out, as well as health and safety recommendations.

Before You Go

A better diaper bag. I highly recommend the Lands' End (www.landsend.com, or 800-356-4444) diaper bags; they come in several different sizes and styles, and they're made of sturdy nylon so they don't get dirty as easily. They're not as cutesy or feminine as traditional diaper bags, and Dad won't mind carrying it, either. Mine has a nice big changing pad and lots of room to stash everything for baby, including a detachable water-resistant pouch for wet clothes or soiled diapers. And there's a separate compartment for the parents' things, too. Also, the strap is adjustable and is long enough so that you can carry the bag more comfortably over your shoulder.

Angela Allen Willner, Christiansburg, VA

Try the backpack diaper bag. I like the Lands' End backpack diaper bag. It's great because it frees both of your hands.

Deanne, Herndon, VA

Two's better than one. It's better to have *two* diaper bags at your disposal—a smaller one to hold a couple of diapers, a few wipes, and a bottle for when running a quick errand, and a larger diaper bag for all-day outings or overnight trips.

Donna M. Condida, Archbald, PA

Don't forget to restock. Always restock your diaper bag as soon as you get home so that it's ready the next time you're rushing out the door.

Allison DeWitt, Jacksonville, FL

AFTER RESTOCKING MINE, I WOULD IMMEDIATELY RETURN IT TO THE CAR SO THAT I WOULDN'T FORGET IT THE NEXT TIME.——MJM

Snacks keep baby content. Don't go anywhere without healthy snacks. Whether you're taking your baby for a stroller ride around the neighborhood or an airplane ride across the country, have something healthy and easily accessible for baby to eat in case he gets hungry. Doing this has saved me time and time again!

Marian Gormley, Falls Church, VA

Stash a twenty-dollar bill. After three babies and two grand-babies, this still holds true: Keep an extra set of car keys, a house key, and a twenty-dollar bill hidden in the bottom of your diaper bag. There will come a day when you'll be happy you did. (The Extra Strength Tylenol is optional!)

Kimberly R. Harris, Fairview, NC

Hand sanitizer keeps little hands germ-free. A relatively new item on the market that you will want to be sure and include in your diaper bag is a travel-size bottle of antibacterial hand sanitizer. No water is required and no wiping, either. You need only to rub a small amount on your baby's hands to kill 99.9 percent of germs instantly.

Nancy Ablao, Kalamazoo, MI

Zip in a Ziploc. I always kept a few freezer-size Ziploc bags in my diaper bag to store poopy diapers or "blown-out" outfits in. I always kept a spare set of baby clothes.

Elizabeth, New York City

Don't leave home without it. If your baby is dependent on a pacifier, have several extras stored for travel; keep them in your diaper bag, glove compartment, purse, and your parents' or in-laws' homes. It will cause major problems if you're away from home and find yourself without one.

Elizabeth Palmer Hale, Lorraine, Quebec

Make an emergency bag for your car. Always keep an emergency bag in the car containing diapers, washcloths, wet wipes, juice or bottled water, extra pacifiers, toys, and so forth. You'll forget your diaper bag one day, and your emergency bag will save your life.

Sharyn Lonsdale, Englewood, FL

Get yourself ready first. Before leaving the house, dress yourself first, then finish dressing baby; that way, after you dress baby, you can immediately get in the car. If you don't, you'll find that your baby—who *was* ready to go thirty minutes ago—is getting fussy, or in need of a diaper change, feeding, or change of clothing.

Sue Menna, Coatesville, PA

Strollers

Stroller/car-seat combination saves work. I highly recommend the stroller/car-seat combination stroller. Being able to bundle baby up and buckle her in once (especially in the wintertime) was very helpful. Plus, since baby usually falls asleep in the car, once you arrive at your destination, you won't have to wake baby up—just pop out the car seat and snap it onto the stroller.

Sheryl McCarthy, North Stonington, CT

"Test-drive" strollers before buying. I didn't like the travel system (stroller and car seat in one), because usually either the stroller or car seat is not the same quality as when you buy each piece separately. Make sure the stroller you choose reclines fully for a newborn and has at least a three- or five-point seat belt. Test-drive the stroller in the store by loading the seat with thirty pounds of something—they steer differently empty and loaded. Check the basket; is it easily accessible? This is a must!

Alexia Weber, South Lyon, MI

Umbrella strollers are lightest. Invest in an umbrella stroller! They are cheap, lightweight, and easy to use with an older baby. You can buy them with baskets and canopies, too. Extra-long handles are also available at large retailers for taller mommies and daddies. After baby number two can sit up on her own, you can just buy another umbrella stroller, along with the brace that connects two strollers together side to side, giving you a cheap double stroller.

Rebecca Vogel-Pitts, Longmont, CO

Accessorize, accessorize, accessorize. I think it's worth investing in a few stroller accessories: the sun canopy or umbrella, to keep the sun out of baby's eyes; the plastic rain cover for unexpected cloudbursts; and the net bag to store toys and essentials. Note to new moms: Be careful how much stuff you pile onto the back of the stroller, or your baby might go bottoms up when you let go of the handle!

Betsy Rapoport, White Plains, NY

Taking Baby Out

Shield baby from germs. I wouldn't recommend traveling with baby much before the first two weeks or so—you'll probably still be feeling sore anyway and won't feel like getting out yourself. Taking baby out too soon will also make him more susceptible to the germs of other people (and people are always drawn to new babies). Besides, you won't like the disapproving looks you'll get. Not that public opinion necessarily matters, but in your fragile postpartum state, the smallest criticism can make you cry.

Wendy R., Tooele, UT

Getting some fresh air is fine. I took my baby out at one week. It was springtime and a nice day, so we went for a walk in the carriage.

Debra S. Fair, Waltham, MA

The baby's out already. We asked the hospital pediatrician when we could take our newborn son out. He smiled, pointed at my collapsed belly, and said, "Guess what? He's out! You can take him out right away. Just use common sense and keep him away from anyone who's sick." We took his advice and took our son out in a Snuggli when he was three days old. We all needed the fresh air!

Lisa, NY

Doesn't do any good to fight it. If your baby gets increasingly fussy, overly tired, or sick, call off the trip and go home. Things usually won't improve until baby has eaten and has napped . . . and that goes for you, too!

Heather Petit, Newark, DE

Avoid crowds. I regret that we took our one-month-old daughter to a family gathering where one of the children had a nasty flu virus and we all caught it, including our baby girl. We felt so helpless to do anything for her and felt guilty for exposing her tiny body to all of those germs. It's best to keep babies away from large groups of people until they're older and their immune system has had a chance to mature a bit.

Donna Schwartz Mills, Los Angeles, CA

Schedule wellness checkups for after lunch. If you're taking baby to the pediatrician's office for a wellness checkup, schedule the appointment for one P.M., so that you'll be seen right away (after the office lunch break) and you'll avoid being around sick babies (who are usually brought in first thing in the morning). Also, if you feel the need to get out—especially if it is cold or rainy—try your local mall; it's a great place to stroll your baby. Just be sure to take him out early in the morning when it's not so crowded.

Wendy Blumberg, Plano, TX

Baby sling is ideal for outings. Two words: baby sling! I loved my NoJo baby sling, especially when my children were newborns. Baby stays safe and secure in a sling next to Mom when out, which means no fussing. It also means that you can nurse discreetly, whether you're eating out, at the movies or the store, or anyplace else. I believe they work so well because baby has everything he wants: his mommy, a comfortable place to rest, and a meal close at hand.

Rebecca Vogel-Pitts, Longmont, CO

Sling protects baby. Everyone wants to see and touch your new baby. I found that with my second child, carrying him in a baby sling when we were out greatly reduced any contact. I felt much more comfortable about taking him out early on, unlike my first son, whom I carried in an infant car seat and found people were constantly touching him.

Amy Allred, Woodstock, GA

"What, again?!" Expect to be late everywhere you go for the first two months. As soon as you're ready to head out the door, you'll discover that the baby has a poopy diaper or has spit up all over his clothes and needs to be changed.

Sheryl McCarthy, North Stonington, CT

Count on being tardy. I found that, for the first year, it takes about thirty-five to forty additional minutes (after Mom and Dad are ready to leave) to get baby ready to go out—even if you're just going for a walk! This is why you'll be at least half an hour late for any appointment that involves your baby— you'll think it will only take you fifteen minutes to get the baby ready, and that's what you plan for, but in reality it will take twice as long.

Heather Petit, Newark, DE

Best to leave baby at home. If you're a fond subscriber to the "shop till you drop" philosophy, plan your shopping for special days when you can get a sitter for the baby. Babies and toddlers can only take so much before they begin to make everyone within earshot miserable. It's not fair to them, and it's not fun for you.

Jane A. Zanca, Atlanta, GA

Car-seat safety. Check with your local police and fire departments to see if they provide a free car-seat check service. In our town, both do this. An officer comes to your home and checks to ensure that your child's car seat is installed correctly. I'm glad we did this—we found that our baby's seat was incorrectly installed, and we now feel safer knowing that our daughter is snugly restrained.

Lori Peters, PA

Monitor baby while driving. Get one of those clip-on mirrors (which attach just below the rearview mirror or on the visor) so that you can safely check on baby without having to turn your head or adjust your rearview mirror. If your baby is rear-facing, there is a backseat mirror available, too, which attaches to the backseat and can be positioned so that you can view baby from your rearview mirror.

Susan Flannery, Louisville, KY

❦ *Motor-Vehicle Occupant Injury*

According to the National Safe Kids Campaign (www.safekids.org, or 202-662-0600), motor-vehicle crashes remain the leading cause of unintentional injury-related death among children ages fourteen and under. Riding unrestrained is the greatest risk factor for death and injury among child occupants of motor vehicles. Approximately 29 percent of children ages four and under ride unrestrained, placing them at twice the risk of death and injury as those riding restrained. Furthermore, the misuse of child safety seats is widespread; it is estimated that approximately **85 percent of children who are placed in child-safety seats and booster seats are improperly restrained. This includes 63 percent of seats not installed tightly, and other cases in which the safety belt was not locked.** Here's what you can do to prevent motor-vehicle-related injuries:

- Always use child-safety seats and/or safety belts correctly every time you ride. Restrain children ages twelve and under in a backseat.
- Infants, until at least one year old and at least twenty pounds, should be in rear-facing child-safety seats. Never put a rear-

facing infant or convertible safety seat in the front passenger seat of a vehicle with an active passenger air bag.

• Children over one year old and between twenty and forty pounds should be in forward-facing child-safety seats. In addition, children ages four to eight (about forty to eighty pounds) should be in a car booster seat and restrained with lap/shoulder belt every time they ride.

• Read your child-safety-seat instruction manual and your motor-vehicle owner's manual for directions on proper installation.

• National Safe Kids Campaign has partnered with General Motors Corporation (GM) to develop the Safe Kids Buckle Up program. This child-passenger safety initiative provides hands-on instructions through car-seat checkup events, where trained child-passenger safety specialists inspect your infant and infant/child car seats to ensure proper installation and use. You can find a listing of upcoming car-seat checkup events in your area by visiting the National Safe Kids Campaign Web site listed above. ✍

Baby in back. I knew I was supposed to keep my daughter in the middle of the backseat, but she fussed and cried constantly if she couldn't see me, so I cheated and put her car seat up front with me. Then I was in a car crash; and the taxi bashed in the passenger seat. Miraculously, she was unharmed, but I'll never make that mistake again. The backseat is safest!

Betsy Rapoport, White Plains, NY

Extra clothing saves embarrassment. We found that when taking baby out, it was best to pack several large plastic bags in the diaper bag, as well as a couple of T-shirts and one-piece outfits. That way, if an accident occurred while we were out, we could put the soiled clothing in the plastic bags and dress her in clean clothing. It seems like common sense, but as new parents we didn't know to do this, and on our first outing to a restaurant, our baby had an accident, leaving us with a half-dressed child and a few odd stares.

Valerie Turner, PA

Easy parking at grocery store. When taking baby to the grocery store, don't try to find a parking space closest to the door; instead, park near the shopping-cart corral. You can get a cart instantly, which allows you to load baby from your car directly into the cart. Also, you'll be able to return the cart to the corral as soon as your groceries are loaded, rather than having to leave the baby and walk to the corral.

Angela Allen Willner, Christiansburg, VA

Safety harness keeps baby secure. I found it very cumbersome to lug my baby's carrier into the grocery store every time I needed to go shopping. Then one day, while traveling the aisles at our local baby store, I found a great product called the Ecology Kids Two-in-One Safety Sitter Guard (800-247-9063)—it's a padded harness that attaches to the shopping cart (and can also be attached to a high chair or restaurant chair) and holds baby securely in place. I liked using it for the shopping cart because it held my baby upright and also had a wrap for the shopping-cart handle to protect her from germs and tooth damage. I used this product for months, taking it everywhere I went with my children. Then one day last spring, I learned firsthand how truly useful a safety harness can be. I had just strapped my daughter, who was six months old at the time, into the safety harness and was fumbling for change in the bottom of my purse to buy a canned drink from the vending machine. While my eyes were diverted, my five-year-old son decided to climb onto the side of the shopping cart for a "free ride," which caused the entire cart to tip over with the baby in it! Needless to

✽ *Shopping-Cart Injuries*

National Safe Kids Campaign reports that the number of children ages five and under injured in shopping-cart-related incidents has increased by 30 percent in recent years. Over twenty-five thousand children are treated in hospital emergency rooms each year in shopping-cart accidents. Children ages four and under account for 83 percent of these injuries, suffering mostly head injuries. Shopping carts have a high center of gravity and a narrow wheel base, making them top-heavy when loaded and easy to tip over. When children stand up, their chances of falling or tipping the cart over increase. Here are some injury prevention tips:

- Always use safety belts to restrain your child.
- Consider bringing a harness or safety belt with you when shopping.
- Always stay close to the shopping cart.
- Don't let your child stand in the shopping cart.
- Never let a child push or steer the shopping cart. ✽

say, I was absolutely frantic! I bent down to pick up my daughter and saw that she was still tightly snuggled into her harness—miraculously, there was not a scratch or bump on her. I really believe that, had I not used a harness, she would have slid across the floor or suffered a fractured skull, laceration, or who knows what else.

Karen S. Thomas, Birmingham, AL

No substitute for a watchful eye. As a mom of two boys who were very active, and as a pediatric nurse who sees children after they have been injured, I would tell parents that although restraints/harnesses are great, nothing can replace the watchful eye of a parent. Even safety belts can be used inappropriately and give parents a false sense of security. Children left alone in car seats, carriages, infant seats, or shopping carts are just accidents waiting to happen.

Nancy Kuehner

Backpacks go anywhere you do. Our baby backpack has been worth its weight in gold! I can put baby on my back and he's a happy camper. It's convenient for going shopping, to the park, or hiking; there is also a shade you can buy for the top to shade baby from the sun. Some have a mirror kit, too, so you can see your baby while he's on your back. My husband loves wearing it, and it makes us both feel closer to our son.

Rebecca Vogel-Pitts, Longmont, CO

Baby Bjorn carrier gets high rating. One item I found useful for travel is the baby carrier by Baby Bjorn. It's more expensive than other carriers, but it is much better than most. It doesn't hurt your back, holds baby upright, and accommodates a baby from eight to thirty-three pounds. It's perfect for walks and for going into little boutiques and stores where strollers don't fit.

Kathryn A. Varuzza, New Paltz, NY

Nonslip high chair. To keep baby from slipping in the high chair in restaurants, bring along a rubber jar-lid gripper or a piece of rubber shelf liner and place it on the seat. Both will keep baby in place while eating.

Andrea R. Cartwright, Stuyvesant, NY

Use coffee cup to warm bottle. Restaurants will usually be happy to comply with your request for a cup of hot water for warming baby's bottle.

Debra S. Fair, Waltham, MA

A full baby is a satisfied baby. Feed your baby or toddler *before* you go out to eat at a nicer restaurant. Your child will not be cranky because he's hungry, and he can entertain himself with toys or nibble on a special treat while you're enjoying your meal.

Angela Allen Willner, Christiansburg, VA

Sanitary dining for baby. When baby is old enough for finger foods, I highly recommend bringing along disposable place mats when eating out; they come in paper or plastic and are self-adhesive. When my girls were little, I never wanted them to be served food on a ceramic plate because they most likely would have knocked the plate onto the floor, and food placed directly on a restaurant table was susceptible to bacteria. The disposable place mats are sterile and safe; just throw them away after each use.

Wendy Pisciotta, Stafford Springs, CT

Traveling out of Town

Traveling long distances with a baby is much easier than traveling with a restless toddler, and the younger the baby, the easier it is; after all, for the first few months, baby's needs consist primarily of feedings, diaper changes, and sleeping. I traveled quite a bit by plane in my youngest son's first year and found that he mostly entertained himself by watching the people around him and the changing scenery along the way. But I do remember one unfortunate flight, at holiday time, when my then five-month-old son cried from sea to shining sea. I learned a valuable lesson that day: When traveling with a baby by plane, travel off-peak if possible, avoiding the crowds at the airport and overbooked flights. I also discovered that flying during the week was usually less crowded than flying on the weekends, and traveling mid- to late morning was easiest on me (I had the most energy in the mornings) and my son (the morning was his happiest time of day).

Plane travel is definitely fastest, but sometimes taking a trip by car is the best way to go. You'll have room to pack more of baby's comforts from home, and you can decide what departure time is best for baby, most likely coinciding with a nap or bedtime. Or, as one mom suggests, leave a couple of hours before baby's normal wake-up time in the morning to get a quiet start to the trip. The downside to car travel, though, is trying to keep baby from getting restless hour after hour. In the past you may have been accustomed to driving straight through to your destination or making infrequent stops, but with baby in tow, you'll fare much better if you stop every two or three hours to give her some fresh air, stroll her a bit, and feed her. It adds time to your trip, but the trip will be much more pleasant overall.

Whatever your mode of transportation, as you'll hear from other moms in this chapter, the keys to successful long-distance traveling are to slow yourself down, maintain baby's normal schedule as much as possible, and be flexible. Continue reading for useful tips on preparing for your out-of-town trip, including what to pack and what to leave behind; advice on making long car trips more enjoyable and air travel less challenging— including how to change a dirty diaper at thirty thousand feet!—and things you can do once you've arrived at your destination to make the adjustment easier and happier for baby.

Packing for Your Trip

Make a list, check it twice. Start by making a list of everything you think you will need for baby several days in advance of your trip—go through an entire day in your head and write it all down. Then decide what you will pack and what you will purchase at your destination.

Francine deFay, Rochester, NY

Don't be sorry later . . . If you think you'll need it, take it!

Lauren McMenimen, Tempe, AZ

Tidy up before you go. As difficult as it may seem, try to get the house in order before you go away for a few days. There's nothing more discouraging than getting home with a tired baby and several days of travel laundry and facing the dishes you left in the sink, the trash you forgot to take out, or the stale sheets on the bed.

Jane A. Zanca, Atlanta, GA

Pack by the outfit. When packing my children's clothes for a trip, I assemble complete outfits—shirts, bottoms, socks, and so forth—and place them in separate clear plastic bags in the suitcase. Each day of the trip, I need only to take out one plastic bag for each child, rather than endlessly searching the suitcase for matching clothing. After your trip, empty the plastic bags and store them in the suitcase for your next trip.

Marian Gormley, Falls Church, VA

Divide clothing when packing. On our last trip to San Francisco with our two children, the airlines lost our son's bag. The experience taught me a valuable lesson: Never pack all of a family member's clothing in one bag. Instead, pack a mix of

HAVE BABY, WILL TRAVEL

everyone's clothes in each bag, then if one bag gets lost, you'll still have some backup clothing for that person.

Kathryn A. Varuzza, New Paltz, NY

Separates are easiest. When packing, plan the baby's outfits as you would your own; pack several different tops for each pair of pants or jumper. Then, if one top or a pair of pants gets soiled, you won't have to change the entire outfit.

Mary Czajkoski, Joliet, IL

Mail ahead baby items. If you're traveling to a rather expensive vacation destination, consider mailing a box of necessities ahead of your trip to save money and time. We recently took our twins to the Virgin Islands and mailed ahead all of their food, formula, diapers, and wipes, all items we planned to use while on vacation but would not require repacking for the return trip. Most hotels are happy to store guests' packages until their arrival. You may also wish to send bulkier items, like toys, beach gear, and other baby equipment, in advance—it's less of a hassle than trying to pack everything into suitcases.

Laura Witek, Milwaukee, WI

Take along comforts from home. Definitely bring the familiar comforts from home; for my son it was his blanket. We took it with us when we stayed in hotels so that even if the crib was different from the one at home, he still had his familiar blanket.

Jamie Kennedy, Midland, MI

Traveling by Car

An ounce of prevention . . . Preventive treatment for diaper rash is especially important when going on a long car trip—be sure you apply a thick layer of diaper cream *before* you start.

Kimberly R. Harris, Fairview, NC

Don't forget to bring a change of clothing. While driving to a photographer's studio for a baby-modeling job, my daughter had projectile vomiting a block before the studio! Needless to say, the photographer and I were aghast at the messy baby I brought in!

Cindy B., Island Park, NY

Early departure is easiest on baby. For longer car trips it's best to leave very early—no later than four-thirty or five A.M.—and don't bother waking, changing, or feeding the baby. Just load up the car, and when you're completely loaded and ready to pull out of the driveway, take baby from his crib—still asleep and in his pajamas—and place him in the car. Even if he wakes up, he'll quickly go back to sleep and should stay asleep until feeding time.

Sue Menna, Coatesville, PA

In the still of the night . . . Or, if leaving at the crack of dawn is too hard on you, wait until just before baby's bedtime and then drive at night. That's what we do; our baby sleeps and we have a quiet ride.

Jodi Detjen

No rest for the weary. The only problem with driving all night is that when you finally arrive—worn out and ready for a nap—your baby will be raring to go!

Linda Alderman, Kanab, UT

Try leaving at naptime. When my son was two months old, we drove eight hours to a vacation house. We left around ten P.M., which was his bedtime, and drove through the night, arriving around six A.M. We were completely exhausted when we arrived, and it took us the entire week's vacation to recover. We vowed to never do this again. For the drive home, we decided to leave around our son's afternoon nap, around two P.M., and he slept for two hours. Then for the times that he was awake, one of us would sit in the backseat and keep him entertained. When he became fussy, we pulled off at a rest area and took him out of the car; by the time we left the rest stop, it was time for his next nap. Repeating this cycle meant that the trip took a little longer, but it was easier on us physically and mentally.

Meghan Collins, Chelmsford, MA

Break up long car trips. Keep in mind that on long car trips, you will have to make frequent stops for the sake of your children. On our trips, we stopped every two hours to feed, change diapers, and just get out and stretch. We kept milk and fresh fruit in an ice chest for healthy snacking at the stops. The best you can do is to be patient with your children and try to enjoy the breaks—use them as an opportunity to have fun and explore new surroundings.

Paula, West Dundee, IL

The shock of the new. I store away various little toys and books at home and pull them out specifically for long car trips. To the baby, they seem like new toys each time, and they keep her entertained.

D. Walker, San Diego, CA

Backseat fun with Mom. I found that my toddler and infant traveled long distances better if I sat in the backseat with them. I would read stories to them, hand them new toys to play with, sing songs, and talk about what we were seeing outside the window. (There is a downside, however—by sitting in the backseat, Mom never gets a break!)

Sandie Fitzgerald, Lakeville, MN

Get good mileage with Cheerios. It's an endless battle while driving to keep baby entertained and parents headache-free. The trick is to keep baby from getting bored—my baby was happy with sock puppets, silly voices, peekaboo, picture books, and an endless supply of Cheerios. Also, call ahead to hotels to ask if they have a special room for parents traveling with infants or children; many hotels do. Locate the best family restaurants in the area, too. All babies love animals, so if there is a nearby zoo, try to make a visit.

Donna M. Condida, Archbald, PA

Container of fun. Babies love taking things out of containers. We put Cheerios or other nonsugary cereal in a four-inch plastic Cheerio or plastic Pepperidge Farm goldfish. The baby had as much fun opening and snapping the lid as eating the treat.

Joanne, NY

Tackle box is a good organizer. When vacationing by car, a fishing tackle box works great for storing everything needed for first aid or illness. Here are some of the first-aid supplies I keep in mine: Band-Aids, antibiotic ointment, 1 percent hydrocortisone cream, travel cold packs, thermometer, Red Cross first-aid book, copies of the children's medical histories, health-insurance information, immunization records, common medications (like ibuprofen [Advil], acetaminophen [Tylenol]), sunscreen and sunburn lotions, flashlight and batteries. The one vacation that I forgot to pack my box was when our daughter became very ill, and I really missed my special box.

Myra Lowrie, Sugar Land, TX

CALL YOUR LOCAL RED CROSS CHAPTER TO OBTAIN A COPY OF THEIR *FIRST AID FAST* BOOK.——MJM

Music, music, music. Keep a supply of tapes on hand. We loved Joanie Bartels best, but also introduced our kids to folk guitar and bluegrass.

Elizabeth, New York City

Shade baby from the sun. Be sure and put shades on the windows in the backseat before you leave on your trip. Baby shouldn't have the sun on his face for hours at a time.

Debra S. Fair, Waltham, MA

Comfy cozy. Remove baby's shoes for traveling and dress her in 100 percent cotton, top to bottom—she'll be much more comfortable and less irritable. Also, splurge on the premium diapers to keep diaper rash away. Pampers Premiums are more expensive, but they're worth the price when traveling long distances.

Julie Zmerzlikar, Pacifica, CA

Bring along a changing pad. We drove from Pennsylvania to Arizona when our daughter was five months old. I expected the trip to be a nightmare, but it was actually very fun! One tip I'd like to pass along is to always carry your own changing pad when traveling. We found that gas-station restrooms were usually not very clean, and if they had a baby-changing table at all, it was unsanitary. If you can, stop at national chain restaurants—most of their restrooms have baby-changing tables that are reasonably clean.

Marie M. Bassili, Tucson, AZ

Reserve a room *and* a crib. Call your hotel ahead of time to make sure that they have a crib for the baby. Most hotels charge only a nominal fee for cribs, if they charge at all. However, bring your own crib bumpers—hotels never have those.

Dawn M. Casella, Westland, MI

Drawer makes cozy crib. If you are unable to secure a crib in a hotel room, use a dresser drawer and line it with a towel and blanket. We did that with our baby daughter on one trip, and she slept well.

Julie Zmerzlikar, Pacifica, CA

Portable bassinet is versatile. Invest in a Graco *Pack 'N Play* for long trips. They have one that converts to a portable bassinet, changing station, and play yard. It folds easily into a carrying case, and aside from making an excellent bed for baby, the play yard can be used for corralling her in a nonchildproof house.

Heather Petit, Newark, DE

Routine helps baby feel more secure. When you travel with baby, keep the same routine you do at home as much as possible—this will help her feel more secure. I brought along my daughter's crib bumper pad when we traveled. Her bumper pad was familiar to her, and she would stare at it as she drifted off to sleep.

Melissa Hill, Kent, England

Take a lap. When camping with two young children, we found that naptime and bedtime were a real challenge, as it was not possible to continue the normal routine. We finally got them to quiet down by putting them in the car and driving around the campground. It took only a couple of laps before they would fall asleep, then we transferred them into our tent.

Patty Kartchner, Dayton, OR

Arrange for a baby-sitter. Most resorts have baby-sitting services available; call ahead to inquire. It's nice to have a relaxing dinner with your spouse while you're on vacation.

Laura Witek, Milwaukee, WI

Traveling by Airplane

Infants are easiest when traveling. The easiest time for traveling with a baby is from about six weeks to five months, especially if you're breast-feeding. Once baby is mobile, long-distance traveling becomes much more challenging.

Cynthia, Palo Alto, CA

Sling is best for airports. Life is much easier when going through the airport security gates if you carry your baby in a sling. If baby is in a stroller or backpack, you will have to take her out each time for a security check.

Elizabeth Vroom, Leiden, The Netherlands

Babies are easiest in the air. Don't be afraid of traveling with an infant. We traveled transatlantic with our daughter and found that she slept for most of the flight.

Donna Schwartz Mills, Los Angeles, CA

Mile-high cries. My travel experiences with my babies were anything but easy. I've traveled several times with both of my children alone, coast to coast, and I remember my kids taking turns crying for no apparent reason. On one trip, by the time I landed back in California, I was crying and apologizing to the people around me—of course, everyone said that they understood and had been through it themselves. Truly, each trip was stressful.

Ann Wells, San Diego, CA

Travel during off-peak times. Babies do best when traveling if you remember to respect their schedules. The airlines aren't set up with your baby's schedule in mind, so it's up to you to work the system. When possible, schedule your travel during off-peak hours and off-peak days. Extend out-of-town visits over major holidays so that you arrive and depart before and after the crush. If there's a chance of bad weather, cancel your plans—nothing is worth a sleepover in a jammed airport!

Jane A. Zanca, Atlanta, GA

Try a backpack for plane. The best diaper bag for airplane travel is a backpack on wheels. They are as portable as a diaper bag, but the weight and bulk are easier to carry on your shoulders or to pull behind you with one hand. They now come in a variety of sizes, and you can get one big enough to hold the essentials, along with snacks and toys, yet small enough to fit under your seat.

Cindy, Palo Alto, CA

Travel light in the air. Take as little as possible on the plane—you'll be loaded down enough. Purchase the bulk of your baby supplies at your destination.

Debra S. Fair, Waltham, MA

Bring extra for delays. It is a good idea to pack light, but by the same token, take along a few more bottles, diapers, wipes, and snacks than you anticipate needing for the duration of your total travel time (including to the airport, in the air, and to your final destination). You never know when you'll be delayed or bumped by the airlines. Also, try to book a nonstop flight when flying with a baby; it's much easier than changing planes.

Christine S. Simonson, Sumter, SC

Book a row of seats. If you're traveling with an infant and you don't wish to purchase a seat for him, try to book an aisle seat and a window seat for you and your partner. This will leave the middle seat open for your baby if no other passenger is assigned to sit there (be sure to take along your baby's car seat, too). If the plane happens to fill up, the passenger with the assigned middle seat will usually be more than happy to swap his seat with one of yours, since window and aisle seats are physically less restrictive.

Susan Sarnello-Harrison, Itasca, IL

Bulkhead seats offer more room. For longer flights, press for the bulkhead seats (bulkhead seats usually cannot be reserved in advance but can be requested at the ticket counter or gate)— you and your baby will have more room. We were able to get the bulkhead on our last flight, and our son slept on the floor and played at our feet during the flight. It was so much easier than trying to hold him for seven hours.

Jodi Detjen

More room in the rear. I found that sitting in the rear of the plane was the best place for my baby and me. Frequent flyers and business travelers, who typically board first, fill up the front section of the plane so that they can exit quickly after landing. If you sit in the back, you'll find it's less crowded and you'll see other moms doing what you're doing: changing diapers in the aisles!

D.B.

Wait to board. Although the gate attendants will offer boarding to families with small children before general boarding, I found it is best to wait until all other passengers are boarded first. The boarding process can take twenty minutes or more,

and that is too long to be sitting on a hot airplane with a baby.
Just make sure you're positioned near the boarding ramp so
that you don't miss your flight.

Joan Quigley, Kingston, NY

"Really, you're *too* kind . . ." If someone gets a bit too impatient with you and your baby, ask—or should I say "volun-
teer"—them to assist you. When you're all settled into your seat,
be sure to thank them, letting them know that if it wasn't for
their kindness, you could not have managed. This makes them
feel good while forcing them to consider their rude behavior.

Donna M. Condida, Archbald, PA

Feeding baby relieves painful eardrums. Babies often cry
during takeoff and landing due to increased pressure in their
ears. Nurse your baby, or give baby a bottle to drink during
both takeoff and landing to relieve the pressure.

Michelle Pool, Red Oak, TX

Happy flying with airplane surprises. Here's a tip my sister-
in-law gave me for keeping baby contented on airplane flights,
and it really works: Wrap small toys, or even boxes of juice or
raisins, in colorful gift wrap or tissue paper and give them to
baby one at a time during the flight. The wrap works to build
up the mystery of the treasure inside and takes some time to
unwrap. My daughter would spend twenty or thirty minutes
playing with each toy, and between toys, we took juice breaks,
ate meals and snacks, read interactive books, and (thankfully)
slept!

Nancy Ablao, Kalamazoo, MI

Wikki Stix. A friend introduced me to these waxy pieces of
multicolored strips that come in a lightweight packet. You can
bend them into any shape on top of the fold-down airline tray,

or stick them onto the window. They peel right off and don't feel sticky.

Beth, New York City

String of toys. You can keep baby's toys from rolling down the aisles by linking them together with a plastic link chain or tying them together with some yarn, making one long string of toys.

Shelly Nordlinger, Woodstock, GA

Request special meal for baby. If your baby is eating solids, order a special meal for him on meal flights; most airlines offer special baby and kiddie meals. There is no additional cost, and you can get foods that he will eat, like strained meats, vegetables, crackers, and fruit.

Heather Petit, Newark, DE

"Just to let you know . . ." If you're traveling by airplane, explain to passengers sitting next to you, prior to takeoff, that you will be nursing your baby—this gives them the option of sitting elsewhere if it makes them uncomfortable.

Lee Firlus, Marietta, GA

Deplane last. If you're traveling with baby by yourself, it's easier to wait until all other passengers have deplaned before exiting yourself. You'll need the extra time and space to gather up all of your belongings and get them organized before picking up baby.

Tracy Murtagh, Long Island, NY

Flight attendants are moms, too. As a flight attendant and mom of two, I have learned a few tips about traveling by airplane with babies and children:

1. Always bring food already prepared. There are no microwaves or can openers on the airplanes.

2. There is no prepared baby food onboard the aircraft, but there is juice.

3. The flight attendant can warm up a baby bottle with hot water in a clean "airsick bag."

4. Many flight attendants are moms, too! They are usually eager to help in any way that they can. Don't be afraid to ask for help, including if you have to use the lavatory. We especially like to hold babies; it helps us when we are missing our own children.

5. Borrow a blanket from the overhead compartment to use for diaper changes. If there are no vacant seats available, you can lay the blanket on the toilet with the lid down and change baby there.

6. Most of all, give yourself plenty of extra time upon arriving at the airport, so that you aren't stressed out before you even board the airplane.

Robin, Atlanta, GA

Cab watch! When my daughter and I arrived at the airport, I was so distracted that I didn't realize until it was too late that the cab had left with my daughter's suitcase. I had to buy all new baby clothes when we arrived in London—and it was expensive!

Cindy B., Island Park, NY

How to Change a Dirty Diaper at Thirty Thousand Feet

"Would you excuse us, please?" I smile to myself when I think of the great lengths to which parents go to provide comfort for their children. Things we ordinarily would think twice about are done without a moment's hesitation. Take, for example, my first airline flight with my then four-month-old son: We were about an hour into the flight when I realized that he had a poopy diaper, and I thought, *Now, where do I change him— the lavatory? Disgusting! The aisle? Too busy!* So I decided that I would just have to change him in my seat . . . and the sooner the better. I turned to the starched business suit sitting next to me and asked him if he wouldn't mind giving up his seat momentarily. As he abruptly headed down the aisle, I put up the armrest and proceeded with the diaper change. It only took a minute or two, and then everyone was happy again. The rest of the trip went smoothly, and I discovered that the stranger next to us even had a name. We laughed out loud about how our seats, 11A and B, made such a great changing table!

Heather A. Bergner, Poulsbo, WA

Use your lap. If your baby is small enough, change him on your lap while *you* sit on the toilet seat.

Laurie Dickan, Carmel, NY

Jump seat easier for Mom. Behind the last row of seats is a wall that separates the cabin crew's space from the passengers. Behind this wall, there is a jump seat that folds down into a bench, and with the flight attendant's permission, I've changed my baby on that bench. I liked the fact that it was located in a semiprivate area, offered an adequate amount of room for changing my baby, and was high enough to make it comfortable for me.

Bernadette F., West Chester, PA

Back of the plane is less crowded. If the plane isn't full, go to the back of the plane—which is usually less crowded—and lay a receiving blanket down on a couple of empty seats to change baby's diaper. Open the scented wipes first, to help scent the air.

Stacie L. Bryant, Two Rivers, WI

You'd cry, too! If someone gives you "the look," just smile and say, "What if it were *your* diaper?"

Kimberly R. Harris, Fairview, NC

Once You've Arrived

Helping baby feel settled. When vacationing, most babies will feel unsettled and become fussy with the change of routine and sleeping arrangements. Try to maintain her schedule as much as possible by feeding her, bathing her, reading to her, and putting her to bed at the same time you would at home. Also, make every effort not to change locations again—stay at one house and have people come to you for a visit.

Peta Gjedsted, Perth, Western Australia

Baby-proofing away from home. It's a good idea to pack your own baby-proof supplies when traveling away from home. Spend the first day following your baby around *at his level* to see what dangers lie in his path. Rearrange the house as necessary: Put away breakables, cover outlets, lock kitchen drawers and doors, cover doorknobs, gate stairs, and close toilet-seat lids and bathroom doors.

Andrea R. Cartwright, Stuyvesant, NY

Don't forget the sunscreen. We live in southern California, which is quite a mixed blessing. The sun shines most of the time, but our two fair-skinned boys sunburn quickly. I apply Coppertone Water Babies Sunblock 45 daily, even on cloudy days. If you're going to a sunny vacation spot, be sure to bring along sunscreen; a stroller top or hat isn't enough to protect baby from the damaging ultraviolet light of the sun.

Ann Wells, San Diego, CA

❦ Sunburn Protection for Baby

The American Cancer Society (www.cancer.org, or 800-ACS-2345) warns that baby's skin is thin, tender, and more susceptible to sunburn than an adult's. Here are some things you can do to protect your baby from the sun's harmful ultraviolet (UV) radiation:

• Avoid sun exposure between the hours of ten A.M. and four P.M., when the sun's UV rays are strongest.

• When outdoors, keep baby in the shade as much as possible and out of direct sunlight.

• Sunscreen is not recommended for babies under six months. For babies six months and older, apply a sunscreen with an SPF of 15 or more (SPF 30 is recommended for fair-skinned babies) thirty minutes before going into the sun, and reapply frequently.

• Dress baby in comfortable, loose-fitting cotton clothing. Cover baby's head with a protective hat, such as a floppy hat that has a visor and flaps, protecting baby's face, neck, and ears. ❦

Flexibility is key on vacation. The first vacation we took with our daughter was a three-day, two-night vacation to Florida in February. When we got to the beach, it was very windy and a little chilly. My daughter did not like the water one bit, so I spent most of that vacation sitting under an umbrella, holding and nursing her. I learned to enjoy what I had, rather than thinking about all of the things I wanted to do but couldn't. Our next vacation was to a small island in Mexico. Shortly after our arrival, our daughter came down with a fever and was very cranky. She did not want to do anything; she only wanted Mama to hold her. I was disappointed that I couldn't go sightseeing or swim much, but I decided to focus on the positive instead—like the fact that I was sitting on a beautiful, warm beach looking at turquoise-blue water. I didn't have to cook or clean; I could just rest quietly while holding my child. I guess the best advice I can give is before you leave the house to go on a trip with your children, take into account their needs and abilities. Don't make a big list of things you're going to see or do; think about what you would like to do, then take it one day at a time and, above all, be flexible.

Kathryn A. Varuzza, New Paltz, NY

CHAPTER 10

Home Safe Home

Safety and Baby-proofing

I used to bathe my son in an infant tub that fitted nicely over the kitchen sink. The height of the sink made it easier for me, and I had plenty of room on the adjacent island countertop on which to undress my son and lay out his bath supplies. Then one afternoon when my son was about thirteen weeks old, I undressed him for his bath and placed him on a blanket on the countertop while filling his bathtub with water. I *thought* my right hand was resting on one of his legs as I tested the temperature of the water with my left wrist, but that must not have been the case. After I filled his bathtub, I turned back around to pick up my baby, only to find he was gone. It took a full five seconds before I realized that he must have pushed himself off the counter with his feet and was lying on the floor on the other side of the counter! Even worse, he was making no sound whatsoever. I was almost too paralyzed with fear to even move—I thought I would find my beautiful baby in a pool of blood.

But when I got to the other side of the counter, I almost

couldn't believe what I saw: Somehow my baby had stayed perfectly positioned on top of the thick, double-folded afghan receiving blanket on which I had placed him, and the blanket had provided him a soft (and safe) landing. When I screamed his name, he just gave me an inquisitive look, as if wondering what all the fuss was about. Although it was embarrassing to have to relate the story of my inattentiveness a short while later to his doctor, I was relieved when, after examining my baby, the doctor reported that he had no apparent injuries. From that day's near-tragic accident, I learned firsthand two critical rules of in-home safety: *Never* leave a baby unattended in high places and *continually* reevaluate baby's abilities on a week-to-week— even daily—basis. What my son couldn't do at twelve weeks of age—push off with his feet—he *could* do at thirteen weeks.

The American Academy of Pediatrics reports that unintentional injuries are the number-one cause of death in children under five, and more than one million children are treated each year because of it. These are sobering statistics for sure, but the good news is that you can do plenty to keep your baby safe and out of harm's way. The first thing is to get educated. Ask your baby's doctor for reading material on baby safety and first aid. Know that danger lurks in every room of your house. Baby-proof *before* your baby starts to move around, and assume that he will eventually figure a way to get around your best defenses. Don't mistakenly think that you can keep your child out of trouble with a close eye on him; even the most vigilant parent can't monitor their child's every move throughout the day. Get down on your hands and knees and look at each room in your house from his level—if it's potentially harmful, store it away, lock it up, or get rid of it. Once your child starts cruising and walking, take the child's-eye-view baby-proofing tour again; there are plenty of new safety hazards for vertical kids.

Moms relate their own baby-safety stories in this important chapter and talk about the importance of getting educated on baby safety and emergency care, the best ways to baby-proof your house, pet safety, and safety must-haves for keeping baby away from danger.

Getting Educated

It's a lifesaver! Was I ever glad I took an infant/toddler safety and CPR class: My son had just started crawling when he found something on the floor and tried to swallow it. He began gasping for air and turned pale. Before I even had time to panic, the things they taught me in class kicked in and my instincts took over: I scooped him up, turned him over in my lap, and slapped him hard on the back, and the object flew out of his mouth. He took in a deep breath and started crying. Had it not been for the training I received in class, I would have panicked in that situation, but instead I felt prepared and informed, and it helped me to make a calm and quick decision.

Dawn M. Oliveri, Saunderstown, RI

Try your local fire department. One phone call to our local fire department hooked me up with a firefighter who also taught CPR classes. I picked a date for him to come to teach a group of ten new moms, and we all split the cost, so it was very reasonable.

Susan Sarnello-Harrison, Itasca, IL

ᵂᵉ Learn How to Keep Baby Safe

The Consumer Products Safety Commission (CPSC) (www.cpsc.gov, or 800-638-2772) is an independent federal regulatory agency that acts to keep American families safe by reducing the risk, injury, or death from consumer products. Visit the CPSC Web site to obtain publications on a variety of in-home baby-safety topics, including nursery equipment, infant bedding and SIDS prevention, household furniture, household products, fire and burn protection, carbon-monoxide poisoning, toy safety, and much more. The site also keeps a current listing of product recalls and invites consumers to report injuries and unsafe products. ᵂᵉ

Get the lead out. Lead—found in older paint, water, and some crystal and ceramics—poses a real risk to baby's developing brain. Hardware stores carry kits you can use to test paint on walls and windowsills, crystal, and ceramics. Your local water-treatment plant can test a water sample from your pipes for free or a nominal fee. Ask your pediatrician if he or she recommends periodic blood tests so you can be sure your baby is safe. And if you have to have lead removed from a home built prior to 1979, hire a professional who specializes in lead abatement. I had a friend who hired a regular housepainter who sandblasted the old paint off her home's exterior, contaminating the house inside and out! The EPA had to evacuate the whole family!

Betsy Rapoport, White Plains, NY

Consider hiring a baby-proofing service. When we moved into our new house, we had a baby-proofing company come to our house. For $25, the safety expert spent about an hour going through the house and suggesting ways to make it safer for

❧ *Baby-proofing Products and Services*

Here are a few good national resources for baby-proofing products
and services:

SAFETY 1ST

Safety 1st (www.safety1st.com, or 800-723-3065) has over three
hundred child-care products to help keep your baby safe in the
home, including baby-proofing items, tubs, bath seats, bed rails,
gates, nonmobile walkers, and more. They also offer referrals to
childproofing companies in your area.

SAFE BEGINNINGS

Safe Beginnings (www.safebeginnings.com, or 800-598-8911)
offers a wide selection of baby-proofing and family-safety products, all designed to withstand continuous use. Baby-proofing items
such as brackets, guards, straps, and latches can be found in the
online catalog.

INTERNATIONAL ASSOCIATION FOR CHILD SAFETY (IACS)

IACS (www.iafcs.com, or 888-677-IACS) promotes child-safety
awareness and educates parents on ways to help reduce and prevent
household injuries. Visit their Web site for child-proofing and
safety tips, as well as to locate a child-proofing service near you.

THE SAFETY GUY NETWORK

The Safety Guy Network (www.askthesafetyguy.com, or call 888-
388-3811) is a national home-safety company offering safety information and tips, a safety checklist for the home, and referrals to
baby-proofing and home-safety experts in your area.   ❧

babies and toddlers. Some of the suggestions involved things that we could do on our own, while other things required purchasing safety supplies or equipment. The consultation fee was applied toward our purchases, and we even scheduled their technician to install some of the trickier items.

Jan Harrison Furlow, Alexandria, VA

Poison Control

Keep Poison Control Center number handy. Get the telephone number to your regional Poison Control Center and keep it near your telephone. You may need it one day but not be able to find it in a panic situation—that's exactly what happened to me. I was holding my ten-month-old and giving her what I *thought* was her medicine, but I was distracted talking to my sister and instead gave her her older brother's asthma medication! I realized what I had done and fortunately found the number for Poison Control on the inside of the front cover of the telephone book. Thankfully, everything turned out okay, but what a scare!

Dawn M. Casella, Westland, MI

Prevention better than anticipation. Sure, there are developmental guidelines, but you'll never know when your baby will flip, push off, crawl forward, or stand. Our son flipped off his changing table (thank God he fell into the open drawer and wasn't hurt) weeks and weeks before he was "supposed to" and certainly without any "preflipping" behavior. From then on, I kept one hand on him while changing him. Practice preventive safety from the get-go.

Elizabeth, New York City

🦢 Poisoning

The American Heart Association (www.americanheart.org, or 800-242-8721) states that childhood poisoning is a common problem in our society. We have access to more than two hundred and fifty thousand household products; it is not surprising that curious, exploring children are often victims of poisoning. Some common poisons found in the home include:

- Prescription and nonprescription medications, most importantly iron pills, vitamins containing iron, Tylenol, and aspirin
- Plants
- Cleansers, polishing agents, ammonia, and detergents
- Cosmetics and hair-care products
- Alcohol and liquor
- Insect and rodent poisons, mothballs
- Gasoline, kerosene, and other petroleum products
- Pesticides, weed killers, and fertilizers
- Lye and acids
- Paint and paint thinners

Syrup of ipecac (to cause vomiting) should be kept in every home with young children. It is a helpful treatment for various types of poisoning but should be used *only when prescribed by a doctor or Poison Control Center*. For some poison ingestions, inducing vomiting is *not* indicated and may be harmful. Always check with the Poison Control Center or your doctor *before* giving ipecac.

Reproduced with permission © *Pediatric Basic Life Support,* 1997 Copyright American Heart Association 🦢

MANY MOMS RECOMMEND MAKING A LIST OF THE POISON CONTROL CENTER, PEDIATRICIAN, HOSPITAL, AND POLICE AND PUTTING IT NEAR EVERY PHONE IN THE HOUSE.——MJM

Keep *all* medications out of reach. I had a scare when my husband thought my daughter was sucking on a tube of infant toothpaste, only to find out that it was Benadryl cream. There was a warning on the tube to call Poison Control in case of ingestion. We had to estimate the size of the glob in her mouth so that they could recommend treatment. Fortunately, she had not ingested a harmful amount. It taught me how easily a child can mistake products that look so much alike.

Natalie Tabet, NM

Post your address and phone number near the telephone. In addition to the Poison Control number, write your address and home telephone number on a card and keep it by the phone. This is useful for you in a panic situation, because you may not be able to remember your address if your child isn't breathing; also, it's vital if you have a sitter, who may not know your address or remember your phone number if it isn't listed on the phone. If you live in an apartment or condominium with numbered buildings, write your building number down, too.

Jane A. Zanca, Atlanta, GA

Baby-proofing and Safety

Store it away. You may intend to keep some of your valuables displayed in your home after baby arrives, but believe me, you will get very tired of constantly telling her *No!* Instead, make your house a *Yes!* house, making everything within her reach okay to touch. You'll both be happier.

Amy Lanhardt, Orange, CA

Seeing his point of view. When baby begins to crawl and pull himself up, get down on your hands and knees and see what your baby sees from his level—it's a whole different world down there, and you will see all kinds of hazards you never knew existed. Also, a baby's reach is two to three feet from the floor, so be sure to baby-proof at least three feet up.

PoLee Mark-Yee, Kirkland, Quebec

Assign "safe" rooms for baby. So that you don't drive yourself crazy, rather than trying to make every room in your house safe for baby, completely childproof those rooms designated for him, then lock or gate off the other rooms. That way, you can relax with your baby and not have to be nervous about what he's getting into when he's momentarily out of your sight.

Julie Zmerzlikar, Pacifica, CA

In the Kitchen

Kitchen knives especially hazardous. Put the baby down while you're preparing food. I'll never forget how close I came to injuring my baby one day while preparing a meal. My daughter was crying, so I picked her up and held her while cutting cheese. All of a sudden, she flung her body forward, and I barely missed impaling her head with my sharp paring knife. After that, I always put her down—no matter how hard she cried—before preparing food in the kitchen.

Sheryl McCarthy, North Stonington, CT

Keep baby busy in the kitchen. When you're in the kitchen, your baby will most likely want to be there, too. To keep baby occupied, let him have one "safe" drawer—a drawer low to the floor that is his only. Fill it with safe things that will keep his attention, like colorful plastic containers, wooden and plastic utensils, and empty food boxes.

Lauren McMenimen, Tempe, AZ

Magnetic lock and key are best. Although most of the inexpensive plastic door/drawer locks available on the market are fine for a baby, by the time he's a toddler, he'll have figured out how to unlatch most of them. For critical areas, like under the kitchen sink, get the Safety 1st Tot Lok (www.safety1st.com, or 800-723-3065); it's a strong magnetic lock that disengages only when its magnetic key is used. It will cost you more, but you won't have to worry about your child being able to unlatch it on his own. Since the key is a magnet, too, you can store it high on your refrigerator out of your child's reach.

Tina Evans, Marietta, GA

Cook with back burners. Never use the front burners on your stovetop—your baby will soon be able to reach the handles of hot pots and pans. Get in the habit of using only back burners.

Sheila Billick, Gillette, WY

IF YOU MUST USE THE FRONT BURNERS, TURN ALL HANDLE POTS IN, (AWAY FROM BABY) OR CONSIDER INSTALLING A STOVETOP SHIELD. IF STOVE KNOBS ARE ACCESSIBLE, INVEST IN BABY-PROOF COVERS FOR THEM.—MJM

Oven doors can burn. Never underestimate what your baby might be capable of. My son was about nine months old and was just learning how to pull himself up and take a few steps. One day he was standing next to me in the kitchen as I was preparing biscuits; the oven was behind me and preheated to 350°F. My son walked about four steps to the oven, grabbed hold of the door handle, and pulled it open. Before I realized what he had done, he placed his tiny hand on the hot, hot glass

☞ Kitchen Hazards

The Consumer Product Safety Commission reports:
· An estimated 9,300 injuries to children under age five are treated in U.S. hospital emergency rooms in a given year.
· Annually, there are about 22,000 thermal burn injuries involving stoves.
· There are 16,000 injuries to children involving kitchen knives in a given year.
· Each year, many children under age five are injured or die from household chemicals and medicines. ☞

on the inside of the door. I learned after rushing him to the hospital that he had suffered a second-degree burn on his palm; he was treated and we had to return for checkups every other day for several weeks. That night of his accident, we went out and purchased an oven-door safety latch that secures the oven door. What's ironic is that we had planned on buying a safety latch but thought we had plenty of time and that our son was still too young to harm himself.

Judith Schneider, Ingomar, PA

Place chemicals and cleaners up high. You can't count on childproof locks when you're talking about dangerous chemicals and liquids like household cleaners; if your baby is able to get to them even once, it could prove fatal. Plus, many older babies and toddlers can open many kinds of childproof locks. Move all cleaning products out from underneath the sink and onto a top shelf.

Jaki Thomas, South Australia

MANY MOMS HAVE STARTED TRYING GREEN, ALL-NATURAL HOUSE-
HOLD CLEANERS FOR THIS REASON; MANY ARE LESS TOXIC THAN
STANDARD CLEANERS.—MJM

Don't use tablecloths. Burns from hot foods and beverages
can occur when a toddler pulls a place mat or tablecloth off the
table. Teach your child right from the start not to reach for
things on the table. Don't use tablecloths (place mats are better),
but it's really best to keep baby confined while you're eating.

Mirka

Decals ideal for glass doors. For sliding glass doors, buy colorful vinyl decals with cartoons on them—available at most
baby stores—and adhere them to the glass at your toddler's eye
level so he can't run into it. Toddlers get distracted when playing and can forget that the doors are even there.

Karen D. Menna, Dunwoody, GA

Other Rooms in the House

Slide outlet covers are user-friendly. You should cover all
electrical outlets, but I would not recommend the cheap, flat
plastic safety covers that plug in; they're much too difficult to
remove when you need to use the outlet. Instead, get the slide
covers; they cover the entire outlet and automatically slide
closed when you pull out the plug. They're a bit more expensive
than the other kind, but they're a lot more user-friendly.

Julie, Moorpark, CA

"I think it landed in Africa." Buy the kind of safety gates that
screw into the wall. Your six-month-old may be contained just
fine with the pressure-lock type, but I guarantee you that once

he's eighteen months old, he'll kick any pressure-lock gate from here to Timbuktu!

Lara Joudrey, London, Ontario

Walkers are more harmful than good. Don't use baby walkers! The American Academy of Pediatrics has suggested banning them due to the high volume of injuries—over twenty-eight thousand a year! Most accidents occur when the walkers tip over, which happens more easily than you may think; walkers can tip from changes in floor surfaces, when area rugs bunch up, from running over toys or other objects in its path, and most certainly when baby connects with a flight of stairs. And, because baby is at eye level with furniture in a walker, it's not uncommon for him to walk himself into sharp corners of furniture and other dangerous objects. With stakes this high, why take the risk?

Holly Glennon, Anchorage, AK

Cushion furniture. An inexpensive and effective way to protect young toddlers from pointed furniture is to wrap sharp edges and legs with bubble wrap, newspaper, paper towels, or clean rags and secure with packaging tape. It doesn't look particularly great, but who cares? Your baby will be little for such a short while, and you can have your house back the way you want it later.

Sue Menna, Coatesville, PA

Gives your baby more room to play, too. Coffee tables are a big hazard to little ones just learning to walk; they can be injured by sharp edges and many times bump their heads on them. Why not do what I did and just remove the coffee table altogether? What do you really use it for, anyway?

Linda Alderman, Kanab, UT

Secure freestanding furniture. Attach all unsteady pieces of furniture (dressers, entertainment centers, freestanding book-cases, baker's racks) to the wall or floor. One time my daughter decided that she wanted something from the top of her dresser and proceeded to pull open each of the dresser drawers and climbed up. But the dresser could not support her weight and it toppled over on her! She was momentarily trapped underneath but, luckily, unhurt. After that, we bolted all of the dressers to the floor.

Amy L. Burrell, Sharon Hill, PA

Unstable TV stands can tip. We currently have a TV stand that we realize we're going to have to get rid of before our ten-month-old daughter gets much older. It would be too easy for her to tip the TV over onto herself. We plan on investing in a full-size entertainment center—it will be much safer.

Erin Khan

Tie up hanging cords. Keep hanging blinds and drape cords bundled up and out of baby's reach. If your cords are knotted together, unknot or cut them so that they cannot form a noose

❧ Furniture Tip-over

The CPSC estimates that eight to ten thousand victims are treated annually in U.S. emergency rooms for injuries associated with the tip-over of furniture. The majority of these injuries and deaths are to children when they climb onto shelves, bookcases, dressers, bureaus, desks, chests, and television stands. Place televisions on lower furniture, as far back as possible, and use angle braces to secure tip-over furniture to the wall. ❧

and make it possible for baby to strangle himself. Never place baby's crib or any furniture near blinds, which can make cords too easily accessible.

Tina Golden, Coldwater, MS

SOME BABY-SAFETY CATALOGS HAVE TUBES YOU CAN FIT ALL THE CORDS INTO SO THEY'RE OUT OF REACH.——MJM

Towel prevents doors from closing. To prevent fingers from getting caught or slammed in doors, hang a bath towel over the top of each of your doors; that way the doors won't be able to fully close.

Jaki Thomas, South Australia

Pen off hazardous areas. Use large, multisectional "yards" (plastic pens) to keep baby away from electronics or other dangerous areas. Instead of using them to cage baby *in,* use them to keep baby *out.*

Heather Petit, Newark, DE

Eyes on the changing table! Be careful when your baby is on the changing table. I turned away for one second to get a wipe and my daughter fell onto the diaper pail! Luckily she didn't get hurt.

Cindy, Long Island, NY

Make high places off-limits to baby. Don't leave baby on high places unattended. My five-month-old was just learning to roll over but wasn't quite able to do so. Then one day, my husband and I took him to the basement with us so we could do the laundry, placing him on a futon mattress (it was about a foot off the floor). We were watching him, but in just a split second, before either of us could dive for him, he rolled off the mattress and landed on his head on the cement floor! He started wailing right away. He had a small red mark on the side of his head, but it didn't seem that bad at the time. Well, the next morning he woke up with an enormous lump on his head about the size of an orange cut in half. It was absolutely terrifying to discover. Luckily, a doctor's check verified that everything was okay. We were like many people who assumed that an injury such as the one our baby suffered only happened to inattentive parents, but that's not true. It happened to us, and it can easily happen to you.

Meghan Collins, Chelmsford, MA

Future Olympians take note. Our daughter, at ten months, figured out how to push a kitchen chair up against the counter, climb up on the counter, and get at high shelves. Little climbers can be very enterprising, so be on the alert.

Betsy Rapoport, White Plains, NY

Gate stairways early. I learned this lesson the hard way. My baby fell down a flight of stairs the very day she sat up and moved for the first time on her own. It was quite a shock, but fortunately, she wasn't badly hurt. I would tell new moms to be sure and install safety gates at the top of the stairs *before* they think they'll need them.

Elizabeth Vroom, Leiden, The Netherlands

Common houseplants can be poisonous. Know what kinds of plants you have in your house and if they are poisonous. My nine-month-old daughter put a leaf in her mouth, and I realized that I had no idea what kind of plant it was. I quickly called Poison Control and was told that if the plant was poisonous, it could make her mouth burn and possibly cause her to vomit. They told me to take the plant to a nursery in order to have it correctly identified. As it turned out, the plant was not poisonous and everything turned out fine, but it was a frightening experience. If you're the least bit unsure about the types of plants you have, I suggest that you take a clipping of each to a local nursery for identification. Then do some research as to whether or not it is poisonous to children.

Natalie Tabet, NM

YOU MAY WANT TO DO WHAT I DID AND GET RID OF YOUR HOUSE PLANTS ALTOGETHER.—MJM

Strict supervision near water. A baby can drown in just a few inches of water; don't leave your baby alone around *any* water—not even for a second! This includes the tub, toilet, swimming pool or wading pool, or even a seemingly harmless bucket of water.

Paula, West Dundee, IL

Top your toilet. Kids can fall into toilets, and they also adore launching toys into the bowl, so we always used toilet-lid locks.

Betsy Rapoport, White Plains, NY

Curling irons are a common cause of burns. One day while I was fixing dinner, I heard a horrific cry from my daughter. I went into the bathroom and saw my curling iron lying on the floor—I hadn't realized until I touched it that I had forgotten to unplug it that morning. I found my daughter in the bedroom crying, with her entire palm blistering fast. I hurried her into the kitchen and ran cool water over it (I had just completed a first-aid refresher course and knew that this was the first thing to do, as the cool water prevents the heat from continuing to burn the skin. *Never* use butter or ice). My husband joined me, and we put a wrapped ice pack on it and telephoned her pediatrician. I felt terrible. I learned a valuable lesson that day: Never leave a curling iron—plugged in or not—within a child's reach.

Deborah Baska, Kansas City, MO

Lock drugs away in a fishing tackle box. A good idea for keeping medicine out of the reach of small children is to put it under lock and key in a fishing tackle box. Keep the tackle box on a high shelf.

Sheila Billick, Gillette, WY

Traction makes cruising safer. When baby starts to walk, dress her in nonslip socks (with rubber on the bottom), or leave socks off completely. Wooden flooring and other flooring surfaces are dangerously slippery when baby is wearing regular socks.

Lynne Morgan, London, England

Miscellaneous

Ban all latex balloons. One thing all children want is a pretty balloon. However, the most common balloons, made of latex, are especially hazardous because if a child swallows a piece, it can completely obstruct the airway and is virtually impossible for an adult to remove (the Heimlich maneuver most likely won't work). Mylar balloons are a safer alternative because should it burst, the Mylar breaks into large pieces. However, if either type pops, dispose of all pieces immediately.

Kimberly Cushman, West Windsor, NJ

Kick the habit (or take it outside). Never smoke around baby, or even in the house. It takes about six hours for a room to clear of smoke, and children, especially newborns, develop chronic ear infections and respiratory problems from second-hand smoke. This is a must!

Katherine W. Manning-Pinotti, Houston, TX

Pitch the plastic. Dry cleaners' plastic bags and balloon fragments are smothering and choking hazards. We removed dry cleaners' bags as soon as we brought our clothes home and walked them outside to the trash. We used Mylar balloons for parties so we wouldn't have balloon scraps from popped balloons.

Joanne, New York City

Monitor pets closely. If you have a pet that is dear to you and accustomed to getting all of your attention, watch for signs of jealousy or aggression when baby comes home. Many otherwise gentle family pets can suddenly feel displaced by a new baby and may bite, or worse, maim your baby. It's best never to leave your pet unattended around your baby, and be especially careful as baby grows that she does not put her face close to the

✻ Pet Safety

The Humane Society of the United States (www.hsus.org and www. nodogbites.org, or 202-452-1100) reports that an estimated 4.7 million people in the United States, most of whom are children, are bitten by dogs each year. Although some dogs are more genetically predisposed to be dangerously aggressive, *any* breed of dog has the potential to bite. Contributing factors other than breed include the quality of care, the degree of socialization to people, and the level and type of training the dog has received.

Whether your family pet is a dog or cat (or both), changes brought on your pet prior to the baby's arrival can stress your pet. It's often the change in your pet's routine, and not the baby itself, that causes your pet to be stressed when baby makes four. You can minimize the stress by introducing the changes gradually; that way, your pet won't associate them with the arrival of the baby. It's equally important that good things happen to your pet when your baby is present. Start making these changes now, before your baby is born.

- Ask your veterinarian to examine your pet for good general health and ensure that vaccinations are current. Routine care prevents the transmission of intestinal and external parasites to baby.
- If you haven't spayed or neutered your pet, do so now. Sterilized pets have fewer health problems, are less likely to bite, and are more loving and calm.
- If you allow your pet to pounce, swat, or nibble on parts of your body, redirect that behavior to toys. Keep nails and claws trimmed to prevent accidental scratches.
- Your pet should no longer be allowed in your lap uninvited, since this will be the baby's place. Instead, train him—using positive techniques and rewards—to remain calmly on the floor at your side.
- If you haven't been through a training class with your dog, or

it's been a while, consider enrolling in one. Training allows you to safely and positively control your dog's behavior. If your pet is fearful or anxious, ask your veterinarian for advice or for a referral to an animal behaviorist or trainer.

• Carry around a swaddled baby doll to familiarize your pet with bathing and diapering. If you acquire a mechanical swing, turn it on. Sit in the rocking chair and offer your pet a treat, or play with him to make it a positive experience.

• Apply lotion or baby powder to your skin to get your pet familiar with the new scents.

• To keep pets off certain furniture, apply double-stick tape to the furniture. If your pet has been allowed in a room that will now be the baby's room, install a sturdy screen door or gate to prevent your pet from entering unsupervised.

• If your dog enjoys walks, get yourself and your dog used to walking with the stroller.

• Before coming home from the hospital, send an article of clothing or blanket ahead for your pet to investigate. When you return from the hospital, have someone else hold the baby so you can give your pet a warm welcome.

After you bring baby home:

• Never force your pet to interact with your baby, and always supervise any interactions between them. An excitable pet can easily injure a baby, if only by accident when baby kicks and grabs. Don't allow baby to disturb your sleeping pet or touch the pet without the pet seeing the baby first.

• Teach your baby, using positive reinforcement ("I like how gently you're petting the cat; that feels good") to treat your pet with gentleness. Babies have a tendency to grab animals very forcefully, leaving them little option but to react aggressively.

pet's, or try to take the pet's food or toys. We chose to have our dog—who is big and muscular and lives primarily in the house with us—neutered before our daughter was born. We were told that neutering would help ease aggressive tendencies, especially in male dogs. To help introduce our baby daughter to our dog, my husband first brought home one of her blankets from the hospital, then laid it in the doorway to the nursery so that he would become familiar with her scent. We found it was important, too, that my husband spend some one-on-one time with our dog each day to reassure him that he was loved and not forgotten.

Angela J. Byrnes, Stanford, CA

Check for recalls. It's a good idea to check baby products for recalls, especially if you buy secondhand items. A good Web site for recalled baby products is the U.S. Consumer Product Safety Commission (www.cpsc.gov). You can also visit parenting sites—ParenthoodWeb.com (www.parenthood.com) and About.com's Parenting: Babies and Toddlers (http://babyparenting.about.com/)—and type "product recall" in the search field.

Tammy W., Anchorage, AK

YOU SHOULD ALSO CHECK TOYS AND STUFFED ANIMALS FREQUENTLY FOR LOOSE OR FRAYING PARTS.—MJM

Firearms should be locked up or removed. If you have a gun in the house, now is the time to lock it up in a strongbox. Then place the strongbox in the trunk of your car. Next, push your car off a high cliff located above a deep levee. Seriously!

Kimberly R. Harris, Fairview, NC

✿ Gun Safety

Common Sense (www.kidsandguns.org, or 877-955-KIDS) is a nonprofit group working to protect America's children from gun deaths and injuries. They warn all parents who own guns to:
- Unload and lock it up.
- Lock and store ammunition separately.
- Hide keys where children can't find them.
- Teach young children not to touch guns and to tell an adult if they find one. ✿

No substitute for a watchful eye. Although safety equipment is a good idea, don't completely rely on it; it can give parents a less attentive attitude, possibly putting the child in danger. There is *no* substitute for a watchful eye. In the long run, it's more important to change the behavior of your little one as she grows, teaching her to avoid dangerous objects and situations, rather than to always try to put up safety barriers.

Debra Z. Ackley, Hammondsport, NY

Spring forward, fall back. Make sure you have smoke detectors on every floor. Check them once a week and change the batteries twice a year. We do it when the clocks get set back and forward. Carbon-monoxide detectors are a good idea, too, and should be placed outside of the bedroom(s).

Betsy Rapoport, White Plains, NY

Get a choke tube. If you're worried that a toy might pose a choking hazard, insert it into a choking tube, a plastic cylinder you can get from most retailers. If the toy fits inside, it's too small to play with at your baby's age.

Joanne, New York City

CHAPTER 11

Chasing the Blues Away
— ❧ —
The Postpartum Adjustment Period

Postpartum Adjustment

There's nothing easy about it. The postpartum period—the first few weeks and months following your baby's birth—can wipe you out physically and emotionally. First-time moms often find that their otherwise sunny disposition is sent packing with the arrival of fluctuating hormones, postpartum pains and discomfort, sleep deprivation, the relentlessness of around-the-clock baby care, and feelings of inadequacy in caring for a helpless newborn. It's a temporary situation, but when you're in the throes of it, you feel like there's no end in sight.

Women who are used to being "in control" often find the postpartum period especially onerous. That was the case with me. As a former regional sales manager for a large food company, I was accustomed to a carefree lifestyle that included setting my own schedule, hopping on an airplane week in and week out, socializing with my peers, eating out several nights a week, and meeting the demands and challenges of the job. Once home with a newborn—who spent most of his day sleeping—

I felt restless and anxious, and badly yearned for mental stimulation. It was pretty apparent from the start that this new little person in my life controlled my every waking moment, and I was going to have to figure out how to cope or else go crazy! I felt better when I got out of the house with my baby, so I made sure I did so once a day. Eventually, I found the mental challenge I was looking for through my writing; it made me feel connected again to the rest of the world.

As you'll hear from other moms, there's little you can do about the exhaustion and fatigue in the first few weeks. Try to rest as much as possible and arrange for postpartum help—your spouse, a relative or friend, or even a postpartum professional to assist you for the first couple of weeks at home. Let the housework and the cooking go. Talk to other moms about what you're feeling; chances are, they've been down a similar road themselves and can offer support and advice. Finally, you'll feel better if you get up and get out; take a walk, go grocery shopping, or visit a friend.

The first half of this chapter addresses the postpartum adjustment period, while the last half focuses on the "baby blues" and postpartum depression. Be sure to read "Taking Time for Yourself" in the next chapter, too; there you'll find lots of useful advice on taking care of yourself during the weeks and months following baby's arrival. Keep reading as moms talk about their own postpartum adjustment experiences and things you can do to prepare beforehand; keeping the exhaustion and stress to a minimum; when to keep visitors at bay and when to accept help; things you can do to pick yourself up; and finding postpartum support.

Supermom means super exhaustion. I had fallen into the Supermom trap, thinking that, because I was on a six-week break from work, I needed to fill in all of the holes at home, like having a home-cooked meal every night for my husband, making the beds, doing the grocery shopping, cleaning the house, and running errands. Trying to maintain this kind of schedule added up to a lot of stress and put a damper on what should have been a beautiful time in my life. The situation was further aggravated by my husband, who really didn't understand the demands of a new baby; he would come home and ask me what I did all day. *Well . . . I fed the baby, changed diapers, dressed the baby, held the baby, put the baby to sleep, and bathed the baby.* When you say it out loud, it doesn't sound like it can possibly take twelve hours out of a day, but believe me, it does!

Deborah Baska, Kansas City, MO

It's when the hard work *really* begins. Maternity leave is not a vacation—as some of my coworkers implied—it is a very important time for you and your new family to learn about each other. Taking care of a new baby at home alone is a tremendous undertaking. There were many days when I felt a great sense of accomplishment in just taking a shower and getting dressed.

Angela J. Byrnes, Stanford, CA

Strive for progress, not perfection. So many women buy into the motherhood fairy tale. The stage is set with crisply ironed white-eyelet bonnets and cradle drapes. The baby coos softly, sleeps soundly, and eats and naps regularly—everything is cuddly and idyllic. But the truth is, babies are a chaotic reality, and someone should tell you to be prepared for things like sleep deprivation, hormonal roller-coaster rides, a delay in the

208 ~ CHASING THE BLUES AWAY

much-touted bonding process, ear infections, colic, and fevers. Also expect strangers to give you advice and everyone—even your doctor—to contradict your most basic instincts. In the beginning, don't even hope for good days—appreciate good moments when they come; after a while, they add up. Strive for progress, not perfection.

Linda Federman, Randolph, NJ

Home alone. It took many years of marriage and many children to get my sweet husband to understand this basic principle: A new mom feels a great deal of isolation. It takes so much work to go out of the house with the baby that sometimes it's easier to stay home. I used to feel completely overwhelmed and trapped if I didn't get enough breaks from the baby-care routine.

Patty Kartchner, Dayton, OR

Hotels are a new mom's best friend. If it's going to add stress to an already stressful situation, don't be shy about asking your in-laws and other visitors to give you some time before visiting and possibly even find alternate accommodations. The first six weeks of my son's life were extremely hard for me. I'm glad my in-laws waited three weeks before visiting (though a few weeks longer would have been even better), and although this was a point of contention between my husband and me, we requested that they stay in a hotel. We were worried at first that they would be insulted, but they were fine with it, and I didn't have to stress out about cleaning linens, changing the beds, getting the bathrooms clean, or our crying baby waking them at night.

Meghan Collins, Chelmsford, MA

Couldn't have done it without you, Mom. If you have a good relationship with your own mother, by all means ask her for help after the baby arrives. When I first announced my first pregnancy to my mother, she said that of course she would come to help . . . I couldn't understand what she was talking about. Then I brought my daughter home—I never would have survived the first two weeks without my mother cooking, doing the laundry, and offering moral support. She made it clear from the start that this baby belonged to me and she never once—nor has she since—criticized a decision I've made as a parent (and I've made some pretty boneheaded ones!). Not everyone has a mother like mine, but every woman needs help postpartum. If you can't import a close relative to help, then hire someone for housecleaning and meal preparation.

Cynthia, Palo Alto, CA

Have Dad stay home at first, too. Having the father home with Mom and the baby in the initial weeks promotes family bonding, as well as a greater understanding by the father of the difficulties of life with an infant. Plus, Mom is less overwhelmed.

Paula Bobbett, McKinney, TX

Tag-team parenting. My husband and I can get six weeks of parental leave. I took the first six at home, and he took the second six. It made us feel less stressed to know that a parent was on duty, even if I would have liked to have both of us at home those first two weeks.

Beth, New York City

Give yourself time to heal from C-section. I've had two C-sections, and I would advise a new mom facing the same prospect to try to get her husband or partner to stay home for at least a week. Continually getting out of bed prolongs the healing process; having a little extra time to yourself will help you recover more quickly. If you know ahead of time that you will be having a C-section, plan ahead by making extra at mealtimes and freezing foods like casseroles, pizza, pasta sauces, and so forth. If your C-section is a surprise, have hubby bring home takeout at night.

Karen Rudolph Durrie, Calgary, Alberta

Say hello to the new you! Things will fall into place after you bring your baby home. I cannot explain it, but there's something inside you that knows just what to do—call it mother's intuition. As for feeling like your old self again, you won't . . . you'll feel even better!

Kimberly Cushman, West Windsor, NJ

Time softens the hardships of motherhood. I was overwhelmed! I adored my baby, but I was exhausted. I was anxious during the day when my husband was away at work, then at five P.M. every afternoon, I expected him to walk in the door and take over. All I wanted was to go to bed. I remember rocking my baby and thinking, *My poor baby is going to be an only child. There is no way I could ever go through this again! What was I thinking?* Now, of course, it's funny to me—I'm seven and a half months pregnant with our second child, and I can't wait!

Natalie Tabet, NM

"Could I get some recognition around here, please?" I had been good at my professional job, but I had no clue how to do my "mothering" job. I was so used to being a part of a professional organization, being recognized and receiving accolades for my work. Then suddenly there I was, "working" alone at home. My responsibilities went from the important to the mundane, and I got no satisfaction from doing housework. I found being a new mom was a lonely experience that made me feel isolated.

Janelle Goossens

Find an understanding ear. Avoid talking to "friends" who constantly have only "dreamy" things to say about the first few weeks with a newborn. If all someone can say is "Isn't it wonderful?" and "Don't you just tear up every time you look at your beautiful baby?," then she is not someone with whom you can share your insecurities. A good friend is someone who knows that, while you have fallen madly in love with your sweet, new baby, there are moments that are not so blissful and times when baby doesn't act so sweet.

Jan Harrison Furlow, Alexandria, VA

Take a lesson from the opposite sex. It's funny how we women have this perception that we are expected to carry on as if we didn't just have a baby. If it were a man who had just had a baby, do you think for even one minute that he would clean the house instead of napping when he had gotten only one hour of sleep the night before? Of course not! He wouldn't clean the house at all. He wouldn't cook. He would eat take-out food and lie down as much as possible. So my best advice is . . . *pretend you're a man!*

Kathryn A. Varuzza, New Paltz, NY

I'LL ADMIT THAT SOME MALE READERS THOUGHT THIS WAS SEXIST, BUT IT MADE A LOT OF MY MOMMY FRIENDS NOD THEIR HEADS VIG-OROUSLY!——MJM

Cornflakes taste just as good for lunch. I would have bene-fited from talking with someone who had recently had a baby. I was almost afraid to go to sleep, because I thought I wouldn't hear my daughter; so, consequently, I never really allowed myself to sleep. I would tell other sleep-deprived moms not to worry if they find themselves still in their pajamas at noon.

Sheryl McCarthy, North Stonington, CT

Passing in the night. I am a mom of identical twin girls, and for the first few months, my babies had their days and nights mixed up. My husband and I began accusing each other of get-ting more sleep. Each time one of us would get up at night to check on the babies, the other one would be asleep, so we both believed that only one of us was taking care of the babies at night. It wasn't until we sat down and talked about it that we realized that we were taking turns getting up. It was tough duty for a while. My husband would have to get up at six A.M. to go to work, and until our twins got their days and nights straight, we were both like the walking dead during the day.

Dina Dell Odom, Andalusia, AL

Just ask any mom. *Everything* gets better when your baby starts to sleep through the night.

Gabriella Marshall, Houston, TX

You've heard it before . . . It's true, but until your baby sleeps through the night, the best thing you can do for yourself is *sleep when the baby sleeps*. The newborn period is the time when your baby will sleep the most, so take full advantage of it—you can clean the house later.

Erin Khan

Sleep for your health. New moms, especially moms like me with sick babies, should definitely sleep every minute that they can. Everyone told me to do this, but I didn't follow their advice; instead I tried to get things done while my baby slept. Thus, I got almost no sleep, which contributed to me feeling run-down and becoming very ill.

Meghan Collins, Chelmsford, MA

Love takes time. It may have been because I was very young when I had my first baby, but it surprised me that I didn't automatically love my daughter. In fact, I did not begin feeling like I loved her until she was about four months old. I think it had more to do with my young age and the difficulty I experienced in labor and delivery. Also, I went back to school to complete my degree. I was exhausted! I felt guilty about feeling the way that I did, but then I learned that it's not uncommon for a first-time mom to experience these same feelings.

Kelley Raney, Marvell, AR

Bonding begins with a touch. All through my pregnancy I had visions of my delivery. I pictured this little person being laid upon my stomach and me bursting into tears of joy as an overwhelming wave of love washed over me. Well, that didn't happen. They did lay my son on my stomach, but honestly it was like touching a stranger. The intense feeling of love and bonding took time to develop; it grew stronger each time I touched his little fingers and toes, each time I nursed, each time I cuddled him.

Amy Allred, Woodstock, GA

Like after the Macy's Thanksgiving Day parade. I had a lot of difficulty dealing with what pregnancy did to my body. It took three months before I was willing to really look at my belly in the mirror, and when I did, I thought it looked like an old balloon that had been blown up until it nearly popped, then had the air let out of it. Although I hadn't gained a lot of weight in my pregnancy, it was five months before I could even put away my maternity pants and scrunch all of my baggy skin into my *husband's* jeans. A part of me still interprets my saggy belly as some kind of failing on my part.

Evelyn O'Donnell, Alameda, CA

Bod by Mom. Don't be too hard on yourself—you will tone up, it just takes time. My advice is to give yourself at least six weeks until you start exercising again and at least nine months to get the weight off. It took nine months to put it on, it takes nine months to take it off.

Rebecca Vogel-Pitts, Longmont, CO

You'll miss it when it's gone. You'll be so tired in the first few weeks after the baby is born that you won't even know yourself anymore. It is critical to understand that these difficult weeks *will* pass and that—although you're exhausted—this time is precious. Reflect, however blearily, on the gift that you've been given. I wish someone had shared this with me before my first child was born. I didn't fully appreciate how magical the newborn period really was until my second child was born—only then did I relax and treasure that short, short season.

Debra M. Gelbart, Phoenix, AZ

It's tiring being so tired. Everyone told me how little sleep I would get and how hard it was going to be, but I thought, *It can't* *be that bad.* Boy was I wrong. My daughter will be one year old next month and I'm still tired!

Laurie Dickan, Carmel, NY

I REMEMBER ASKING MY SISTER-IN-LAW, WHO HAD TWO SCHOOL-AGED CHILDREN, WHEN I WOULD SEE EIGHT HOURS OF SLEEP AGAIN, AND HER REPLY WAS, "NEVER."—MJM

Accept offers of help. After the baby arrives, people will call and ask if there is anything they can do for you. So before baby comes, while you still have some free time on your hands, write down on a pad of paper, to be kept near the phone, ten to fifteen things someone can do to help: *Would you run to the pharmacy . . . grocery store . . . post office . . . vet . . . for me?; It would be a big help if you would run the vacuum . . . load the dishwasher . . . fold a load of clothes for me; I would love for you to make your famous taco casserole so I don't need to fix dinner; Do you think you could baby-sit one Saturday night six weeks from now?; The lawn sure could use mowing . . . plants need pruning . . . garden needs weeding.* Something else you can do in the early weeks when well-meaning visitors drop by unannounced is to keep a bathrobe near the front door and don the robe when you hear the doorbell ring. Now you can answer the door armed with an excuse: *I was just getting dressed . . . getting up . . . about to take a shower . . . lying down for a nap.* This gives you a great excuse for telling someone that now is not a good time without being rude or causing hurt feelings.

Judy Fleck, Tigard, OR

Make meals in advance. One thing we did with the second baby that we didn't do with the first was to prepare and freeze a number of meals—lasagna, spaghetti sauce, soups, and casseroles—ahead of time, along with stocking up on frozen meals and vegetables from the grocery store. After the baby came, all we had to do was heat and serve! Also, for a couple of months, we used only paper plates, plastic cups, and disposable utensils at mealtime—this made for less work and cleanup. We stocked up on soda, paper towels, toilet paper, packaged foods, and snacks months in advance of baby's arrival, too, and I was glad we did. My house may have looked like a bomb shelter, but my daughter was six weeks old before I had to run to the store for anything except for milk, eggs, and bread.

Amy L. Burrell, Sharon Hill, PA

"The nursing station's in the backseat." I'm still grateful to my sister-in-law for the "tough love" she gave me when she visited me four weeks after I delivered my son. I was breast-feeding, and not only had I never nursed him outside the house, I had barely left the house at all. When she arrived, she suggested that the three of us go to a nearby store to buy me a comfy pair of jeans. I agreed only after I timed our trip so that I would return home with my son before the next feeding. But once we got to the store, she suggested lunch. I panicked, protested, and finally gave in when she convinced me that it would be all right to nurse my son in the backseat of her car. I did so and within a couple of minutes realized that it really wasn't so difficult. Afterward, we had a nice, relaxing lunch. From then on I gradually gained more courage to venture out of the house with my baby. I quickly learned that even a short trip outside the house each day did a lot for my sanity and confidence.

Jan Harrison Furlow, Alexandria, VA

Sift through unsolicited advice. One of the most difficult things about being a new mom is trying to please everyone. You might find that your mother, mother-in-law, siblings, neighbors, and friends are all telling you the best way to care for your baby—I remember feeling completely overwhelmed by all of the advice I was receiving. Then I made a decision: This is *my* baby and I am going to care for my baby the way that *I* see fit! From that point on, when I received any advice, I would thank the person and then decide whether or not to incorporate it.

Judith Burnett Schneider, Ingomar, PA

"The doctor says . . ." When a know-it-all (your mother-in-law?) questions everything you're doing and the way you're doing it—taking baby out too soon, taking baby to a crowded restaurant, not dressing baby properly—just say, "Well, the doctor says," then insert your point of view. Nothing will silence a parenting critic faster!

Daylle Schwartz, New York City

Take the pressure off yourself. The moment someone places your new baby into your arms, you need no one to tell you how to love this little creature that God has so richly blessed you with. What you wouldn't mind hearing is how to love him in the wee hours of the morning when sleep has abandoned you and your spouse for three nights running. When you are stressed and tired—*never* a good combination—even a mother's love can feel like it's too much to expect. New mothers try very hard to be relaxed, assuring one and all that everything is under control. In many ways, of course, everything *is* under control, but the great responsibility and overwhelming workload of caring for a newborn can produce periodic twinges of anger and frustration, which can be accompanied by guilt and shame. As a mother and grandmother, I have run the gamut from colic to sibling rivalry. I have stayed up all night with one sick child only to awaken to an even sicker one who required my attention and energy for the rest of the day. Looking back at those early years, I now see the undue pressure I placed on myself to always appear calm, cheerful, graceful, and completely competent to the outside world . . . the perfect mother! In actuality, I was a zombie most of the time, and the closest thing I ever came to perfection was in sterilizing bottles. I would lie in bed at night, too tired to even fall asleep, and think about my shortcomings for the day: I would remember whining at the sound of my baby waking from his nap. I would visualize how uncomfortable my baby looked sleeping in his baby swing, all curled up in a ball, while I stole fifteen minutes to myself before the old swing crank woke him up during my attempt to get fifteen minutes more. I felt guilty about feeding my baby too fast or propping his bottle. Now, from my lofty position as grandmother, I can see that all of those pressures of being a perfect mother were completely self-imposed. From here I can see that I *was* perfect in the eyes of my baby, and as his mother, no one could have done a better job.

Carla Bioni, Moline, IL

Single mom, double workload. I was ecstatic to be a mom at last, but I quickly ran myself into the ground trying to do everything myself. If you're a single mom, you're going to be doubly overwhelmed without help. Call in family and friends, build a support network. You can be a mom alone, but you don't have to be lonely.

Beth, New York City

Mothering the new mom. There are lots of baby-care books on the market, but a good *mother*-care book I would recommend to all first-time moms is *The Year After Childbirth,* by Sheila Kitzinger. This book gives women a realistic picture of what life is like after the birth and through the first roller-coaster year.

Carol M Smith, Williamsburg, VA

Unflinchingly honest. My favorite account of life with a new-born is the brave, hilarious, exhilaratingly candid book *Operating Instructions,* by Anne Lamott. She understands perfectly how you can fawn over your precious sleeping angel, then want to brain him when he raises that "loathsome reptilian head" to your exhausted eyes.

Betsy Rapoport, White Plains, NY

Postpartum Support

Mothers' groups extremely valuable. I started attending a new-mommies group at two weeks postpartum; it was one of the benefits offered by the birthing center where I delivered my baby. Our group was comprised of the same people who attended my childbirth class, and we met once a week for about six weeks (then continued to meet on a rotating basis in our homes). The meetings were supposed to last for an hour and a half, but most of us stayed for three hours! I found the group discussions incredibly valuable, especially in the first few weeks postpartum when the discussions were along the lines of: *My baby is doing X, is that normal?; How much milk do you get with that brand of pump?; I don't really want to go back to work, does anyone have any ideas on how I can make money while at home?;* and *Is anyone else terrified to leave her baby, even with someone she trusts?* To find a new-mothers' group where you live, contact your birthing center

❧ La Leche League (LLL)

The La Leche League International (www.lalecheleague.org, or 800-LALECHE) offers lots of mother-to-mother support, encouragement, and friendship in their monthly support groups held in communities all over the world. For every mothering and breast-feeding question or problem brought before the group, there are usually several mothers at the meetings who are able to offer solutions and suggestions. Visit their Web site or call for a referral to a local LLL group. ❧

or hospital, your OB, or your baby's pediatrician; also, try the local La Leche League, YWCA/YMCA, community centers, or churches in your area.

Heather Petit, Newark, DE

Postpartum doulas aid new parents. A new professional to aid parents is the postpartum doula. Postpartum doulas offer support for everyone in the family. Some of the things a doula can help you with include: giving you some much-needed rest time; teaching you baby-care skills (including what's normal behavior and when it's time to call a doctor); answering your questions about your recovery period; breast-feeding support; light household tasks; meal preparation; running errands; sibling care; an ear for listening; and anything else that will help Mom and the entire family feel nurtured while easing postpartum adjustment.

Tammy McGraw, Wasilla, AK

Find an accredited agency or specially trained individual. I am a mother and president and founder of a twenty-woman doula service in Cleveland, Ohio, called Birth & Beyond, Inc. Birth & Beyond provides Labor Support Doulas and extensive

Postpartum Doula services to assist new mothers and families from conception for up to twelve weeks following birth or adoption. About 20 percent of our services are paid for or given as a gift by family members (especially husbands and grandmothers) or friends. We recommend that a woman seeking a Postpartum Doula should contact NAPCS or DONA [see sidebar] for a referral to an accredited agency or individual in their area.

If a mother cannot locate an accredited doula service or certified Postpartum Doula in her area, it is highly recommended that she thoroughly check all of the prospective doula's references and credentials, including past clients, relevant education, experience and training in relation to postpartum mother and infant care (breast-feeding training, infant CPR/First Aid, safety, and philosophies on key issues), and the types of services offered. It is also recommended that prior to engaging the doula's services, a contract be signed outlining the services to be provided, length of service, and payment arrangements.

Noreen M. Roman, Cleveland, OH

Free lunch. Mutual friends threw together six of us who all had newborns. We met once a week and took turns hosting and providing lunch. It was great. Everyone vented, shared tips, laughed, and cried—and we all left knowing we'd get at least one lunch that week! It saved my sanity.

Elizabeth, New York City

The Baby Blues and Postpartum Depression (PPD)

The National Depressive and Manic-Depressive Association (National DMDA) estimates that 50 to 80 percent of all women

✐ Doulas

A doula (pronounced dóo-la) comes from the Greek word for "handmaiden." Doulas are professionally trained (but not medically trained) to provide women with information, and emotional and physical support during labor and/or postpartum. Postpartum care includes mother care, breast-feeding support, baby care, companionship, preparation of meals, doing errands, light housework, and so forth. Below are doula-certifying organizations, which you may contact for referrals in your area:

NATIONAL ASSOCIATION OF POSTPARTUM CARE SERVICES (NAPCS)

NAPCS (www.napcs.org, or 800-45-DOULA) is an association that provides accreditation and certification for postpartum doulas exclusively. NAPCS postpartum doulas are required to complete a postpartum training course, do fieldwork, and pass a written exam. Once certified, doulas must also complete continuing-education classes each year and provide client evaluations.

DOULAS OF NORTH AMERICA (DONA)

DONA (www.dona.org, or 801-756-7331) is an international nonprofit organization of nearly three thousand members. Although they offer certification for their birth doulas, at this time they do not offer accreditation or certification for their postpartum doulas. However, DONA does maintain an active referral listing of close to six hundred postpartum doulas.   ✐

who have had a baby experience the baby blues, a mild form of depression occurring most often within two weeks following childbirth. Women who suffer the blues frequently complain of sadness, unprovoked crying, anxiety, mood swings, and feelings of unworthiness. For most new moms, the baby blues is a temporary condition and will usually clear up within one or two weeks, although sometimes they can persist for up to six weeks. If you find yourself suffering from the blues, know that they are a normal part of the postpartum period and that you are in the company of millions of other women.

Some new moms find that their blues darken instead of lift, signaling postpartum depression (PPD). Depression After Delivery, Inc., an information and referral resource for women who suffer from PPD, reports that at least one in ten new mothers experience various degrees of PPD. Symptoms can occur within a few days of delivery, or even months later, and include depression, hopelessness, extreme fatigue and exhaustion, appetite and sleep disturbances, poor concentration or confusion, memory loss, uncontrollable crying and irritability, lack of interest in the baby, guilt, worthlessness, and fear of harming the baby or yourself. PPD differs from the baby blues in that women who suffer from PPD will usually have more than one symptom, and the symptoms don't go away but continue to build over time. A visit to your OB/GYN or family doctor is the first step toward diagnosis and treatment of PPD. Your doctor will probably first want to conduct a thyroid screening (a thyroid condition can make you feel extremely fatigued also) and, if the diagnosis is PPD, may prescribe an antidepressant or refer you to a mental-health professional trained to treat depression. PPD support groups can be especially helpful at this time, too. PPD is not something you have to live with; it can be treated.

In this half of the chapter, you'll hear what moms have to say about this important subject, including combating the baby blues, getting help for PPD, and the treatments that really work.

"What about *me*?" When I went home from the hospital, I no longer felt "special"—I actually missed my big belly and the wonderful movements inside of me. The initial flurry of attention I received—people calling and visiting—quickly disappeared, and reality set in. I was afraid to care for my son because I had never been around babies before and lacked confidence. I wouldn't let him out of my sight, not even to go to the bathroom. To make matters worse, I had trouble pumping my breast milk and didn't feel comfortable with my huge breasts. I felt empty and like a failure. My husband wasn't very supportive at first, which only fueled my depression. It can feel lonely out there when you don't know anyone else going through the same thing.

Debra S. Fair, Waltham, MA

A disappointing birth can trigger PPD. When my first son was born, I was disappointed that his arrival was by cesarean birth. During my second pregnancy, I had planned for a vaginal birth but ended up with another C-section. Within a week, I found myself feeling numb and sometimes crying for no reason at all. I felt removed from everyone and void of any emotion. My husband tried to be supportive at first, but as the days wore on, he started to become impatient at my inability to handle things and urged me to "move on." I went to see the nurse at my doctor's office, and she told me that it was merely the "baby blues," advising me to get lots of rest and call the doctor if things became worse. Well, things did become worse, but I was in no shape to call the doctor. It got to a point where dark thoughts began to creep into my mind, and I became detached from my family. After one heated argument with my husband, I searched through the telephone book and newspaper until my eyes rested on a small ad about an organization called the International Cesarean Awareness Network (ICAN). The ad indicated that a local group was meeting that week, so I attended it. I received a lot of support and help from that meeting and, over time, was able to address some of the issues that were causing my negative emotions, especially the circumstances surrounding the C-sections. Looking back, I think that medication perhaps would have helped me to respond quicker, but at the time, the counseling and the emotional support of other moms is what got me through. There's also a wonderful book I would highly recommend called *Laughter and Tears,* by Elisabeth Bing, that deals with PPD in detail.

Karen Putz, Boilingbrook, IL

The Burlington Express arrives at nine. No one told me that the baby blues could come within twenty-four hours of delivering—I had read that it could develop any time in the first few weeks, but not the first few hours! The night my son was born I was totally elated and psyched that the delivery was over; I didn't have much soreness, and I was on an adrenaline high. But the very next morning, I felt like I had been run over by a freight train. People were coming into my hospital room and

🌀 International Cesarean Awareness Network (ICAN)

ICAN (www.childbirth.org/section/ICAN.html, or 310-542-6400) is a nonprofit organization that primarily seeks to educate women on how to prevent an unnecessary cesarean. Local ICAN chapters across the country provide the opportunity for women who have had a C-section to express their childbirth-related feelings and help plan future VBAC (vaginal birth after cesarean) births. 🌀

calling all throughout the day. It was all very nice, but I began to feel a bit overwhelmed, and by late afternoon, I was extremely tired and cried at the littlest things. By the evening, I was sobbing for no reason at all and couldn't stop. A nurse came by and asked me if anyone had talked to me about postpartum depression, and that set me off crying again. This went on for about three days, and gradually it began to wane over the next two weeks. Had I been better prepared for baby blues, I might have been able to deal with it better.

Meghan Collins, Chelmsford, MA

Walking in sunshine. My first suggestion for chasing the blues away is to open the curtains and windows and let the sunshine in! I was amazed at the difference such a little thing did for me. The whole atmosphere of the house changes when there is natural daylight shining in from all sides. Plus, the fresh air was great for all of us. My second suggestion is to get up! No matter how hard or overwhelming it may feel, just do it: Wash your hair and get dressed—it will help you to feel "normal" again.

Bernadette F., West Chester, PA

Opt for shows that lift you, like *Oprah*. One thing not to do if you're suffering from the postpartum blues is to watch shows like *Baywatch*. I remember when my daughter was about ten days old, sitting frozen in front of the TV, watching *Baywatch* and crying. I laugh about it now, but back then I thought I would never fit into a bathing suit again. (But you know what? I did!)

Robin, Atlanta, GA

It *does* get better. My first few months with my first daughter were dreamy—watching her little smiles, night feedings, and cuddles was great—I was so proud to show her off. Postpartum depression and I lived on different planets . . . then along came my second daughter. She was fussy and had painful reflux. I couldn't face night feedings because I was so exhausted. I was so often in tears, feeling depressed to the point of not wanting my baby anymore—I was a wreck! But the depression began to lift at about six weeks, and I've been feeling great ever since. My advice is don't try to get through it on your own. Go see a friend, family member, doctor, or counselor for advice and encouragement. Try to remember that it *does* get better.

Jaki Thomas, South Australia

Help is just a phone call away. I had PPD, but it took a long time before I sought help because I felt like a failure as a mother—but then I learned that I wasn't. On the contrary, I was a *good* mother who was reacting to her hormones being all out of whack. I got help from a nationwide PPD support group called Depression After Delivery (DAD), who put me in touch with other women in my area who had PPD. At the meetings I found support, mentoring, friendship, and, most importantly, understanding. It helped me to not feel so alone; I could see that others had gone through it and survived! My doctor also put me in touch with a program offered by the nursing school at a local university. A student nurse came once a week to check on my daughter's development and well-being, chat with me, and help me in any way necessary. She offered suggestions about medication, therapy, and stress management. Since both DAD and the university's programs were free, I didn't have the additional worry about money. Don't wait to get help—the longer you wait, the worse you will feel. You may want to get a copy of a PPD self-help book called *This Isn't What I Expected,* by Karen R. Kleiman, M.S.W., and Valerie D. Raskin, M.D. This book gives solid advice for new moms suffering from PPD and talks about ways that spouses can help, too.

Amy L. Burrell, Sharon Hill, PA

❧ *Resources for Postpartum Depression*

DEPRESSION AFTER DELIVERY, INC. (DAD)

DAD (www.behavenet.com/dadinc/, or 800-944-4PPD) is a nonprofit organization that provides support for women with postpartum depression. Call to obtain information on postpartum disorders, professional referral lists, telephone volunteers, and local support groups.

POSTPARTUM SUPPORT INTERNATIONAL (PSI)

PSI (www.postpartum.net, or 805-967-7636) is a postpartum social support network and information center working to bring together women who suffer from PPD with professionals in their area, including local support groups. This site also includes links to postpartum chat rooms, new-parenting Web sites, and bulletin boards.

NATIONAL DEPRESSIVE AND MANIC-DEPRESSIVE ASSOCIATION (NATIONAL DMDA)

National DMDA (www.ndmda.org, or 800-826-3632) is an association with a grassroots network of nearly three hundred chapters and support groups around the country. They also publish written materials and videos about depressive disorders, including the helpful video *Woman to Woman: Finding Help for Depression.* ❧

Finding the right doctor is critical. My most important advice to a new mom would be to read about postpartum depression and find out in advance which doctors in your area specialize in treating the disorder. It's not pleasant to think about, but if you find yourself suffering from PPD, the search for a qualified doctor who truly understands the disease can be daunting—it's not a task you will want to undertake after the baby is born and depression sets in. I was not prepared when

PPD struck me, and as a result, I saw six different doctors, all taking their best guess as to how to treat me. Finally, the seventh doctor I saw—whom I was referred to by DAD—was able to make a proper diagnosis and recommend treatment.

Kathy Shaskan

History of depression means higher risk for PPD. Women who have struggled with depression at a younger age are at a higher risk for PPD. My PPD is viewed by my doctor as being related to an incident in my teens and the resulting depression at that time, as well as my low self-esteem. The best way I can describe PPD is to say that everything has become, well . . . harder. I can look at my son with ease, but I cannot look at myself; I worry about the least little thing and tend to be impulsive. When I go out of the house, my mind races; I go over and over all of the bad things that could happen. The thing that worries my doctor most is the fact that I cannot sleep well. I get an average of about three hours of sleep per night, until, several exhausting nights later, I sleep long and hard and can barely get out of bed the next day. I'm on antidepressants, but I don't particularly feel better (or worse, for that matter). The only advice I can impart is *don't give up;* take things slowly, and remember that PPD is not something you should be embarrassed by—it is not your fault that this has happened to you.

Donna Wilson

Medication can work wonders. I had just enough energy to care for my daughter, and then I was *spent.* I saw my family doctor, who diagnosed me with postpartum depression and prescribed antidepressants. He told me that postpartum depression was nothing to feel ashamed about; it's a hormonal imbalance, and our emotions are chemically driven. There was nothing that I did wrong to get PPD, and the antidepressants made a *world* of difference. My husband was worried that I was going to be a wife and mother "floating" on drugs, but instead, the drugs corrected my imbalance and restored the old me! If you are feeling overwhelmed to the point of feeling almost paralyzed, then go see a trusted doctor and let him determine if you suffer from PPD. Don't try to convince yourself that it's just you and that you have to just get through it.

Janelle Goossens

A natural solution to PPD. I had postpartum depression with my first child but didn't realize it for quite some time. I had been run-down and very sad for the first four months following her birth. I was tired all of the time and cried a lot. I thought all new moms experienced this until I went to see my doctor. She checked my thyroid, did some blood work, and spent some time talking with me. After diagnosing me with PPD, she put me on Saint-John's-wort (Hypericum herb); it's a great alternative to prescription drugs and worked wonders for me. Although Saint-John's-wort is available over the counter, be sure to consult your physician first, as it can have side effects. I don't like to be medicated, so I was thrilled to learn of this natural solution to PPD.

Rebecca Vogel-Pitts, Longmont, CO

NEVER TAKE SAINT-JOHN'S-WORT OR ANY OTHER HERB WITHOUT CONSULTING YOUR DOCTOR. ALSO, NEVER STOP TAKING A PRESCRIBED MEDICATION IN FAVOR OF AN ALTERNATIVE THERAPY; YOUR DOCTOR NEEDS TO BE SURE THE ALTERNATIVE IS APPROPRIATE FOR YOU, AND SOME MEDICATIONS CAN PRODUCE SERIOUS SIDE EFFECTS IF DISCONTINUED SUDDENLY.——MJM

CHAPTER 12

Fizzle to Sizzle
You and Your Spouse

After all of the planning and anticipation, your baby is finally here. What a beautiful expression of your love for each other. You both trumpet in delight as you discover familiar family features in your newborn's wrinkly little face. At home, the order of the day is making baby comfortable and settling into new parenthood—it's a busy, happy time. And with a little bit of work, it can remain that way! Surprised to hear that it may not?

The reality is that having a baby can strengthen the bond between couples or sour it. It may be hard to understand why having a baby can jeopardize the spousal relationship when starting a family is something both partners often so badly want in the first place. But it's not the baby who creates distance between a married couple; it's the monumental workload in caring for a totally dependent infant, a reshuffling of priorities from spouse to baby, and one too many nights of interrupted sleep. A common scenario goes something like this: Mom's at home while Dad returns to work. Week after week, Mom's get-

ting buried in diapers, dirty dishes, and laundry; her life has changed and not in the way that she had expected. Dad, on the other hand, is busy back at the job where almost nothing has changed. Mom's getting tired—she's feeling underappreciated and overworked and yearns for a break. She can't understand why Dad doesn't relieve her burden, take more initiative to help out with the baby, or do more around the house. Dad doesn't grasp the depth of Mom's plight and is left wondering why she has become so unhappy. As time goes on, tensions mount, and discussions turn into arguments.

Although this is a reality for millions of new parents, it doesn't have to be yours. There is plenty you can do to keep your marriage strong, like discussing ahead of time how you plan on divvying up the baby-care responsibilities and other household chores. Studies show this is the hottest area of contention for new parents and the more each partner is willing to share in the family duties, the less burdened the other partner will feel. It's important, too, to keep communications flowing after the baby is born by having regular discussions about what each of you is experiencing in your role as a new parent. Whatever the difficulties, together you can find workable solutions to your problems and, given time, gain confidence in your ability to parent. Making a conscientious effort to invest in one-on-one time with each other every day will also foster a lasting partnership, whether it's swapping foot rubs on the couch, taking the baby for a walk, having a quiet dinner together, or meeting for a tub full of bubbles after the baby goes down. As you'll hear from one mom, another great way to reconnect with your spouse is to keep a regular "date night" for just the two of you—"and *never* cancel." (This may be tougher for Mom to do in the beginning; it's not easy leaving baby, but it's the baby who reaps the biggest benefit when Mom and Dad return home happy and rejuvenated.) Expect that sex may take a holiday for a period of time after the baby comes—nothing kills romance faster than swollen breasts, a flabby belly, and a foggy mind. Be honest with your partner about how you feel, but at the same time, don't forget him. There are lots of other ways to be intimate—like hugging, kissing, caressing, and cuddling—until you feel up to having sex again. (Then again, there are lots of ways you can give your libido a boost, and you'll get lots of good suggestions in the last third of this chapter.)

Finally, don't forget about *you*. This is easier said than done when you become a new mother; doing for everyone else seems to be what is required and expected. But it's vitally important that you nurture yourself, too. Taking a break at least once a day, if possible, and doing something you enjoy—reading, exercising, needlepoint, working on a scrapbook—will help ease the stress of new parenthood and make you feel more relaxed and rested. You'll return to your family with renewed vigor, and *that's* good for everyone.

Read on as moms who've been through it talk about the changes in how their relationship with their spouse changes after the baby comes; ways you can foster a more loving, less stressful relationship with your partner; scheduling time alone as a couple and keeping the sizzle alive in your marriage; making yourself a priority and things you can do to give yourself a lift; and getting back in the groove for SEX!

Adjusting to Parenthood

You may have to help clue hubby in. Accept one thing: The father of your child may very likely have no clue what to do after the baby arrives. Now, this was an amazing discovery to me, because I didn't have a clue what to do either, but that didn't seem to matter. I found myself constantly asking my husband to do what I considered to be obvious tasks: fold the wash, empty the trash, wash the dishes, vacuum the floor, walk the dog, and so on. I love my husband dearly, but when it came to knowing how to help in the critical postpartum period, he was a little in the dark. This quickly became a problem for us in our marriage, because I felt like I was doing everything and he was doing nothing. I would love to say we quietly discussed it, worked it out, and everything was wonderful again, but that's not the way it happened. With hormones raging and sleeplessness quickly overtaking me, our discussions were heated, and it wasn't until I reached the point of tears that he understood this was a serious issue. We eventually worked it out by talking about it, but it wasn't easy.

Bernadette F., West Chester, PA

Your spouse will never look the same again. You'll see your spouse as a whole different person after the baby arrives, and if you're lucky, you will really *like* that new person! (chuckle) There is something very sweet about a good and loving daddy, and fortunately, my husband is one of those guys. Our time alone is very limited now, but neither one of us seems to mind it too much—we've become family-oriented and have put our personal needs on the back burner for a while.

Natalie Tabet, NM

You're in good company. We were like every other couple with a new baby: happy, tired, sleepy, broke, proud, thankful, and blessed.

Kimberly R. Harris, Fairview, NC

Fatherhood can be a heavy burden. Expect Dad to be as scared as you are after the baby comes home. In many cases, he'll feel a weighty responsibility for the financial stability and physical safety of the family. This is an enormous burden and not one to be taken lightly. I didn't understand it until I went back to work as our only source of income (my husband stayed home with our baby). The responsibility I felt was terrifying.

Heather Petit, Newark, DE

It can pull you together and push you apart. Having three babies permanently changed my relationship with my spouse of twenty-three years. On one hand, it has brought us closer: There is no greater love than the love we jointly share for our children, and no one else but my husband feels the way that I do about each of them. On the other hand, I was exhausted and cranky right after each of their births, and that put a strain on our relationship. No longer was it just two of us; but three, four, and now five of us. We no longer have alone time, time to love without inhibition, or time for carefree play. We are working hard to try to get back what we once had and become the lovers we once were.

Jane Garrard, Portland, OR

No time for "vegging." When my husband gets home from work, all he wants to do is sit on the couch and veg. I've been home all day with the baby, and all I want to do is turn her over to her daddy and veg myself. We decided that instead of fighting about it, we would share the baby-care responsibilities: I make dinner while he feeds the baby. He cleans up while I change her. He bathes her while I do chores around the house. We relax. I nurse the baby, but I have a bottle handy so he can feed her, too. Bedtime is family time. Everything has become easier and much less stressful this way.

Rebecca Vogel-Pitts, Longmont, CO

Give dad some credit. It took a while, but I finally "learned" that my husband was a capable parent. He did not do things exactly the way that I did, but what he did worked and our baby survived.

Amy L. Burrell, Sharon Hill, PA

Dad's making adjustments, too. Sharing your feelings with your husband will make the postpartum adjustment period easier. Realize that Dad is also adjusting to new fatherhood and may be feeling incompetent with baby or perplexed by the changes he sees in you. By sharing your experiences and anxieties with each other, you'll get through it with less strife while building a stronger bond.

Donna M. Condida, Archbald, PA

Moms are the glue of the family. The relationship with my spouse was rocky at first. We were well into our thirties when we had our son and were used to coming and going as we pleased, but then there was someone else to answer to. We argued a lot, and it was hard on both of us—I was depressed and exhausted; he was angry and tired. He wouldn't let my mother come over as often as I wanted her to because he wanted us to take care of our new baby ourselves, only he wasn't helping me enough. Then one day I yelled at him so badly he stormed out of the house and ran to his mother's house. Well, he came back with a totally different attitude a few hours later! He was sympathetic, supportive, and attentive. His mother told me later that she told him he had better change, or I would have a nervous break-down. She said that I was the glue that holds our family together and that he had better grow up and help out the way I needed him to. Our relationship improved greatly after that.

Debra S. Fair, Waltham, MA

Talk it over later. You will be emotional for the first few weeks after birth. Assure your partner that any outburst is not to be taken personally; at the same time, recognize that your partner will be making adjustments, too.

Angela Dove, Singapore

Discuss, don't blame. Don't blame each other when things go wrong—blaming only creates more stress.

Susan Flannery, Louisville, KY

Father knows best. I would recommend to new moms that they empower their baby's father with confidence in his parenting intuitiveness; when he is alone with baby, he is *parenting*, not baby-sitting. You will find that the baby will demonstrate different cues with the father than with the mother to have his or her needs met. When Mom constantly criticizes Dad on his parenting skills, it can erode his confidence as a capable caregiver, and he will no longer listen to his instincts and subtle nuances that baby generously provides him.

Julie

Bow out. It's true! Nothing is harder on a marriage than when your partner feels left out or unimportant. When baby is screaming and Daddy is changing the diaper, trying to figure out if he's got it right, you will feel a strong urge to rush in and save the day. *Don't!* Just as you had to learn your way through trial and error, Daddy does, too; taking part in caring for baby will help him bond with her.

Tina Golden, Coldwater, MS

Parenthood is a co-op. When our first baby arrived, my husband was mesmerized. He just couldn't believe that he was holding a little bit of himself in his hands, and immediately he wanted more. At first our daughter brought us together, deepening our relationship and dependence on each other. But soon the newness wore off, and I was doing everything from bathing to changing diapers to waking up for middle-of-the-night feedings. My husband would wake up in the morning feeling refreshed and rejuvenated, while I was bleary-eyed and disoriented from lack of sleep. He would say, "I didn't hear the baby at all." Exactly one year later to the day, our second daughter was born. It put a significant strain on our marriage because he was working a lot of hours and again didn't help much. I loved my husband but resented the fact that he got eight to twelve hours of "free time," as I saw it. Then one day, when my pressure cooker was about to explode, I confronted him. I told him that parenthood should be a cooperative effort, and that we were *both* parents, not only me. He could no longer be just another playmate for our kids and needed to take a more active role in caring for them. Shortly after, I went out for an entire day one weekend, leaving him alone with the girls. He quickly saw that life at home was more than just watching TV and napping. Not ten minutes after I left, I was getting frantic phone calls pleading with me to come home. It was the eye-opener I had hoped for; from that point forward, my husband began changing diapers, cleaning, feeding, and bathing the girls, and even cut back on the amount of time he spent at work. We began to enjoy each other's company again, too.

Tina Pavich, Noblesville, IN

Keep your sense of humor. When we brought our first baby home, it was a trial-and-error period. It's a lot easier on Mom if Dad takes the initiative to pitch in and help; unfortunately, my husband did not do this. I found that I had to be very explicit about how, when, and what I needed him to do. He was willing to help but didn't notice the ten loads of laundry piling up. We got through it by communicating and keeping our sense of humor. We also made time to be alone after the baby was born; if we couldn't get a sitter, we put our baby to bed and went out on the deck. We both still believe that one of the best things you can give your children is a strong relationship between the two parents.

Deanne, Herndon, VA

Finding support can help relieve tension when baby has disabilities. If your baby is born with a developmental disability, you and your spouse will experience extra stresses. Mixed in with your joy and excitement may be worry, anxiety, disappointment, sadness, blame, guilt, and anger. If you don't communicate with each other, your feelings about this new challenge in your life may strike at the heart of your marriage.

Jane A. Zanca, Atlanta, GA

Caution: Hormone Landslide Area. Better warn your husband now: Occurring shortly after the baby is born—and lasting for the better part of the first year—is a time I call the female "descent off hormones," leaving husbands off guard as to which mood their wives will be in at any given moment!

Christine S. Simonson, Sumter, SC

Stressful day, dear? My son had reflux when he was born. Reflux is when the flap between the esophagus and stomach does not shut properly, and it caused my baby to projectile-vomit and have terrible heartburn. He cried and screamed a lot. One day as my husband was walking in the door from work, I greeted him with "Take off your clothes." I don't know whether it was the look on my face or the sound of my voice, but he did it. I then pulled off our son's diaper and handed him to his father, saying, "The tub's already full." My husband looked sorrowfully at our suddenly quiet baby and said, "Now you've done it. She's going to drown us both!"

Marie White, Ottawa, Ontario

Let hubby know you still need him. If you forget your husband after the baby comes, he can become jealous. This is especially true when your spouse is used to getting all of your attention. That's what happened in our marriage. I just figured that he could make his own way. I found myself so wrapped up in the baby's needs that I forgot my husband needed to feel important, too.

Debbie Wiltse, Tempe, AZ

KEEPING THE HOME FIRES BURNING ~ 241

The invisible man. After the birth of our son, I remember my husband saying that he felt like he had vanished from my life. He would get home from the college where he taught, and I would fill him in on everything that our baby and I did that day but forget to ask him about what was going on in his life. One day my husband confronted me about my absorption in our son and lack of attention to him, and to us as a couple. It took time to achieve a happy balance, but eventually we did.

Sally Rowan, Baltimore, MD

Renewed appreciation. To me, there's nothing more wonderful than watching my husband comfort one of our children; seeing each other in the role of parent has really helped our relationship mature. Remember, now that you and your husband have a child, you are truly related to each other. This realization has deepened our marriage immeasurably.

Kaleigh Donnelly, Memphis, TN

Keeping the Home Fires Burning

Initiate togetherness. Here's my advice to new parents:
1. Keep a date night just for the two of you and *never* cancel.
2. Turn off the TV and the computer; this forces creativity.
3. Go to bed early . . . on purpose!
4. Be spontaneous! Lighting candles, and just being together and talking, can be intimate.

Nancy Ablao, Kalamazoo, MI

Make a conscious effort. It's important to keep the love flowing and the affection going after baby is born. Take a peaceful stroll through your neighborhood while your children are little—it will help you feel close. Or pack a picnic lunch and spend the day at the park; that's what we did when our children were babies. I would tote along a book, and my husband would catch a little nap. It was a wonderful way to spend the day being a family. Keep the surprise in the marriage by being impulsive with your affections; give your spouse an unexpected kiss or hug, or a pinch on the bottom! Greet him with a hello and a kiss every day, not with negative news as soon as he walks in the door. Give him time to unwind from work and have dinner, and then relate the day's events. Always remember that no matter how mad you are at your spouse, he is the person you love and can count on for love, support, and friendship.

Mary Jo Rulnick, Pittsburgh, PA

Thinking of you. Don't forget what your mate likes (flowers, CDs, back massages); an occasional small gift or gesture can put the spark back into a marriage.

Kimberly Cushman, West Windsor, NJ

"My couch or yours?" For a long time my husband and I couldn't afford a baby-sitter, so we kept a regular Saturday-night date at home: After the kids were in bed, we met on the couch for a favorite TV show, conversation, or whatever else we had time for. Now that our favorite show is off the air, it's been too easy for us to spend Saturday nights doing catch-up house-work and other projects apart from each other. Hmmm . . . maybe it's time to revisit that tradition.

Cynthia, Palo Alto, CA

A little gratitude improves the attitude. After the twins were born, life became much more stressful, and our communi-cation suffered. We were too busy to notice all of the little things we each did during the day, and we each started to resent the other because of it. Then we decided to try the Oprah Win-frey (www.oprah.com) Gratitude Journal each night: writing down five things we were grateful for each day that the other person had done ("Thanks for bringing the laundry upstairs"). We found that the things we appreciated after the baby came were simple things like household tasks or taking the baby for a while, but it didn't matter; what was important was the fact that we recognized the other's contributions and no longer took each other for granted.

Wendy Pisciotta, Stafford Springs, CT

Just be a couple again. Plan a date night and let Grandma, an aunt, or a neighbor watch the baby for a few hours. You don't really have to go out; rent a movie, order pizza, or pop some popcorn.

Laura Bell, Roseville, CA

Be social. We were too nervous to turn our newborn over to a baby-sitter, but we craved our old social life. Finally we just decided to stop caring whether *House Beautiful* would pop in for an impromptu photo shoot. We called up friends and said, "The apartment looks like it's been bombed, we look like zombies, but we miss you. Come for dinner—and bring takeout." We'd all eat on the bed while our son slept out in the living room, and had a blast. Lower your entertaining standards and keep socializing as a couple.

Elizabeth, New York City

Vacation breathes new life into a marriage. Over the summer I was so drained from the responsibilities of being a full-time mom and had just about had it with my husband. So we planned a ten-day trip together and asked my parents to stay with our baby. When the time came to go, I felt extremely reluctant to leave the baby, but I forced myself to go anyway. As it turned out, I had a wonderful, relaxing time—in fact, I felt like a honeymooner again! The trip not only did wonders for our marriage, but it also made me realize that the stress I was feeling was of my *own* doing, and not of my husband's. Away from home, I saw that my husband was—and had always been—the same wonderful man I had fallen in love with. It was the added stress of a new baby that made me see him as a bad guy who couldn't do anything right. I would tell new parents not to feel guilty about taking some time for themselves—it can revitalize your marriage in ways you never thought possible.

Kimberly Cushman, West Windsor, NJ

Good for baby, too. If you can't get away for a vacation, even going away for an occasional weekend is good for everyone. My husband and I have cherished our weekend retreats; they not only refresh us, they also help our son better deal with separation.

Jodi Detjen

Nurturing your relationship now pays off later. Your children can quickly monopolize all of your time, attention, and energy, but don't let it happen or you may find that your marriage will suffer for it. I feel very strongly that—as much as you love your children totally and completely—children should be number two in priority, and your spouse should be number one. This doesn't mean that you neglect your children, it simply means that you *don't* neglect your spouse. Continue to grow together as a couple and share. Develop common interests and spend time together alone: These are the things that will keep a marriage strong. I can guarantee you that the next eighteen years will fly by faster than you can imagine, and when your children have left the nest, it will be just the two of you alone again.

Joanne Nichols, Winterset, IA

Taking Care of Yourself

No points for martyrdom. Don't be a martyr, placing everyone else's needs above your own—you will get sick and become angry and resentful. The old adage is true: *If Momma ain't happy, ain't nobody happy!* You must make yourself a priority and pamper yourself whenever you can.

Kathryn A. Varuzza, New Paltz, NY

Keep yourself interested and interesting. On the first postpartum visit to my obstetrician, he ushered me into his office, sat me down, and stopped me dead in my tracks with this question: "What are you doing to keep yourself interested and interesting?" I had to admit that I wasn't doing very much in that regard, since I was too overwhelmed with the seemingly endless responsibilities of being a mom to my beautiful new son. He counseled me to make some time for myself and the activities that I had loved in my "previous life" or I might wind up resentful and depressed. And so I took his advice. I was lucky enough to have an older neighbor who was willing to care for my son in her home for a few hours a couple of times a week. I resolved *not* to use this time for errands or household chores. Instead, it was to be discretionary time for me—reading a book, taking a bath, gardening, practicing the piano. It didn't take long before I realized that this "selfish time" made me a happier woman and a far better mom.

Anne Hawkins, Hollis, NH

Take a stress reliever. Leave baby with Dad and take a walk around the block or a trip to the grocery store, or read a book— a few minutes a day for yourself will do wonders. This is especially true in the first six months when sleep is a precious commodity, tempers get short, and patience is tried. Putting a few minutes aside will help you keep everything in perspective and relieve a lot of tension.

Danielle Furr, Belmont, NC

Swap baby-sitting time with friends. Consider forming a baby-sitting "co-op" with your friends, so that you can swap baby-sitting time at least once a month.

Lesley Spencer, Austin, TX

Write it down. Keep a diary. Record your feelings about parenthood, both the joys and the trials. Rehashing your thoughts and getting it down on paper will help relieve some of the tension and give you perspective.

Valerie S. Turner, PA

Set aside some extra time. Get up a bit earlier in the morning—before anyone else—or stay up an extra hour or so. I found that getting even fifteen minutes of "me" time was better than getting none at all.

Lori Peters, PA

Just do it. Get out and exercise at least three times a week for twenty minutes. Take a stroll with the baby, walk the treadmill, swim a few laps . . . you'll feel better and sleep better. This especially helps in the first few weeks when fatigue sets in.

Rebecca Vogel-Pitts, Longmont, CO

Calgon, take me away! I recommend a long bubble bath every other week. Schedule it for after the baby goes to sleep so you won't be interrupted. Treat yourself to bubbles and a glass of vino to relax.

Andrea R. Cartwright, Stuyvesant, NY

Get together with friends. Girls' night out! Once a month, leave baby with Dad and spend an evening with some friends (don't forget to include your childless girlfriends, too).

Heather Petit, Newark, DE

Indulge yourself. Get a haircut, and let them style it, too.

Alexia Weber, South Lyon, MI

Catch up on your sleep. In our house, Daddy takes baby out on Saturday morning and lets Mama sleep in!

Debra S. Fair, Waltham, MA

Getting Back in the Groove for Sex!

A return to intimacy takes time. It's been almost thirteen years since our first baby arrived, and if you ask my husband, the first thing he will tell you is "Less sex for a while." That's true; there was no sex for close to six weeks after each of our children's births. This is one of those areas where a good husband is transformed into either an ogre, because he demands it too soon, or a prince among men, because he patiently works with his wife to reestablish intimacy gradually.

Christine S. Simonson, Sumter, SC

It might feel different. I had an episiotomy, and sex really didn't feel good for almost nine months. Plus, I felt stretched out after the birth, and that felt different, too. Tell your partner about what does and doesn't feel good and don't feel guilty if you're not in the mood for a while.

Joanne, New York City

Surprise him with quips of love. Take the initiative to reconnect with your partner: Write love notes to him and leave them where he will be sure to find them (bathroom mirror, sock drawer, briefcase, lunch bag); give each other dual foot massages with one rule: *No* talking!; prepare a bubble bath for him, complete with candles and soft music; have a picnic on your living room floor.

Cindi Howard Castle, Lake Park, FL

Get energized with exercise. When we see our bodies as flabby, our breasts as milk machines, and our primary role as mom, it's hard to feel sexy. After my six-week checkup, my husband and I invested in home gym equipment—it was probably the best investment in our marriage that we ever made. We exercised together in the evening when the baby was getting close to bedtime. The noise from the stair-step machine and the movement of the weights up and down were calming to the baby and quieted her. By the time our workout was over, the baby was ready to sleep, and my husband and I felt great! The glow of exercise, combined with a positive body image, improves your sexual energy, not to mention all of the other health benefits.

Susan Sarnello-Harrison, Itasca, IL

Snuggling feels good, too. Snuggle when you are just too tired for sex.

Heather Petit, Newark, DE

Try a little tenderness. Sex is emotionally as important for women as for men, so even if you're tired, it's worth making an effort. We gave each other massages—complete with candles and aromatherapy oils—when we felt too tired for anything else. It always amazed me that no matter how tired we felt, with the right ambiance and a little touching, things would start to sizzle again.

Jaki Thomas, South Australia

Put it on the calendar. After five children in eight years, there was little time for intimacy, let alone a desire for it. But as my dear husband and I discussed the subject, we found that, although my physical needs were less after the birth of our children, his needs were the same as before. I came to realize that some of my need for close physical contact was somewhat met by the little ones, since I got a lot of touching, snuggling, and hugging from them throughout the day. I further realized that although *I* got a lot of hugs and loving during the day, my husband did not. So we made a plan: We set aside a specific time each week for intimacy. It was my responsibility to be well rested and ready to give him my undivided attention, and to even be sexy—it was the one time a week when I was a wife and a lover, not a mother. In return, he would agree to be respectful of my wishes for the balance of the week by not expecting sex. By taking the pressure off of me during the week, I found that I was much more relaxed and affectionate—I didn't have to worry about whether a hug, a kiss, or a little cuddling would turn into more than I had time or energy for.

Patty Kartchner, Dayton, OR

Ready when you are! If he's in the mood but you're not, tell him. Don't let him pressure you—if he pressures you each time, you will only come to resent him for it. Let him know why you don't wish to be intimate, but reassure him that you still love him and find him desirable. On the other hand, when you're ready for a little action, don't be embarrassed to let him know—he'll probably be ready whenever you are!

Lauren McMenimen, Tempe, AZ

Nothing captures attention like lace. Even if you think you're still carrying too much "baby fat," wear sexy underwear—it will get the imagination going!

Angela J. Byrnes, Stanford, CA

Arte de flesh. Discover body paints!

Donna M. Condida, Archbald, PA

Happiness in an eight-room house. If you use the family bed in your home, there are lots of other rooms in the house where you and your hubby can be intimate. It also adds to the experience!

Deborah, St. Louis, MO

Rockin' around the clock. Plan a "sex date" with your mate during the day, when you know baby will be sleeping. The anticipation will drive him wild!

Jane Garrard, Portland, OR

Invite Fabio into your bedroom. One helpful hint: Since your whole life revolves around your baby, consider buying a romance novel and reread the sexiest parts to stimulate your brain (and other body parts) and take you to a place far, far away from dirty diapers.

Sherrie Glogosh, Alpharetta, GA

You'll find it next to the luncheon meats. Keeping the *sizzle* alive? Isn't that the noise the bacon makes when you're cooking it for everyone else but yourself? As for sizzle, I have none. As for love, compassion, trust, and respect, I have plenty. Who needs sizzle when you have everything else?

Lara Joudrey, London, Ontario

CHAPTER 13

Either Way, It's a Full-time Job
Staying at Home or Returning to Work

I remember sitting around with a few coworkers one day when the subject of having children was brought up. I matter-of-factly announced, "Believe me, when *I* have kids, they will not *want* me to stay at home with them—I would be miserable, and so would they!" But that was when I was in my twenties and early thirties, "married" to my work and on the fast track up the corporate ladder. I always knew I wanted children, but I didn't believe that I could ever slow down enough—or have enough patience—to be at home with them 24/7.

But I was wrong. At thirty-six years old, I gave birth to our first son and became a full-time stay-at-home mom. It didn't take long to realize that I had made the right decision. Regardless of what I thought was best for me, it became immediately apparent that it was best for my son to be with his mommy; I knew that with the exception of his father, no one could love him as much or care for him as lovingly as I could. But I was lucky that I had a choice. For millions of new moms today, returning to work is a necessity—these women would happily welcome the opportunity to stay at home with baby, but are unable to do so for financial reasons. Giving up their income means more than forfeiting personal luxuries: It means that the family will fall short of critical monthly obligations. Other women make a conscientious choice to return to work; they seek the intellectual stimulation and socialization that the workplace provides them. Others choose to work because they feel they don't have the patience or emotional stamina to be at home with a baby, opting to place their babies with caregivers who can manage the trials of motherhood with fewer frays. Many seek a balance of work and home and want to model that balance for their children. Ask a hundred moms about their choices and you'll get a hundred reasons—and all of them are valid.

If you are still undecided about whether to be a full-time mom or working mom, it may help to lay out all of your options on paper and prioritize your personal, career, and financial goals. Here are some things to consider:

STAYING AT HOME

1. Would you be miserable or constantly worried if someone else—most possibly a complete stranger—cares for your baby? How will you feel when your baby develops a strong emotional attachment with the caregiver?

2. Does returning to work mean that most or all of your income will be spent on child care? Are you able and willing to sacrifice your current level of income? For how long?

3. Is your job demanding, requiring travel or a long work-

week? How do you think you will feel about precious bonding time spent away from your baby?

4. Do you feel the energy required to work full-time *and* be a wife and mother in the evenings will leave you overly fatigued and unhappy?

RETURNING TO WORK

1. Is it vital to your sense of self-worth to return to work?
2. Is your income vital to the family's financial stability?
3. Are you able to find acceptable, affordable care for baby?
4. By not returning to work, will you slip or lose your current position or career aspirations? Is that important to you?
5. How family-friendly is your workplace? Do you feel you will be treated respectfully if you must stay home to care for a sick baby? Or will you feel pressed to come into work against your better judgment?
6. Will work bring you the intellectual stimulation and break from household drudgery you need to be more fully present and engaged with your child?

POSSIBLE COMPROMISES

- Toss the career, but only for a year or two.
- Negotiate an extended maternity leave with your current company. The Family and Medical Leave Act of 1993 allows eligible employees the option of taking up to twelve weeks of unpaid leave.
- Work part-time for your current employer, or seek a new company offering part-time work.

- Work from home for your current company, start your own in-home business, or become a freelancer.
- Expand telecommuting, using e-mail, phone, and fax to work more out of your home on a permanent or flexible basis.
- Become an in-home caregiver or family care provider. This would enable you to be with your baby while earning income by caring for one or more additional children.
- Have Dad stay at home. Or go into business with your spouse and integrate shared child care into your business strategy.

Moms in this chapter talk openly and frankly about the choices they made to stay at home or return to work, and reflect upon their decision; pass along career alternatives for moms who want to work less and spend more time with their families; and offer advice for staying satisfied with staying at home, including maintaining a healthy self-esteem, useful coping skills and reducing stress, achieving a happy balance between work and home for moms who return to the workplace, and tips for the working mom searching for child care.

The Pros and Cons

Have confidence in your decision. Deciding to work or not is the most personal of decisions. It's like choosing the baby's name. Only you can do it. There are no right and wrong absolutes and at any time the circumstances could change.

Keep all judgment out of it and do what's best for you. A happy mother is a good mother. An unhappy mother has a big mountain to climb. If the answer to this question is too big for you, consider seeking the advice of a good therapist or dear friend. Often others who are less personally involved can add a new perspective to a situation.

Linda Republicano, Alameda, CA

Just can't say good-bye . . . Up until my son was four weeks old, I had every intention of going back to work full-time, but then decided that it was too many hours to be apart from my baby each week. I called my work to explain and after some juggling they offered me a part-time position closer to my home. I accepted the position, but then called the day I was supposed to start back and told them that I just couldn't leave my baby. Be sure to give full consideration to your priorities. Is it possible for you to cut back on expenses and stay at home for at least the first year? I sold my car (no car payment and no insurance premiums) so that I could afford to do it. So much happens in the first year of your baby's life that you will never get to see again. Do you want to be the one to witness your baby's milestones or only hear about them from a baby-sitter?

Pamela Bartolotto, Prosperity, PA

Focus on the positive. I was very resentful, sad, and full of guilt about having to work. I felt like I missed so much of my son's life by having to trudge off to a job I didn't like. I had no other choice at the time because we needed the money and the benefits. At one point I felt consumed by regret. Then after some serious soul-searching I realized that I had to let it go. I consoled myself with the knowledge that I was doing the very best I could do and feeling guilty was a huge waste of energy—

energy that could be better directed toward something positive, like my children.

Brenna Cooper

Day care is always open. Day care over in-home care works for me because day care is open every day and I don't have to be worried about the caregiver taking a vacation or being sick. If you opt for in-home care, you have to deal with finding alternate care when these things arise.

Dawn M. Casella, Westland, MI

Every day brings new discoveries. There was never any question for me that I would stay home with my baby. Babies learn something new every day, and I felt that it would be a shame to miss all of those discoveries and milestones. By sharing in his everyday life, I have really come to know my son. I find mothering to be challenging in the best sense of the word, and I'm never bored—we play and learn all day long, and it's great fun!

Evelyn O'Donnell, Alameda, CA

Achy-breaky heart. I had no choice but to return to work, as mine was the only stable job. My mother-in-law watches my son, and up until recently, I was going home every day for lunch and nursing my baby. I spend the time away from my son anticipating the time when we'll be together again—I get a pain in my chest that does not go away until we have been reunited for a while.

Jeanette, Burnaby, British Columbia

Benefits too important to forgo. I returned to work when my babies were three and a half months old because, as a firefighter with over thirteen years of service, I got great medical, dental, and vision benefits, a pension, 401k, and a good salary. My mom and dad cared for my babies while I worked, and my husband was at home on the weekends with them. I felt comfortable leaving them under these circumstances.

Cindy Fagiano, Chicago, IL

Staying at home can be lonely. After the birth of my first son, I tried to stay at home, but I thought I would go nuts! At the time, none of my friends had babies, so there I was, all alone at home, just twiddling my thumbs. I didn't just want to be known as a mommy, and we needed the extra income, so I went back to work. I never regretted my decision, and my son did fine in day care. Now that our second child has arrived—four years later—most of my friends have had one or two babies and we are in a better situation financially, so I'm staying at home. I'm enjoying being at home much more this time around

Julie Anne Cooper, Roswell, GA

In between. I work three days a week. I found I didn't quite fit in with either the full-time stay-at-home moms or the full-time working moms. It took a year to find my place—and it was a long year.

Beth, New York City

Work engages the mind. I don't think I could have coped with being a full-time mom; I have a math degree and like the intellectual stimulation I get from my work. I returned to my job when my daughter was six months old, which I felt was a good age—she did not have the separation anxiety that some older babies experience. I would tell a new mom that if she chooses to work full-time, it should be a job she enjoys thoroughly and one that is relatively stress-free, because it is very difficult coping with a screaming baby at night if you've had a hard day at work.

Mary Sutton, Peterborough, England

Job number one. I feel that raising a child is the most important job that there is in life. You are helping to mold and influence another human being. Being a stay-at-home mom isn't easy—society doesn't give us enough credit for the work that we do. It can be demoralizing and depressing at times, but I'm grateful to be able to stay at home with my children. Your children need you. If you can afford to do it, and if you have the right temperament to do so, you should stay at home to raise your children.

Kathryn A. Varuzza, New Paltz, NY

Second-guessing goes with the territory. I have two kids. I stayed home with the first and went back to work after number two. Every day I found myself second-guessing whatever decision I made. I think most moms do.

Joanne, New York City

Financial independence gained by working. A couple of years after I was married, my parents were on the brink of divorce. My mom never worked a day in her life and found herself in her forties with no marketable skills. I discovered her crying one day, asking herself how she was going to survive. She finally resigned herself to finding a minimum-wage job. From that day forward, I swore I would never depend on a man for financial support and resolved that I would be

a working mom. The thought of being put in a position like my mom terrifies me.

R.M.S.

Transition to full-time mommyhood takes time. I knew I wanted to stay home with my children, but I was surprised by the amount of time that caring for an infant consumed. Unlike my nine-to-five job, which I could leave behind at the office, being a mother required working around the clock. I found myself mourning the life I had, with self-statements like *If I could only sleep in this Sunday,* or *If I could only shower without being disturbed*—it took a full eight months before I made the transition from my old life to my new life as a mommy. And you know what? When I finally accepted my new life, it turned out to be a lot better than the old one.

Tracy Murtagh, Long Island, NY

You'll feel different on the inside. One of the hardest things about going back to work for me was that everyone saw me as the same old person who'd been away on an extended vacation and whose life hadn't changed. But in reality, everything had changed for me—I saw myself as a whole new person. I was now someone with huge new responsibilities and a family who depended on me. I constantly felt then—and still feel today—torn between work and home. If my boss needs me to stay late, it no longer only means that dinner will be late, as it did before I had kids; it also means that I'll be missing out on hugs, story time, kissing boo-boos, and time with my family. I'm not just a worker anymore . . . I'm a mom!

Sheryl McCarthy, North Stonington, CT

These are the formative years. I stayed home with both of my children until they were three years old because I knew that there wasn't anyone out there who could love them and care for them the way I could. Besides, I didn't have children so that someone else could raise them. When I did return to work (for financial reasons), it made me feel better to know that they were old enough to be able to express themselves.

Tori Fugate, Asheville, NC

Happy at work. Maybe I'm different from most working moms, but I never had a problem leaving my child to go back to work. I didn't cry or feel guilty. I didn't even call the sitter to check on them, but then I had a sitter who came highly recommended by people I knew and respected.

R.M.S.

Lurking outside the door. My baby screamed and clung to me when I went back to work after nine months. I waited outside the apartment door every morning for a week to reassure myself that he stopped crying in minutes and became absorbed in games with the baby-sitter.

Lisa, NY

Working can create additional stresses. After my first child was born, I quit working full-time as a systems engineer and worked part-time as a consultant. At the time, we needed the money to pay the bills, so staying at home was not an option. We were fortunate that my mother watched our baby; however, I did not enjoy the guilt that I felt by being away. I felt like I was moving a thousand miles per hour trying to be a good worker, a good wife, a good mother, a good daughter, a good sister, and so on. In the process, I felt like I had lost who I truly was and what I really wanted to be, which was the best mother and woman I could possibly be. So my husband and I sat down and made a plan. We figured out how long it would take us to pay off our current bills and get us back on track so I could stay at home. It took modifying our lifestyle considerably, but I've never regretted my decision. I'm thrilled with staying at home with my children!

Bernadette F., West Chester, PA

It strengthens the bond between mother and baby. I decided to stay home from my teaching career of five years because after ten months of having my daughter in day care, I felt I didn't know her. My teaching job was very demanding, and to make matters worse, I was also attending college part-time to finish my master's degree. I was so spent by the end of the day that I'd arrive home sometimes wishing that my daughter would go to bed early so I could relax. Although it was a very risky step for me to quit my teaching job (good districts like the one in which I taught are hard to come by), I knew it was the right thing to do. If you are debating about staying home, know that it *can* be done. I have been home now for two years, and we have survived on my husband's teacher's salary, while paying off college tuition and an internship.

Nancy Ablao, Kalamazoo, MI

Quantity begets quality. I've never heard a mother say, as she looked back on her childbearing years, that she wished she had worked more and spent less time with her children. However, I have heard many moms express regret for the time they spent working, rather than spending that time caring for their children at home. My husband and I choose to live a very simple lifestyle in order to keep me at home. I spend enough time worrying, *Am I doing a good job raising my children?*; I do not want to add, *Am I spending enough quality time with them?* Quality time comes most readily when there is plenty of *quantity* time.

Patty Kartchner, Dayton, OR

Be a happy mom. I love my baby, and I love my work. I think the greatest gift I give her is showing her that I can contribute to my family and to my community through work. I hope she'll learn that finding passion in all you do—mothering, relationships, work—can be achieved. My job charges my batteries so that when I come home to her, I'm really revved up to be there.

Beth, New York City

A gift that lasts a lifetime. I'm a day-care provider, and I would tell a new mom to stay at home with her child, if at all possible. It's the best gift you can give them.

Juliana Russo, Encinitas, CA

Stand by your choice, and don't feel guilty. I was a full-time stay-at-home mom for my son's first year, then I went back into the workforce full-time. I stayed a full-time working mom following my maternity leave after my daughter's birth, so I've experienced both worlds. My year at home was filled with incredibly hard work and great joy, punctuated by boredom, frustration, and anger—and constant guilt that I wasn't being a good enough mom. I also felt guilty about returning to a job I loved and missed, but I made the decision to focus all my effort on finding the best baby-sitter who could come to my home (the most expensive option, but worth it for my peace of mind and greatest stability for my family). I truly believe that the satisfaction I get from my work makes me a happier, more interesting, and more present mother for my kids. I also believe that all the guilt is nothing more than a huge drain on my energy—and what mom can afford that drain?

My best advice is to be flexible and not let others' advice or prejudices overrule your instincts. My experience in both pairs of shoes has taught me not to judge anyone else's choices; don't let anyone judge yours, and don't judge yourself harshly, whatever route you choose. Moms get dumped on enough. You won't know until the decision is upon you whether you and your child will flourish best if you stay home or return to work. Make a choice from your heart, remind yourself that you can remake it at any time, and know that while you may change what you are, you won't change who you are. As long as you're a loving mom, your kids will thrive.

Betsy Rapoport, White Plains, NY

Do what is right for you. Like they say, "Do what is right for you and it will be right for the baby." Do not feel guilty for working outside the home and do not attempt to "do it all"— you will only set yourself up for disappointment. Try to divide household chores with your spouse, or hire a cleaning service every other week—this gives you more free time to spend with your children.

Tricia Juliano, Hackensack, NJ

Career Alternatives

Part-time work is a good compromise. I returned to work against my will and was very upset; I cried in the ladies' room every day for weeks. When my son was seven months old, I found a part-time position and quit my full-time job. Things got a lot better after that. Now I'm happy that I work—I think I'd be frustrated at home all day long. By working part-time, I still have ample time to spend time with my son each day, reading, walking, playing, and doing lots and lots of cuddling.

Debra S. Fair, Waltham, MA

Consider starting a home-based business. Think seriously about whether you will really go back to a full-time career. I was 110 percent sure I would continue my career—which I dearly loved—but once my newborn baby was in my arms, my priorities changed. As a family, we depended on my salary, so we had to make some big adjustments and sacrifices in order to have me work part-time from home, and I ended up starting a home business in public relations and marketing.

I also found during this time that there was a strong need for support, information, and networking among women who, like me, were working at home or desired to work at home. So, in addition to my business, I started an association called Home-Based Working Moms (www.hbwm.com, or 800-281-8565), which helps bring working moms closer to their children by allowing them to establish a home business. We offer over two hundred home business ideas and opportunities. In addition, we offer a kit called the Mom's Home Business Kit (www.hbwm.com/kit.htm), which was created especially for moms who want to work at home but don't know where to begin or what they want to do.

Some other good resources for moms who want to work at home include:

1. Books: *The Stay-at-Home Mom's Guide to Making Money,* by Liz Folger; *Mompreneurs,* by Ellen H. Parlapiano and Patricia Cobe; *The Best Home Businesses for the 21st Century,* by Paul and Sarah Edwards; *More 101 Best Home-Based Businesses for Women,* by Priscilla Y. Huff.

2. Office of Women's Business Ownership (www.onlinewbc.org, or 202-205-6673), created in partnership with the Small Business Administration, offers a wealth of information for starting and running your own business, networking, resources, and so forth.

3. Small Business Administration (SBA) (www.sba.gov, or

800-U-ASK SBA) provides free counseling on starting your home business.

4. Service Corps of Retired Executives (SCORE) (www. score.org, or 800-634-0245) can refer you to a business counselor in your area; all counseling services are free.

Lesley Spencer, Austin, TX

Maintain a steady work schedule. When opting for part-time work, I've always found it easier to work fewer hours on more days, rather than more hours on fewer days. For example, if you can negotiate a twenty-hour workweek, try to work four hours a day for five days a week instead of two ten-hour days. It's better for baby, because she doesn't have such a long separation from you and can develop a steady routine. And it's better for you because you're seen in the office more frequently.

Cynthia, Palo Alto, CA

Stay-at-home dad's a good option, too. I loved my son, but I hated staying at home—I was depressed and felt like a bad mother for wanting to get back to my job. But I knew that I wasn't functioning normally being at home all day, and that wasn't good for my son, either. We took a hard look at our finances, and after reorganizing our budget, we decided that my husband would quit his job and stay home. We lost two thirds of our income, but it was worth it to us. Knowing that my son's daddy was caring for him made me much more relaxed about going back to work. I didn't have the same guilt that so many other moms had, and I could call three or four times a day to check in without feeling like I was burdening anyone.

Heather Petit, Newark, DE

Consider being a care provider. I was a day-care teacher before I had my baby. I learned firsthand that, in a day-care setting, it's hard to give each infant the time that he or she needs. If the caregiver is responsible for four or five babies and one of those babies is fussy, the fussy baby will get the most attention. If another baby is calm and quiet, he is left alone and not held very much. I also witnessed many of the babies' "firsts" and later related them to the parents; I decided then that I didn't want to miss those experiences with my children. My husband and I share my parents' house so I can stay home. Now that my son is older, I baby-sit another child about the same age two days a week—I'm bringing home good money and I am able to be with my child.

Kimberly Cushman, West Windsor, NJ

Become a home party hostess. For the new mom who wants to stay at home, but could use a little extra money, becoming a home party hostess is ideal. You can sell almost anything in your home (or someone else's home) today and set your own schedule, working as little or as much as desired. Most home party companies have Web sites; here are a few to consider: The Pampered Chef (www.pamperedchef.com), Tupperware (www.tupperware.com), Home Interiors and Gifts (www.homeinteriors.com), PartyLite Gifts (www.partylite.com), Discovery Toys (www.discoverytoysinc.com), and Undercover Wear (www.undercoverwear.com).

Pamela Bartolotto, Prosperity, PA

The job description is endless! To all the stay-at-home moms who thought that being a mom meant giving up your career, think again. A mom is a nurse (caring for a sick child), chef (preparing meals), chauffeur (delivering and picking up your child), accountant (keeping the family budget), secretary (organizing the household and scheduling), teacher (educating baby and helping the bigger ones with homework), referee (sibling rivalry), law-enforcement officer (enforcing household rules), seamstress (mending and hemming clothes), and cleaner (laundry and housekeeping) . . . need I say more?

PoLee Mark-Yee, Kirkland, Quebec

Achieving Satisfaction at Home

Swap child care with friends. Work out a weekly child-sharing program with your friends. I had two best friends when my first four kids were small, and among us we got two half days "off" a week. I used that time to shop, visit my doctor, get my haircut, or even clean the house. It was free day care, worked out among friends. One day a week we designated as "moms' day" and spent our day together solving our parenting problems as a team.

Linda Republicano, Alameda, CA

Play groups are a lifeline for new moms. When you're a first-time mom, it is vitally important to establish friendships with other moms who are in a similar situation, whether you're a mom who will be staying at home, working full-time, or, like me, taking care of twins. It helps to talk with someone who can relate to what you're going through; this is especially true if you are the only one among your friends with children. There are many places—other than your own neighborhood—where you can find a mom's group or play group to join: Contact the churches in your area, YMCA, chamber of commerce (many communities have established play groups that meet on a regular basis), children's bookstores, library, local women's groups and clubs, local hospitals, and women's centers.

Wendy Pisciotta, Stafford Springs, CT

Try the parks. Go to parks in your neighborhood, and I guarantee you will meet new moms (and not-so-new moms) with babies. Other moms are great to talk with!

Debra S. Fair, Waltham, MA

Moms network on the Web. Check out the wonderful parenting support groups on the Internet—you can talk with new moms or old moms, get advice, or simply sound off. I have found stay-at-home-mom groups that are wonderful; one of my favorites is www.femalehome.org.

Amy Allred, Woodstock, GA

Take up a hobby. If you have an interest in a hobby, such as painting, knitting, memory-book making, or writing, now is the best time to start doing it. You'll get enjoyment from it, and you'll feel like you've had a break.

Donna M. Condida, Archbald, PA

Balancing Work and Home

Lay it out the night before. Get everything ready the night before—mornings can be hectic even when you are prepared. I also found that it helps to organize my closet so that only work clothes are in it. I go through the closet every two months to get

🐾 *Helpful Resources for the Stay-at-home Mom*

MOTHERS & MORE

Mothers & More (www.mothersandmore.org, or 630-941-3553) is an international nonprofit organization supporting women who have altered their career paths in order to care for their children at home. Visit their Web site to locate local chapters in your area, to learn more about development of personal and professional growth while at home, and for articles, message boards, links, and chat rooms.

MOTHERS AT HOME (MAH)

Mothers at Home (www.mah.org, or 703-352-1072) is a non-profit organization supporting mothers who have chosen, or would like to choose, to be at home with their children. MAH offers support, information, education, networking, resources, and links for at-home parents through its Web site; they also publish their own books, including *What's a Smart Woman Like You Doing at Home?*, along with their monthly journal, *Welcome Home,* a publication created for and by mothers.

ABOUT.COM: STAY-AT-HOME PARENTS

About.com (http://homeparents.about.com) is an extensive Web site offering information, articles, and a multitude of links to related at-home parenting sites. Stay-at-home parents get encouragement, parenting tips and advice, ways to increase self-esteem, recipes, home-based business advice, ways to reduce stress, plus much more.

PARENTING.COM

This user-centered Web site (www.parenting.com) pulls articles and expert advice from trusted parenting magazines such as *Parenting, Baby Talk, Family Life,* and *Healthy Pregnancy*. Articles address key issues for at-home parents, like answers to baby-care questions, making time for yourself, coping skills, and stories from other at-home parents. The site also has a message board for at-home parents. 🐾

rid of clothes that are out of season, don't fit, are worn out, or are inappropriate for work. This way, all of the clothing in my closet is acceptable and easy to mix and match—no more trying to decide what to wear in the mornings. I keep my "play" clothes in another closet or in my dresser drawers.

Tricia Juliano, Hackensack, NJ

A happy reunion. I found that the best way to reunite with my babies after coming home from work was to nurse, first thing. They were always willing, and it made us both feel good.

Cindy Fagiano, Chicago, IL

Shed your work clothes. I find that if I change into blue jeans and a T-shirt as soon as I come home from work, and put my hair back, I make a psychological transition from my working role as manager to "mommy." I then take my baby for a walk—this is a good way to clear my head and my son gets some fresh air. Plus, it's exercise! Back at home, I read to my son, or just dance around with him. I have about two hours before my husband comes home, and after that things really get hectic (feeding baby, making dinner, preparing for the next day, and so forth). I really cherish our special time together each afternoon.

Tricia Juliano, Hackensack, NJ

Baby swim class a great way to reconnect. One of the best things I did was to enroll my daughter in a mother-baby swim class when she was six months old. I had just enough time after work to pick her up from day care and head to the pool. We got to spend thirty minutes playing and relaxing in the water together. It was a great start to our time together in the late afternoon.

Cynthia, Palo Alto, CA

Finding the Right Care Situation

It's like having a second family. I would highly recommend in-home care, especially for younger children, because it allows the child to be cared for in an environment similar to their own. I found a stay-at-home mom who had a child close to the age of my daughter. They became playmates for one another. There were also older school-aged children in the home, and they took to my daughter like another sister. The downside to in-home care came when they had to move to another part of the state and I lost this very valuable situation. I had to start my search all over again.

Rose Shilladay, Harrisburg, PA

Begin a day-care search while pregnant. Start your day-care search early. I started three months prior to my due date, and it was a good thing I did, since my son was born six weeks early. I found that many day-care facilities either did not take infants or, more commonly, did not have an opening at the time I would need them.

Dawn M. Casella, Westland, MI

Be a casual observer. I started my search by asking the most fastidious mothers I knew which day care their own children attended, and then I paid a personal visit to each facility to check it out for myself. After I toured the facilities and met the staff, I would sit in the staff break room and drink a cup of coffee, which allowed me to observe the staff unnoticed and to chat casually with the teachers. I found that this was a good way to discover the caregivers' real feelings about kids.

Jaki Thomas, South Australia

Search agency saves you time. We contacted a child-care search agency when it was time to find a day care for our son. They charged $70 and did the hardest part of the search for us: They provided us with a complete listing of care facilities, identifying which ones actually had openings, their hours of operation, credentials, programs, cost, and so forth. All we had to do was call the references and visit the facilities. We saved hours and hours of phone calls!

Heather Petit, Newark, DE

Check for complaints. Ask to see a day-care facility's license so you can verify the license expiration data and get the name of the licensing agency. Then call the licensing agent and ask if the facility has had any violations or complaints filed against them.

April Heslar, Indianapolis, IN

Look for accreditation. Look for the National Association for the Education of Young Children (NAEYC)–accredited child care. Besides the basic requirements, the accreditation program considers the quality of the care, whereas many licensing programs only look at minimum ratio requirements.

Cynthia, Palo Alto, CA

Use the baby-sitter network. The nannies in my neighborhood all hang out together and have group play dates, so I went to them first for a good baby-sitter recommendation. I got a wonderful sitter and an instant play group for my son.

Joanne, NY

Check the boards. The preschools at our local churches, temple, and YMCAs are always posting the names of baby-sitters looking for new positions because the children they've been caring for have "aged out" of the need for child care. You can find someone who's been with one family for years—a great reference.

Lisa, NY

Go easy the first few weeks. Don't underestimate the complexity and the impact of handing your baby over to another person for child care—this is one of the hardest milestones you'll have to cross as a mom. You may feel wrenching guilt, worry, sadness, and other distressing feelings that will affect you for a week or more. Prepare for the transition by clearing the board of any other responsibilities for the first week or two, and if at all possible, ease into day care by returning to work part-time, or work from home for a couple of weeks. Have lots of clean laundry and frozen meals on hand so that you can spend the evenings keeping baby on schedule and making up for the snuggles you've missed during the day. Get a good night's sleep and nap on the weekends. Put off paying bills and major house-work so that you can focus on readjusting to the world, letting your baby go without imparting all of your tension and worry to his little being, and maintaining a sane, nonblaming relationship with your partner.

Jane A. Zanca, Atlanta, GA

She loves me, she loves me not. Don't be surprised if even the best care situation leaves you feeling bad. Our daughter loved the woman who cared for her and I was happy that she felt a part of that family. But at the same time, I felt a little rejected when I picked her up at the end of the day and she would cry and say she didn't want to go.

Rose Shilladay, Harrisburg, PA

Schedule surprise visits. Drop in unannounced on the day-care center—you'll be able to observe the staff in "prime" form. Watch to see how the teachers interact with the children

✒ National Child-Care Accreditation Agencies

NATIONAL ASSOCIATION FOR THE EDUCATION OF YOUNG CHILDREN (NAEYC)

Founded in 1926, NAEYC (www.naeyc.org, or 800-424-2460) is the nation's largest organization of early childhood professionals for children, birth through age eight. The NAEYC accreditation program looks at the overall child-care program—including health and safety, staffing, staff qualifications, physical environment, and administration—but places greater emphasis on the quality of inter-actions among staff and children, as well as the developmental appropriateness of the curriculum. For example, one of NAEYC's criteria includes evaluating whether the child-care center stresses all areas of the child's development equally, with time and attention devoted to cognitive development, social and emotional develop-ment, as well as physical development. Visit their Web site to order helpful brochures on child-care options or to locate an NAEYC-accredited center in your area.

NATIONAL ASSOCIATION OF CHILD CARE RESOURCE AND REFERRAL AGENCIES (NACCRRA)

NACCRRA (www.naccrra.net, or Child Care Aware at: 800-424-2246) is a national network of community-based child-care resource and referral agencies and has been in operation for over twenty-five years. The agency's Child Care Aware program provides useful information on the different types of child care available and how to evaluate what's right for you, including the five steps to finding quality child care. Visit their Web site to locate a local NACCRRA Child Care Resource and Referral Agency. ✒

and with one another. Answer these questions: Do the children look contented and happy? Does the staff look happy? Are there stimulating toys and activities in the room? Do the teachers have at least a two-year associate's degree in child development or a related field? Is the facility meeting the legal child-to-teacher ratio for your state? (If there are more than three infants to one teacher [3:1], they may not be within ratio; check with your state licensing facility.)

Rebecca Vogel-Pitts, Longmont, CO

Check for cleanliness. I've worked in day-care centers, and here are some things parents should look for: When you tour the facility, note the level of cleanliness. Toys should be washed and disinfected during the day, mats and cribs should be disinfected periodically, and washable bibs should be clean, too. Check to see if the caregivers wear gloves for diaper changes. Ask about late policies: Is there a late fee? Are there weekend or holiday hours? What are they? Request information on policies for emergencies, such as bad-weather closings. Good child-care centers keep a chart for each child on a daily basis. This should include what time diapers were changed; what time baby was fed; if baby was happy, sad, or playful; and what time naps were taken.

Amanda Battey, Atlanta, GA

Toddlers need room to roam. We looked for large play spaces and little structure. Most of the day-care facilities I observed were cramped and way too structured. I want my toddler to be allowed to play freely or participate in time-limited planned activities—not be told to sit still and color or watch videos for hours.

Jodi Detjen

A book before good-bye saves tears. As an in-home day-care provider, I witness children having a difficult time saying good-bye to their parent when dropped off in the morning. I suggest to the parents that they stay long enough to read one short book to their child, give him a kiss and a hug, and then say good-bye. The child feels special that Mom or Dad took the time in the morning to read to him, and it starts the day off with a smile instead of tears.

Juliana Russo, Encinitas, CA

Always say good-bye. Never, ever sneak out with saying good-bye. We did this once when we dropped our son off at his grandmother's house and will never do it again. He not only spent the whole evening looking for us in every room and crying, but spent the next three weeks following us around to make sure that we didn't "vanish" on him again. After that, leaving became intensely distressing for him. Sneaking out was not worth the cheap escape we got that one time!

Heather Petit, Newark, DE

Observe for an hour before deciding. I am a home family-care provider and a mom, and here's what I would tell new moms searching for family care: First, set up an appointment to meet with the provider when children are *not* present; this will give you a chance to talk uninterrupted. Ask how many children the provider is caring for (remember, the fewer children—particularly infants—the provider cares for, the more attention your child will receive). Make sure, too, that each child has his own crib or bed for sanitary reasons. Ask about how sick and vacation time are handled. Find out if the provider does house-work, takes showers, runs errands, or cooks during sitting hours; you should discuss your feelings about such things. Second, I would strongly urge you to go and observe the provider's home when children *are* present, and stay for an hour. Don't chat with the provider, just be an onlooker. A provider will have a hard time faking it for more than half an hour.

Terry Kopec, Milwaukee, WI

Staff stability is important. The biggest problem in day care today is the lack of pay, coupled with high staff turnover. The first two questions I would ask a day-care provider are what do they pay their teachers and what is their job turnover rate? Your child needs to see the same caring face every day, not the same colored uniform. If the pay is low, just ask yourself how long you would tend to a room full of crying babies at only $7 an hour. Probably not long. I recommend nonprofit day care if you can find it; you'll find that, on average, the teachers receive better pay, benefits, training, and long-term employment. To locate nonprofit day care, contact local churches and other organizations in your area that emphasize child development.

After you've found day care you're happy with, my advice is to—above all else—treat your child's teacher with respect. I once owned a day-care center, and I always hated it when the parents treated my employees like they were the hired help. Your child comes first, and your child's caregivers come second: Be sure to pick up your child on time (regardless of what your boss would like you to first accomplish before leaving the office), or at least call if you're going to be late. Be pleasant and ask about your child's day, and take some time to get to know your child's teacher. Last, but not least, pay on time!

Kimberly R. Harris, Fairview, NC

Mature adults are more stable. Look for mature child-care providers. They seem to stay with one place for years—as opposed to months—providing more stability and security for your child.

Susan Flannery, Louisville, KY

Nannies provide consistency and strong bonding. We have had two different nannies for our kids in four years, and our children loved both of them. There have been some distinct advantages to having a nanny, like the fact that the children could wake up whenever they wanted to and remain in their familiar home environment throughout the day. They didn't have to fight for a teacher's attention, and they learned to get along well with each other. My boys were rarely sick, because they weren't around other sick children, and if they did have a cold or were running a slight temperature, the nanny could stay home with them and I didn't have to miss work. Best of all, they had only one care provider, which allowed them to develop a long-term, loving relationship. Bringing someone into your home makes for an easier transition on the parents, too; it's not quite so upsetting to young children when you leave for work if they are in their own home. But there are a couple of disadvantages to hiring a nanny, too: It is one of the most expensive child-care options available to parents, and your house will most likely be in a constant state of messiness (unless your nanny happens to clean). Also, you *must* be home on time. Still, I would say that if you can afford it, bringing a nanny into your home is the best option and well worth the money.

Ann Wells, San Diego, CA

Your church can be a good referral source. I found that churches are the best referral source for in-home child care. Contact a church in your area and ask for a recommendation, preferably someone they know very well. After two bad (and abusive) nannies, I found some very sweet ladies through a local church with whom I am very happy.

Katherine W. Manning-Pinotti, Houston, TX

Look for day care that feeds on demand. If you plan on continuing to breast-feed your baby after you return to work, look for day care that does not schedule feedings, but rather feeds babies on demand—the good ones do this already. Breast-fed babies are held with greater frequency because they require more frequent feedings (which is a compelling reason to keep up with breast-feeding after returning to work). Before I started back to work, I managed to pump and freeze about seventy-two ounces of breast milk (dated and double-bagged), and maintained that amount for about six months, replacing what I used over that time. My daughter's day care had a small refrigerator available and a small freezer for backup breast milk. The best part was that the day care was only eight minutes from my office, so I was able to nurse over my lunch hour.

Lynne F. Carlberg, Albuquerque, NM

PJs at breakfast. I have a child-care business in my home, and I find that one of the biggest challenges for parents in the morning is getting their kiddos out the door on time. It can be a particularly stressful time for parent and child. I invite parents to leave their children in their pajamas and let me take care of feeding them their breakfast and dressing them after they eat. Breakfast time is much more relaxed and allows some time for play. Ask your child's care provider if this might be an option for you.

Alexia Weber, South Lyon, MI

Mother's Day Out. I have been fortunate to be able to stay at home with my son while working at home (as a self-employed fund-raising consultant). While I am able to get most of my work done in the evenings and on the weekends when my husband is home, I also enrolled my son in a Mother's Day Out program at a local church for three hours a day, two days a week. I have found that having him in this program has made me a better mom; I'm able to truly focus on everything I can't

❦ Helpful Resources for the Working Mom

CHILD CARE NEWS

Child Care News (www.childcarenews.com) is a Web site dedicated to bringing you the latest news of the day in child care.

WORKING MOTHER MAGAZINE

Working Mother Magazine (www.workingmother.com, or 212-445-6100) is a national business magazine for working mothers. Visit their Web site to view the magazine's list of one hundred best companies for working mothers, starting a business, personal finance advice, articles, discussion boards, and links for the working mother.

MOMS REFUGE

Moms Refuge (www.momsrefuge.com) brings you multiple topics for working moms, including single-mom news, the art of juggling work and kids, informative articles on today's family and career issues, as well as discussion boards.

4 WORKING MOTHERS.COM

4 Working Mothers.com (www.4workingmothers.com) is a great starting place with comprehensive links to just about everything for the working mother, including helpful sites for home-based working mothers and telecommuting mothers, mothers making money, child-care options, career moms, professional associations, and househusbands.

CAREFINDER.COM

Carefinder.com (www.carefinder.com) lists almost two hundred thousand individual child day-care centers and homes throughout the U.S. This site helps parents find care providers and offers a variety of other resources for working parents and care providers.

CareGuide.com
  CareGuide.com (www.careguide.com) has a listing of approximately ninety thousand child-care facilities and provides products, services, and networking for parents and caregivers alike. You'll also find articles and tools for screening caregivers. 🖋

do when he's at home with me, and when he is home, I'm able to focus strictly on him. He really seems to enjoy the activities and classmates at his school, too. You can find a Mother's Day Out program (sometimes called Mother's Morning Out) by contacting various local churches in your area.

Jan Harrison Furlow, Alexandria, VA

Swap baby-sitting with other moms. Create a network of moms in a situation similar to yours who would be willing to help out in a pinch, and vice versa. Baby-sitters are not always available, but other moms usually are.

Tina Pavich, Noblesville, IN

Moms of multiples need extra help. Moms with multiples like me (I have triplets) need extra help around the clock for the first two to three months. College students from the area nursing schools are great caregivers and really enjoy caring for multiples. Call your local colleges or universities and inquire with student employment or the instructors in the nursing department.

Stephanie Parrott, Knoxville, TN

CHAPTER 14

Speaking from the Heart
❧
Little Gems of Wisdom

"You're just too good to be true..." When I brought my daughter home from the hospital, I found I couldn't sleep at night—not because she kept me up, but because I just couldn't take my eyes off of her! My daughter has taught me more about love in her short little life than anyone else in this world. I've learned that I am a protective mother and would go to *any* length to protect her from harm.

Heather Allen, Lemon Grove, CA

Cherish the moment. Cherish each and every moment—the good and the bad—all too soon your little baby will be grown, and you won't be able to hold him in your arms anymore.

Deborah Baska, Kansas City, MO

Heaven on earth. My love for my baby feels almost sacred— like being connected to God. Being my son's mommy has given me a sense of completeness I never knew I lacked.

Evelyn O'Donnell, Alameda, CA

Mother knows best. Being a parent is the most rewarding and also the most difficult role you will ever have. Advice comes from many places, sometimes sought out and sometimes forced upon you and delivered with the subtlety of a sledgehammer. Remember that *you* are the final decision maker—do what you think is right for your baby. Just because another parent did something one way does not make it the best way for your child.

Mary K. Beno, WI

Use the old noggin. Your most useful tool as a mom is your common sense.

Denise Campbell, North Providence, RI

"Thanks, Mom." There is no way to explain how much you will love your child—it isn't possible to grasp in advance. Go hug your mom now, because she loves you more than you can know. I bought my mom a card after my son was born, and in it I wrote: *Thanks, Mom, now I finally understand.* Expect your perspective on life, ecology, violence, education, and world peace to change or intensify. Having a baby connects you to the flow of life in a way that nothing else can approximate. You'll become aware of the world in ways you never were before; every news story will move you to tears of joy or pain. You'll grieve deeply when a mother loses her child, and you'll find yourself wondering about the childhoods and mothers of people around you. This isn't hormones, this is motherhood!

Heather Petit, Newark, DE

The heart knows no boundaries. I don't have a special story to tell. Every day is the same uneventful kind of day as the day before: I feed the baby, change him, put him to bed—the routine of a suburban housewife. Yet every day is also different.

Every day I experience something new, every day I discover a new wonder in my dear son, every day is full of trial and error. I never knew I could love someone so much. At first it was scary; I wondered what I would do if I ever lost him. It made me think of my relationship with my own parents: How often did they wonder if they would lose me? Now more than ever, probably, since I moved an ocean away from them. Yet I know I can also go back to them, and they will be there for me. And like my parents have done for me for all these years, I will give as much love as my son accepts without ever asking for anything in return.

Hsiu-chen Lin Classon, Streamwood, IL

Love her tender. You can't spoil your baby with love.

Kaleigh Donnelly, Memphis, TN

Vulnerable. Becoming a mom was so terrifying. My husband and I would tell each other, "I thought I loved you best, but you've just been demoted." I never worried so much in my life; everything seemed a threat to my baby. I realized that *I* was really the vulnerable one—if anything ever happened to my child, I didn't think I could survive it.

Elizabeth, New York City

These are the best years. When my daughter was six weeks old, my husband and I decided to go out to dinner, toting our baby with us. We went to our usual casual restaurant, where our daughter slept during the forty-five-minute wait for a table. Then, just as we were called to our table, our baby woke up and started crying, then shrieking, drawing the attention of everyone in the restaurant! Humiliated and frustrated, we cowered at our table. Just as we were about to sit down, an elderly woman leaned over to me and said, "These are the best years of your life. Enjoy them." At the time, what she said was really

hard to hear. All I could think about was the fact that I could no longer enjoy a carefree life. But now—with our daughter turning nine years old and my having had two more children along the way—I see that the woman in the restaurant was right. The past nine years have gone so quickly, and in just another nine years, our little baby will be leaving home. How much better it would have been to focus on all that we had, rather than all that we lost. What's one spoiled dinner compared to all of the happiness that a child brings to one's life?

Cynthia, Palo Alto, CA

It's infinitely rewarding. Being a mom is the hardest job I've ever loved.

Ann Wells, San Diego, CA

Mission: Shaping the future. The love you'll feel for your new baby is amazing, and it grows as your baby grows. It gave me a new perspective on the world and made me realize that all of the great things that I did before I had a baby (work, travel, and so forth) were nothing compared to giving birth and raising a child. I know that this is the most important work in my life. It is my mission to raise my two children to be wonderful human beings.

Marybeth Danielson-McElroy, Sherwood, OR

Warms the heart. One story I remember from the first year was during an afternoon nursing session with my daughter. She was nursing happily and suddenly stopped, then she looked up at me and gave me the most glorious smile! It was as if she wanted to communicate to me that she knew I loved her and was doing my best for her, and that she loved me, too. I had the warmest feeling in my heart for the rest of the day.

Lori Peters, PA

Toss the guilt. As a new mom, I felt guilty about everything that wasn't perfect, and that was just about everything. Feeling guilty only gets in the way of loving and caring for your baby— it is added stress at a time when you've got stress enough. Being a good parent takes time, patience, and plain old hard work. Don't sweat the small stuff, and enjoy the wonders of your child. Here's to guilt-free parenting!

Carol M Smith, Williamsburg, VA

Each baby is unique. Don't compare your baby to your friends' babies. Everybody's baby is different, and it will only drive you nuts anyway.

Stephanie L. Becker, Traverse City, MI

Was it something I said? My boss called me one day about a week after I gave birth to ask how I was doing. I started crying. He asked what was wrong, but I really didn't know how to respond. I was thinking about the future and the fact that some-day my sweet little angel—who was suddenly the whole reason for my existence—was going to break my heart just by growing up. I felt so vulnerable—I had never before experienced such a deep, all-consuming love. My baby was my flesh, my heart, my blood, and my life. And all of this coming from someone who never really believed she was the "mom" type.

Deborah Baska, Kansas City, MO

Children learn by living. Hold your children, love them, teach them, and learn from them. Look at the world through their eyes. Know that whatever phase your children go through, good or bad, will soon be over; nothing speeds by as quickly as childhood. Be not only a parent, but also a person—your children will be watching you to learn how to "do" life. Don't get stressed; spilling is how children learn to pour, breaking is how they learn to handle, and crying is how they learn to communicate. What may seem like a disaster or annoyance to you is an important lesson to them—the whole world is their classroom and you are their most important teacher. Keep your perspective. Recognize their limitations. Imagine the world as they see it: a forest of knees, a mountain of rules, and things they desire so far out of reach.

Linda Federman, Randolph, NJ

Unconditional love is all a child needs... As a grand-mother, I now watch my daughter struggle with the same feel-ings of inadequacy I struggled with as a young mother. She looks at her baby sometimes with hollow eyes, and I know at those times that she is too tired to even talk, let alone walk across that kitchen floor one more time to make formula. One day I sat down with her and said, "Sweetie, you're a wonderful mother." She shook her head and sighed; tears welled up in her eyes. "Not good enough," she said. "If you only knew . . ."

I took her hand and said, "My darling, you *are* a wonderful mother, and I'll tell you why: because you love your child. Unconditional love is all a child needs to grow. You have not shortchanged your baby because some nights you're too tired and don't feel like getting up with him one more time—you get up anyway. There are times when you may be short-tempered and impatient with your son. It would be nice to be Mary Poppins, smiling and singing throughout the day, but that's not real life. Women are flesh and blood and have bad days: days they don't feel well, or days when they just need a break. That's real life, and that's the wonder of motherhood: Despite a mother's own needs and failing grace, she does what needs to be done. All of his life there is nothing more your son will need from you except your love, and there is nothing he will remember less than the times that his mother was short or impatient with him. Your baby is loved and he knows it; he knows it by the way you talk to him, hold him, and caress him. Your son is happy and will grow up to be a wonderful, caring person like you, and a loving parent himself someday."

Carla Bioni, Moline, IL

Where's the instruction manual? If there is one thing that I've learned about being a mother, it's that *nothing* is written in stone. Children are resilient, and even if we aren't perfect, they will usually turn out just fine. I was one of those judgmental types who would look upon a particular situation between a mother with her child and think, *I'll never do* that *with* my *children.* Of course, once I had children of my own, I promptly did some of those very same things, whether out of convenience or pure exhaustion! I used to feel guilty about my limitations, but not anymore. To all new moms, I say that it isn't as easy as it looks—you may very well allow your children to watch too much TV or eat too few vegetables. All you can do is let your children know that they are loved and do the best you can do for that day.

Carrie Massier, Airdrie, Alberta

Time brings a new perspective. Every new mom feels totally terrified. We all go through it. The baby will not break; the baby will cry. The baby does not have a fatal illness, and you will sleep again. You will get back into those size sixes again, and your mate does find you unbelievably attractive. All new parents feel that they have made mistakes at the lowest point: when you haven't slept in two days, you are barely eating, and the baby hasn't stopped crying for two hours straight. This is normal. When your baby is happy and you're rested, you will get back to normal and realize that you've been given the greatest gift that God could give you.

Donna M. Condida, Archbald, PA

Discipline with love. Discipline is necessary training for children but should serve only to correct misbehavior and teach right from wrong—not to scare, severely punish, or hurt them. Children learn best when you are calm, and it's then that you are best able to reason with them. Parents who yell, scream, hit, scold, threaten, or insult their child will soon have a very unhappy child who will only grow to feel unloved and defiant, making him even more difficult to discipline as he grows. Instruct with mildness. If your child creates a mess, allowing him to clean it up by himself—however long it may take—will make the strongest impression. If he has treated another child unfairly, requiring him to apologize to the other child will correct a wrongful trend. If he gets into something harmful, remove him and provide him with a safe alternative. Remember that you have only about twelve years before the critical teen years set in—establish a healthy discipline base now, and you'll reap the benefits later.

Brenda Martin, Dundee, Scotland

You set the boundaries. Never discipline your child because of what someone else thinks.

Kimberly R. Harris, Fairview, NC

Trust your instincts. One night I found that my baby, who had just finished a bottle, had stopped breathing and was bluish-gray in color, his body lifeless. Fortunately, I was able to resuscitate him and rushed him to the hospital. The doctors at the hospital, and later our own pediatrician, tried to convince my husband and me that our son had simply aspirated and that it was an isolated incident. But I knew it was more than that. Since his birth he had a pattern of spitting up or even vomiting after feedings, along with a somewhat irregular breathing pattern and poor sleeping habits. I couldn't get the doctors to take me seriously and I ended up feeling like a hysterical inexperienced mother who was wasting the doctors' time. It wasn't until I talked to a friend who insisted that I find another doctor and have testing done that I located a wonderful pediatrician who gave us our answers. She questioned us at length, examined our baby thoroughly, and ran a series of tests. The final diagnosis was reflux (his stomach valve doesn't fully close). Now, with medication, he is a much happier, healthier baby and sleeps through the night, and I feel much more confident as a mother. If your baby's doctor is not hearing you, or you know something still isn't right with your baby, trust your instincts and find a new doctor or ask for a referral to a specialist.

Mitzi Ibarra, Cedartown, GA

Let the "stuff" go. One of the hardest things to overcome when you are a new mom is the desire to get things done. Your baby's needs are very real and time-consuming. The stuff that used to be so important pales in significance when compared to the needs of your baby. When you find frustrations building and feel you're not getting much done, read this little poem given to me by another mom:

> *Dust and cleaning can wait for tomorrow*
> *For babies grow up, we've learned in our sorrow.*
> *So quiet down, cobwebs, dust, go to sleep*
> *I'm rocking my baby . . . and babies won't keep!*

Linda Alderman, Kanab, UT

Real Mothers

Real Mothers don't eat quiche; they don't have time to make it.

Real Mothers know that their kitchen utensils are probably in the sandbox.

Real Mothers often have sticky floors, filthy ovens, and happy kids.

Real Mothers know that dried Play-Doh doesn't come out of carpeting.

Real Mothers don't want to know what the vacuum just sucked up.

Real Mothers sometimes ask "Why me?" and get their answer when a little voice says, "Because I love you best."

Real Mothers know that a child's growth is not measured by height or years or grade . . . It is marked by the progression of Mama to Mommy to Mom.

Author Unknown

Resources

———— ❧ ————

WEB SITES

ABCs of Parenting (www.abcparenting.com)
This Parenthood Web family site is a good place to start if you're new to the Internet. This site operates as a pregnancy, parenting, and family search engine, and provides site reviews and ratings. There are numerous categories from which to choose, such as child care, stay-at-home parents, single parents, parents of multiples, parents of preemies, general parenting, safety, and so forth.

Baby Bag Online (www.babybag.com)
Helpful site for parents, including health and safety information, money-saving ideas, baby food recipes, pregnancy and childbirth, and helpful parenting hints. Parents are invited to share their birth stories or birth announcements with other parents.

BabyCenter (www.babycenter.com)
A helpful site addressing pregnancy and baby topics. Expert advice and a personal page available to members. Features include

"Pregnancy and Baby Timeline," giving you information specific to your stage of pregnancy or baby's age, and "Family Photo Center," for sharing your family photos.

Baby Genius (www.babygenius.com)
Give your baby a head start with "genius" products and information. Resources and information on prenatal care, pregnancy, childbirth, and childcare from birth through age six. Money-saving coupons and chat rooms.

Babyonline (www.babyonline.com)
Addresses baby and toddler topics. Online library offers a large source of information written by specialists, including child safety, baby care, and prenatal care. Leading medical experts respond to your personal parenting questions. Also, product tips and chat rooms.

BabyUniversity (www.babyuniversity.com)
Pregnancy and parenting information, baby care, parent-to-parent advice, baby freebies, birth announcements, coupons, humor, games, and baby names.

BabyZone (www.babyzone.com)
Visit this site to set up your own life-stage calendar and journal; also, photo contests, pen pals, free product samples, subscriptions, coupons, and gifts. Features "Mom to Mom," advice from one mom to another; chats and boards.

The CyberMom Dot Com (www.thecybermom.com)
Put on your poodle skirt and cashmere sweater when visiting this

1950s design site. Good stop for connecting with other moms around the world, exchanging ideas, getting solutions to your problems, and making new friends. Also, recipe swaps, tips for family pets, gardening ideas, household hints, and working at home. Chat room and boards.

Family.com (www.family.com)
A Disney site, focusing on almost every topic relating to the family: parenting, baby, pets, health, food, traveling, and so forth. Articles, tips, and expert advice in "Parent Problem Solver"; answering your questions about your child's development and behavior. Chat rooms and boards.

The Labor of Love (www.thelaboroflove.com)
A pregnancy and parenting support center. Tips for conceiving, a database for baby names, money-saving offers, and freebies. "Parents Prose" is a collection of poetry and letters from parents. Also, online pregnancy and parenting magazine, advice, articles, links, chat rooms, pen pals, and boards.

Moms Online (www.momsonline.com)
Fun, '50s-style format with lots of good information. Featuring parenting advice, stress-reducing visualization exercises, homemade gift ideas, family and relationship issues, housekeeping and laundry tips, and working moms' page. Chat rooms and boards.

ParentsPlace.com (www.parentsplace.com)
An iVillage network site; touted as one of the largest, most extensive conception, pregnancy, and parenting sites on the Web, with hundreds of boards, chats, and topics. Features expert chats, inter-

active calendars, home and garden, relationships, baby names, pregnancy after loss, fertility and infertility issues, and parenting children with special needs.

ParenthoodWeb (www.parenthoodweb.com)

Extensive site addressing pregnancy and parenting issues, as well as women's health topics. "Your Baby Today" provides solid "how to" information for baby's first year, including bathing, nursing, baby's development, circumcision advice, feeding, diapering, health issues, and more. "Ask the Experts" answers your pediatric, OB/GYN, lactation, diet, and nutrition questions.

ParentingPlace (www.parentingplace.com)

Parenting information exchange, including parenting articles and essays, book and toy reviews, and solutions to the most challenging baby-care problems. Special sections for the stay-at-home mom, working mom, and military mom. Helpful links, chat rooms, and boards.

ParentSoup (www.parentsoup.com)

One of the largest parenting sites, offering a multitude of features like health advice, articles, expert advice, resource listing, first-year calendar, recipe finder, child-cost calculator, parenting organizations directory, book club, and even a daily crossword puzzle. Numerous chat rooms and boards.

StorkNet.org (www.StorkNet.org)

Pregnancy and parenting site; featuring articles, expert advice, health news, journals, parent-to-parent information swap, columns, freebies, boards, and chats.

ADDITIONAL RESOURCES

The American Academy of Pediatrics (AAP) (www.aap.org, or 800-433-9016) is an organization made up of 45,000 pediatricians dedicated to the health and well-being of infants and children. Visit the AAP Web site or call for the *Parent's Resource Guide*, listing an array of excellent educational books and videos for baby's first year, including: *Caring for Your Baby and Young Child: Birth to Age 5; Caring for Your Newborn: A Parent's Guide to the First 3 Months; Guide to Your Child's Nutrition; Guide to Your Child's Symptoms; Guide to Your Child's Sleep;* and *Guide to Your Child's Allergies and Asthma.*

Index

faucet covers, 114
fennel tea, 85–86
Ferber, Richard, 99–100
firearms, 203–4
first aid, 169–70, 184, 221
foam inserts, 109–10
formula, formulas, 35–36,
38, 40–45, 48–49,
166
colic and, 78, 81
cost vs. convenience of,
42–43, 48
sleep and, 88–89, 96
solid food and, 52–55, 60
switching of, 41–42
see also bottle-feeding
friends, 247, 267
postpartum period and,
211–12, 217–18, 221,
227
fruits and vegetables, 15, 81,
145, 176
introduction of, 55, 57–58,
60–64
furniture, 194–96

gas, 45, 78, 80–86
grocery shopping, 160–62
postpartum period and,
206–7, 215–16

hampers, 141
heartbeats, 72, 94
heating pads, 83
herbs, 16, 85–86, 230
high chairs, 58–59, 162
hobbies, 268
home:
achieving satisfaction at,
267–68
balancing work and,
268–71
breast-feeding at, 8–14, 28
returning to work vs. staying at, 251–81
safety at, 182–204
working at, 254, 263–64,
279
hotels, 166, 169, 171, 208
breast-feeding at, 31–32
hot-water bottles, 22–23
houseplants, 197–98
housework, 232–33
postpartum period and,
207–9, 211, 215–16,
220

ice packs, 23
instincts, 290–91
Internet, 29, 86–87
diapers and, 121–22, 124

Get Your Parenting Tips Published!

———— ❧ ————

You're the "expert"; you've been there and you have the advice other moms are seeking. Share your valuable experience with other moms by forwarding your tips, anecdotes (amusing stories), advice, and words of encouragement for possible inclusion in a companion book to *The New Mom's Manual* (addressing anything in baby's first year); or one of three other parenting "tips" books, addressing the toddler years (ages one to three), early childhood (ages four to six), and childhood years (ages seven to twelve). Request a questionnaire or e-mail/mail your tips to:

Visit my Web site at: newmomsmanual.com

Or,   Mary Jeanne Menna
      c/o Three Rivers Press
      299 Park Avenue
      Mail Drop 6–2
      New York, NY 10171

Please include your name and address so that I may forward a release to you, granting me legal permission to print your tip(s). Also, be sure and let me know if I may include your name, city, and state in my book. Thanks, moms!

About the Author

---- ✐ ----

MARY JEANNE MENNA is an award-winning freelance writer focusing on parenting and children's health issues, whose work has appeared in such publications as *Baby* magazine and *Family Times*. A stay-at-home mom and an active member of Mothers at Home, the National Parenting Association, and the National PTA, she lives outside Atlanta, Georgia.